COMPLETE BOOK OF

DESSERTS

OVER 300 RECIPES, FROM SUMPTUOUS CHOCOLATE CAKES TO FRESH FRUIT SHERBETS

COMPLETE BOOK OF

DESSERTS

OVER 300 RECIPES, FROM SUMPTUOUS CHOCOLATE CAKES TO FRESH FRUIT SHERBETS

International Culinary Society
New York

This 1990 edition published by International Culinary Society
distributed by Outlet Book Company, Inc.,
a Random House Company,
225 Park Avenue South
New York, New York 10003

Published by arrangement with Ebury Press
an imprint of the Random Century Group
Random Century House
20 Vauxhall Bridge Road
London SW1V 2SA

Editor: Barbara Croxford
Home Economists: Janet Smith, Emma-Lee Gow
Designer: Grahame Dudley Associates
Stylist: Sarah Wylie
Illustrations: Linda Smith
Photography: James Murphy
Additional photography: Grant Symon, Jan Baldwin, Laurie Evans, James Jackson,
Charlie Stebbings, Peter Myers, Paul Kemp, and Don Last

ISBN 0-517-03388-7
87654321

Printed and bound in Italy

CONTENTS

THE RECIPES

FRUITS OF THE WORLD

From the exotic guava to the humble apple, the fruits of
the world are now in abundant supply all year round.
Utilize their sweet simplicity and whip up
something sensational from our selection of appealing
fruity desserts.

Soft or crisp fleshed, juicy or firm, sweet or sharp, fruits make perfect crumbles and mousses. Simply washed, peeled and freed from any stalks, pits or cores, they make a simple healthy dessert served au naturel with yogurt, cream or ice cream, or lightly poached in syrup, wine or fruit juice.

Ice Bowl

Serve a plate of perfectly prepared and prettily arranged fruit as a refreshing finale to a meal. For a more extravagant presentation, make an ice bowl: pour about 1 inch water into a large freezerproof bowl. Add flowers and leaves to decorate. Freeze until firm. Place a small freezerproof bowl inside the larger one. Add more flowers and leaves. Place a heavy weight inside the smaller bowl to keep it in place. Carefully fill the space between the two bowls with water. Freeze until firm. Remove the weight. Wipe the inner bowl with a damp hot cloth until it loosens. Repeat with the outside bowl. Return to the freezer until needed. Serve filled with fruit salad, decorated with more flowers and leaves.

Melon Basket

A melon basket is a good receptacle for fruit of all kinds and makes a pretty centerpiece. Choose a firm, ripe, melon. Lay it on its side and cut a small slice from the base so that it will sit securely without wobbling. Insert a sharp knife just above where the stalk was and cut lengthways, almost to the center. Leave a space of 1 inch of the melon uncut, and continue cutting lengthways to the end of the melon. Repeat on the other side. Make the handle by cutting across the melon leaving 1 inch uncut across the center. Remove the two end wedges of melon. Cut away the flesh about $\frac{1}{2}$ inch from the peel, inside the handle. Scoop out the flesh and use to make a fruit salad. Store the melon basket in the refrigerator until required. Serve on a large platter, decorated with herbs, flowers and leaves and filled with fruit or fruit salad of your choice.

Frosted Fruits and Flowers

Frosted fruits and flowers make a pretty decoration for fruit desserts, gâteaux and mousses. Whisk the white of 1 egg and 2 teaspoons cold water together to give a frothy mixture. Using a small paintbrush, brush small firm fruits and flowers with a little of the mixture. Dip in superfine sugar, shake off any excess, then spread out on wax paper. Leave to dry for at least 24 hours.

SUMMER PUDDING

SERVES 8

You do not have to wait until summer to enjoy summer pudding; it can be made very successfully with frozen fruits. Traditionally in England, it is made with bread, but sponge cakes can be used instead. Always make the day before serving.

1 cup redcurrants, stalks removed
2 cups blackcurrants, stalks removed
generous 1–1¼ cups sugar
thinly pared peel of 1 large orange, in one continuous spiral if possible
2 cups raspberries, hulled
2 cups loganberries, hulled
12 thick slices of white bread, about 2 days old, crusts removed

1. Place the currants, sugar and orange peel in a large saucepan. Cover and cook gently until the juices flow and the sugar has dissolved. Add the raspberries and loganberries, and continue cooking for about 5 minutes until they are softened. (Alternatively, microwave in a covered bowl on HIGH for 5–7 minutes until softened, stirring occasionally.) Remove from the heat and leave to cool.

2. Cut a round from one of the slices of bread, large enough to fit in the base of a 6 cup ceramic bowl. Place the round in the bowl, then line the sides of the bowl with slightly overlapping slices of bread, reserve the rest for the center and top.

3. Remove the orange peel from the fruit. Spoon half of the fruit and juice into the lined bowl, then place a layer of bread on top. Add the remaining fruit and juice, then cover completely with the remaining bread.

4. Cover the top of the pudding with plastic wrap, then place a small, flat plate on the top. Stand the bowl on a plate to catch any juices that overflow. Place some heavy weights on top of the plate. Chill overnight.

5. To serve, gently loosen the pudding from the sides of the bowl with a spatula, then turn out on to a flat plate. Serve with Crème Chantilly (see page 248).

Not suitable for freezing.

VARIATION

Fall Pudding   Use 2 pounds mixed autumn fruit such as apples, blackberries, plums. Put the fruit, 6 tablespoons water and scant $\frac{1}{3}$ cup sugar in a saucepan. Cover and cook as above. (Alternatively, microwave in a covered bowl on HIGH for 4–8 minutes, stirring occasionally.) Finish as above.

Previous Page: LAYERED FRUIT TERRINE (PAGE 16).
Opposite: SUMMER PUDDING.

BLACK FRUIT SALAD

SERVES 4–6

Serve this unusual fruit salad in a plain white or glass bowl for the most stunning effect. Other dark-skinned fruits may be added.

2½ cups blueberries or blackcurrants
2½ cups black cherries, pitted
2½ cups seedless black grapes
finely grated peel and juice of 1 large orange
⅓ cup light brown soft sugar

1. Mix the fruits together in a bowl with the orange peel and juice and the sugar.
2. Leave to stand for 3–4 hours or overnight, stirring occasionally. Serve the salad with Frozen yogurt (see page 226).

Not suitable for freezing.

RØDGRØD

SERVES 4–6

Rødgrød is a Danish dessert which essentially is a thick fruit soup. It is always made with fresh soft summer fruit, depending on what is available. An important point to remember is to mix at least two fruits together to provide good flavor and color. In Russia, it is known as Kisel.

3 cups redcurrants or blackcurrants, stalks removed
3½ cups raspberries or strawberries, hulled, or cherries, pitted
2 tablespoons arrowroot
½–1 cup superfine sugar
FOR THE DECORATION
whipped cream
sprigs of mint

1. Place the currants and 4 tablespoons water in a saucepan. Cover and simmer gently for about 20 minutes or until really soft. Leave to cool.
2. Meanwhile, purée half of the berries in a blender or food processor until smooth, then press through a nylon strainer.
3. Blend a little of the purée with the arrowroot. Put the rest into a pan and bring slowly to the boil. Stir into the blended mixture, then return it all to the pan. Bring to the boil again, cook for 4–5 minutes and sweeten to taste. Leave to cool for 10 minutes. Stir in the cooked currants and the remaining raspberries, strawberries or cherries.
4. Pour the Rødgrød into individual glasses and chill for 30 minutes. Top with whipped cream and mint sprigs just before serving.

To freeze: pack and freeze the cold Rødgrød. Defrost overnight in the refrigerator, then finish as above.

TROPICAL FRUIT SALAD WITH PASSION FRUIT CREAM

SERVES 6

The syrup of this delicious fruit salad is flavored with the distinctive taste of fresh lime. It is a perfect background for the exotic mixture of fruit. The passion fruit cream and the fruit salad can both be prepared in the morning for dinner that night.

½ cup sugar
thinly pared peel and juice of 2 limes
1 ripe mango
1 ripe papaya
½ inch thick slice of fresh pineapple
2 ripe kiwi fruit
FOR THE PASSION FRUIT CREAM
4 ripe passion fruit
½ cup thick cream
2 tablespoons superfine sugar

1. To make the tropical fruit salad, put the sugar, ½ cup water and lime peel and juice into a small saucepan. Heat gently until the sugar dissolves, then bring to the boil. Boil gently for 5 minutes. (Alternatively, put all of the ingredients into a bowl and microwave on HIGH for 3 minutes or until the sugar dissolves, stirring frequently. Continue to microwave on HIGH for 3 minutes.) Strain and leave to cool.
2. Peel the mango, then cut the flesh away from the pit. Cut the mango flesh into small cubes. Cut the papaya in half and scoop out the pips. Peel the papaya, then cut each half into two lengthways and cut into slices crossways. Remove all the outer skin from the pineapple, and remove the hard center core. Cut the pineapple into small pieces. Peel and slice the kiwi fruit.
3. Add all of the prepared fruits to the lime syrup. Cover and chill until serving.
4. To make the passion fruit cream, cut each passion fruit in half, then scoop out the pips into a nylon strainer placed over a small bowl. Work the pips in the strainer with the back of a spoon until all of the juice has been extracted into the bowl.
5. Whip the cream and superfine sugar together in a bowl until it holds soft peaks. Gradually fold in the passion fruit juice. Spoon the cream into a serving bowl, cover and chill until ready to serve.
6. Transfer the tropical fruit salad to a serving bowl. Serve with the passion fruit cream.

Not suitable for freezing.

Above: RØDGRØD. Below: CRANBERRY AND ORANGE UPSIDE DOWN CAKE (PAGE 37).

SPARKLING MELON AND LIME SOUP

SERVES 4

A light, refreshing dessert to serve on a hot summer evening.

$\frac{1}{4}$ cup sugar
pared peel and juice of 1 lime
2 cups melon flesh, diced
6 tablespoons champagne or sparkling white wine, chilled

FOR THE DECORATION
julienne strips of mango
raspberries or strawberry slices
tiny mint sprigs, scented geranium or lemon balm leaves

1. Dissolve the sugar in $\frac{1}{2}$ cup water in a saucepan over gentle heat. Add the lime peel, bring to the boil, then simmer for 2–3 minutes. (Alternatively, microwave the sugar and water on HIGH for 5 minutes or until dissolved, stirring occasionally. Add the lime peel and continue cooking for 1 minute.) Leave to cool.
2. When cold, strain the syrup into a blender or food processor. Add the lime juice and melon and purée until smooth. Chill until required.
3. Just before serving, stir in the champagne and decorate with the prepared fruit and leaves.

Not suitable for freezing.

RASPBERRY DESSERT SOUP

SERVES 4–6

A light and refreshing end to a meal on a hot summer's day, this dessert can be made from any soft berries, including redcurrants and even strawberries.

6 cups fresh raspberries, hulled, or frozen, defrosted
1 bottle sweet wine, such as Sauternes, Vouvray or German Auslese
finely grated peel and juice of 1 lime (optional)
1 cup crème fraîche, fromage frais or Greek yogurt
4 tablespoons raspberry-flavored liqueur (optional)

FOR THE DECORATION
mint leaves
edible flowers

1. Pick over the raspberries and discard any damaged fruit. Purée half in a blender or food processor until smooth. Keep the remainder in the refrigerator until needed. Stir the wine, lime peel and juice and icing sugar to taste into the purée. Cover and chill for 3–4 hours to allow the flavors to develop.

2. Spoon the crème fraîche, fromage frais or yogurt into a bowl and add a few spoonfuls of fruit and wine purée. Beat well, then gradually stir in the remaining fruit and wine purée. Add the liqueur, if using.
3. Pour or ladle the soup into chilled soup plates and scatter the remaining raspberries over the top. Decorate with the mint leaves and edible flowers.

To freeze: freeze in a rigid container. Defrost in the refrigerator overnight.

FRUDITÉS

SERVES 6

A light, pretty dessert. Use other fruits in season for something a little different.

2 crisp sweet apples
2 bananas
$1\frac{1}{2}$ cups apricots, pitted
generous 1 cup seedless black or green grapes
$1\frac{1}{2}$ cups strawberries
juice of 1 lemon

FOR THE DIP
$\frac{1}{2}$ cup heavy cream
$\frac{1}{2}$ cup sour cream
2 tablespoons icing sugar, sifted

1. To make the dip, whip the two creams and icing sugar together in a bowl until standing in soft peaks. Pipe or spoon into six individual dishes.
2. Quarter and core the apples, but do not peel them. Peel the bananas and cut into $1\frac{1}{2}$ inch chunks.
3. Arrange the fruit on individual serving plates and sprinkle immediately with lemon juice to prevent discoloration.
4. Place the dishes of cream dip next to the fruit and serve immediately. Use fingers or small fondue forks to dunk the fruit into the cream dip.

Not suitable for freezing.

WILD STRAWBERRY AND CHAMPAGNE JELLY

SERVES 6

The Alpine strawberry is a version of the rare wild strawberry, that is now cultivated in France. Also known as frais du bois, these deliciously flavored baby strawberries do not need to be hulled before they are eaten.

generous ½ cup superfine sugar
pared peel and juice of 1 lemon
4 teaspoons gelatin
1½ cups pink champagne
generous 1 cup Alpine strawberries or frais du bois
edible flowers or sprigs of mint, to decorate

1. Put the sugar, lemon peel and 1 cup water in a saucepan. Heat gently until the sugar has dissolved. (Alternatively, microwave on HIGH for 3 minutes or until dissolved, stirring occasionally.) Leave to cool.

2. Sprinkle the gelatin over the lemon juice in a small bowl and leave to soak for 2–3 minutes. Place the bowl over a pan of simmering water and stir until dissolved. (Alternatively, microwave on HIGH for 30 seconds or until dissolved.)

3. Mix the sugar syrup with the dissolved gelatin and the champagne. Divide most of the strawberries between six champagne flutes. Carefully pour over a little of the jelly and chill until set. When the jelly has set, pour over the remaining jelly. Chill until set.

4. Decorate with the reserved strawberries and edible flowers or mint sprigs.

Not suitable for freezing.

Above: WILD STRAWBERRY AND CHAMPAGNE JELLY.

15

Layered Fruit Terrine

SERVES 6

This luscious-looking terrine is easier to make than you think, but avoid lime fruit and pineapple because they prevent the jelly setting. Do not be restricted by the fruits used here, use any combination in season.

FOR THE JELLY
6 teaspoons gelatin
1½ cups clear grape or apple juice (or half juice and rosé or white wine)
2 cups small even-sized strawberries, hulled
1¼ cups small black seedless grapes
4 large oranges, peeled, segmented and well drained
1¼ cups small green seedless grapes

FOR THE SAUCE
2 cups fresh raspberries, hulled, or frozen, defrosted
icing sugar, to taste
lemon juice
dash of fruit liqueur or kirsch (optional)

FOR THE DECORATION
few extra strawberries or raspberries
sprigs of mint or strawberry leaves

1. To make the jelly, sprinkle the gelatin over ½ cup of the grape juice in a small bowl and leave to soak for 2–3 minutes. Place the bowl over a pan of simmering water and stir until dissolved. (Alternatively, microwave on HIGH for 30 seconds or until dissolved.) Stir the dissolved gelatin into the remaining juice and mix well.

2. Pour a ¼ inch layer of jelly into the base of a 2½ cup non-stick (or non-corrosive) loaf pan or mold. Chill until set.

3. Arrange the whole strawberries in a tightly packed layer over the set jelly. Arrange the black grapes in a thick layer over the strawberries, followed by the oranges, then the green grapes. Make sure the fruit is overlapping or tightly packed.

4. Slowly pour the fruit jelly over the fruit until it just covers the final layer. Tap the mold very lightly on the work surface to remove any air bubbles. Chill for at least 4 hours or until completely set.

5. To make the sauce, purée the raspberries in a blender or food processor until smooth. Press through a sieve if liked, and add sugar and lemon juice to taste. Stir in the liqueur, if using. Cover and chill.

6. To serve, dip the pan or mold in a bowl of lukewarm water for about 10 seconds and invert on to a flat surface. Remove the pan and, using a serrated or electric knife, cut the terrine into thick slices. Transfer each slice carefully on to individual chilled plates.

7. To decorate, pour a little sauce over a corner of each slice and arrange strawberries and mint sprigs on each plate. Serve immediately, with the remaining sauce handed separately.

Not suitable for freezing.

Illustrated on pages 8–9.

Strawberry and Loganberry Jelly

SERVES 8

The subtle taste of puréed strawberries and loganberries combine to make this flavorful jelly. Other fruits can be used in the same way.

1 cup sugar
3 cups strawberries, hulled
3 cups loganberries or raspberries, hulled
2 tablespoons gelatin

FOR THE DECORATION
1 cup heavy cream, whipped
strawberries

1. Put the sugar and 1 cup water into a saucepan and heat gently until the sugar has dissolved. Bring to the boil and boil for 1 minute. (Alternatively, put the water and sugar in a bowl and microwave on HIGH for 3 minutes or until dissolved. Microwave on HIGH for a further minute.) Remove from the heat and leave to cool.

2. Purée the fruits in a blender or food processor, then strain to remove the pips.

3. Sprinkle the gelatin over 6 tablespoons water in a small bowl and leave to soak for 2–3 minutes. Place the bowl over a pan of simmering water and stir until dissolved. (Alternatively, microwave on HIGH for 30 seconds or until dissolved.)

4. Stir the dissolved gelatin into the sugar syrup, then stir into the fruit purée until well blended. Pour the jelly mixture into a 5 cup mold and chill until set.

5. To unmold, dip the mold up to the rim briefly in hot water, then place a plate upside down over the mold. Invert the two, giving them a good shake. Lift off the mold. Decorate the jelly with whipped cream and strawberries. Chill until ready to serve.

Not suitable for freezing.

GERMAN RUMTOPF

A rumtopf is a ceramic pot made especially for preserving fresh summer fruits in rum. Rumtopfs came into being as a result of German seafarers tying to take exotic fruits from the West Indies to Germany about 200 years ago.

Start to make a rumtopf when the first fruits of summer appear, usually strawberries, and continue through the summer months, until the rumtopf is full.

Most fruit can be put into a rumtopf but those with a high water content, such as melon and apple, should be avoided as they can cause fermentation. Also, avoid blackberries, rhubarb and gooseberries, as their sharpness can impart a bitter flavor. All fruits used must be ripe, sound, and very clean.

$2\frac{1}{4}$ cups superfine sugar to every 1 pound ripe strawberries, hulled
1 bottle of rum, no less than 40% alcoholic volume
generous 1 cup superfine sugar to every 1 pound of fruit, such as:
raspberries, hulled
loganberries, hulled
redcurrants and blackcurrants, stalks removed
peaches, peeled, halved and pitted
nectarines, peeled, halved and pitted
apricots, peeled, halved and pitted
plums, peeled, halved and pitted
greengages, peeled, halved and pitted
black and green seedless grapes
cherries, pitted
pineapple, peeled, core removed and cut into small pieces
mango, peeled and cut into dice or slices
papaya, peeled, pips removed and cut into small slices
kiwi fruits, peeled and sliced
pears, peeled, cored and sliced

1. Wash and thoroughly dry the rumtopf.
2. Put the strawberries into a large bowl, sprinkle with the superfine sugar and mix lightly together. Cover and leave to stand for 1 hour.
3. Put the strawberries, sugar and any juices into the rumtopf and cover with rum to a depth of $\frac{1}{2}$ inch.
4. Cover the surface with plastic wrap, then place a saucer on top of the plastic wrap to keep the fruit submerged. Cover with more plastic wrap, then the rumtopf top. Put the rumtopf in a cool, airy cupboard.
5. Continue to add fruits to the rumtopf, soaking them with the stated amount of sugar and rum. When full, cover the rumtopf and store in a cool place for 2–3 months to mature. Serve with cream, ice cream or yogurt.

Not suitable for freezing.

AMARETTI STUFFED PEACHES

SERVES 4

Amaretti are almond macaroons made in Italy. They are available at Italian delicatessens, both in boxes and individually wrapped in tissue paper. Amaretti are delicious served with coffee and liqueurs at the end of a meal. If you cannot find them, use store bought or home-made macaroons instead.

4 yellow peaches, peeled
2 ounces Amaretti or macaroons
1 egg yolk
$\frac{1}{4}$ stick butter
2 tablespoons sugar
$\frac{1}{2}$ cup dry white wine

1. Lightly grease a heatproof dish.
2. Cut the peaches in half and carefully ease out the pits. Make the hollows in the peaches a little deeper with a sharp-edged teaspoon and reserve the removed flesh.
3. Crush the macaroons and mix them with the reserved peach flesh, the egg yolk, butter and 1 tablespoon of the sugar.
4. Use this mixture to stuff the hollows of the peach halves, mounding the filling slightly. Place the peaches in the prepared heatproof dish and sprinkle with the rest of the sugar. Pour the white wine over and around the peaches.
5. Bake in the oven at 350° for 25–30 minutes or until tender. (Alternatively, arrange around the edge of a large shallow dish, cover and microwave on HIGH for 3–5 minutes or until tender. Leave to stand, covered, for 5 minutes.) Serve hot or cold.

Not suitable for freezing.

BRANDIED STUFFED APRICOTS

SERVES 4

Smaller and more unusual than its relations the nectarine and peach, the apricot is highly prized for its unique flavor and aroma. Fresh apricots do not keep well and their season is short. If fresh apricots are not available, this recipe can be made with small peaches or nectarines, but as these are always larger than apricots you will only need half the quantity

16 small apricots
8 tablespoons apricot brandy
2 tablespoons superfine sugar
finely grated peel and juice of 1 lemon
generous $\frac{1}{2}$ cup cottage cheese
$\frac{1}{4}$ cup full fat soft cream cheese
1 tablespoon icing sugar, sifted
chopped roasted hazelnuts, to decorate

1. Place the apricots, brandy, sugar, 1 tablespoon lemon juice and $\frac{1}{2}$ cup water in a saucepan. Poach gently for about 15 minutes until just tender. Remove the apricots and leave to cool for 30 minutes.
2. Boil the poaching liquid for 2–3 minutes until well reduced and syrupy. Leave to cool for 20 minutes.
3. Using a sharp knife, skin the apricots. Slice almost in half and remove the kernel.
4. Strain the cottage cheese into a bowl, add the cream cheese, icing sugar and grated lemon peel, then beat together until well mixed.
5. Sandwich the apricots together with a little of the cheese mixture. Divide the apricots between four individual glass dishes.
6. Spoon a little of the cooled syrup over the apricots. Chill for 2–3 hours, then decorate with chopped nuts before serving.

Not suitable for freezing.

ORANGES IN CARAMEL

SERVES 6

For a sweet, crunchy topping to this classic orange dessert, make caramel chips: dissolve $\frac{1}{2}$ cup sugar very gently in scant $\frac{1}{2}$ cup water. Increase the heat and boil rapidly without stirring until the syrup turns a rich brown caramel color. Pour at once into a greased shallow pan (a jelly roll pan is ideal), then leave until cold and set. Crush with a rolling pin or mallet into fine pieces and sprinkle over the oranges just before serving (not earlier or the caramel will soften).

generous 1 cup sugar
6 large oranges
2–3 tablespoons orange-flavored liqueur

1. Put the sugar and $\frac{1}{4}$ cup water in a saucepan and heat gently until the sugar has dissolved, brushing down the sides of the pan with hot water. Bring to the boil, then boil until the syrup turns a golden caramel color.
2. Immediately, plunge the base of the pan into cold water to prevent the caramel darkening further. Carefully, pour 1 cup boiling water into the pan. Return the caramel to the heat and heat gently until it has completely dissolved into the water.
3. Meanwhile, thinly pare the peel from two of the oranges, taking care not to remove the white pith. Cut the peel into very fine shreds and set aside. Using a very sharp knife, remove the skin and white pith from all the oranges.
4. Put the oranges and shredded peel into the caramel, cover and cook them very gently for 25–30 minutes until the oranges are tender, but do not allow to overcook—they must retain a good shape. Turn the oranges frequently during cooking.
5. Transfer the oranges and syrup to a large serving dish. Add the liqueur and leave to cool. Cover and chill. Serve with Crème Chantilly (see page 248).

Not suitable for freezing.

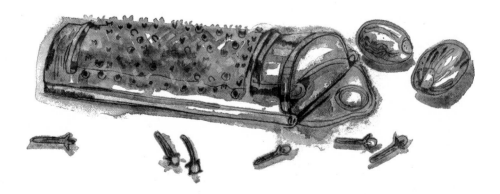

Opposite: ORANGES IN CARAMEL.

BARNSTAPLE FAIR PEARS

SERVES 4

The pear orchards of Devon in England used to supply stalls at the annual Barnstaple Fair. Originally these pears would have been simmered in local cider or scrumpy.

4 large firm pears
¼ cup blanched almonds, split in half
¼ cup superfine sugar
1 cup red wine
2 cloves

1. Peel the pears, leaving the stalks on. Spike the pears with the almond halves.

2. Put the sugar, wine and cloves in a saucepan just large enough to hold the pears and heat gently until the sugar has dissolved. Add the pears, standing them upright in the pan. Cover and simmer gently for about 15 minutes until the pears are just tender. Baste them from time to time with the liquid. (Alternatively, put the sugar, wine and cloves in a bowl and microwave on HIGH for 3–4 minutes until boiling, stirring occasionally. Add the pears, cover and microwave on HIGH for 8–10 minutes until the pears are tender.)

3. Using a slotted spoon, transfer the pears to a serving dish. Boil the syrup in the pan until the liquid is reduced by half. (If cooking in the microwave, uncover and cook on HIGH for 10 minutes or until reduced by half.)

4. Pour the wine syrup over the pears. Serve hot or cold with thick plain yogurt or thick cream.

To freeze: pack in the cooled syrup.

Left: RASPBERRY AND WALNUT SHORTBREAD (PAGE 39).
Right: BARNSTAPLE FAIR PEARS.

Pears Poached in Ginger Syrup

SERVES 4

Use firm or slightly underripe pears for this recipe.

½ *cup dry white wine*
5 tablespoons ginger wine
½ *cup light brown soft sugar*
1 strip lemon peel
1 cinnamon stick
4 firm pears
2 tablespoons preserved ginger in syrup, thinly sliced

1. Pour the white wine into a large heavy-based pan. Add 1 cup water, the ginger wine, sugar, lemon peel and cinnamon. Heat gently until sugar has dissolved, then remove from the heat. (Alternatively, put the ingredients in a bowl and microwave on HIGH for 3–4 minutes until boiling, stirring occasionally.)
2. Using a vegetable peeler or canelle knife, peel the pears from top to bottom in a spiral pattern. Leave the stalks on.
3. Put the pears in the wine and simmer gently for 30 minutes. Transfer to a serving bowl. (If cooking in the microwave, add to the syrup, cover and microwave on HIGH for 8–10 minutes or until the pears are tender.)
4. Boil the liquid in the pan until reduced by half, then strain and stir in the preserved ginger. (Alternatively, microwave on HIGH for 10 minutes or until reduced by half.) Pour over the pears in the bowl.
5. Leave the pears for 1–2 hours until completely cold, then chill overnight, spooning the syrup over them occasionally. Serve chilled, with cream.

To freeze: pack in the syrup at the end of step 5.

Almond Baked Apples

SERVES 4

The almond coating makes these baked apples with a difference.

⅔ *cup dry figs, rinsed and chopped*
grated peel of 1 lime or ½ *lemon*
4 tart apples, each about 8 ounces
½ *cup ground almonds*
1 tablespoon light brown soft sugar
1 tablespoon butter or margarine, melted

1. Put the figs in a bowl, cover with boiling water and leave to soak for 5 minutes. Drain, then mix in the grated lime peel.
2. Peel and core the apples. Fill with the fig mixture, packing down firmly.
3. Mix the ground almonds and sugar together. Brush each apple with the melted butter, then roll the apples in the ground almond mixture. Place the apples in a shallow 4 cups heatproof dish.
4. Bake in the oven at 350° for about 45–50 minutes or until the apples are cooked through and tender when pricked with a cake tester. Serve hot.

Not suitable for freezing.

Flambéed Apples Triberg-Style

SERVES 4–6

This wonderful way of cooking apples comes from Triberg, a small picturesque town in the Black Forest—famous for its kirsch and its clocks! The apples are cooked with honey and lemon, then flambéed with kirsch, and may be cooked on a spirit burner at the dining table.

6 large sweet apples
3 tablespoons sweet butter
2 tablespoons superfine sugar
thinly pared peel of 1 lemon, taken in one continuous spiral if possible
juice of 1 lemon
3 tablespoons clear honey
4 tablespoons kirsch
½ *cup heavy cream, lightly whipped with 1 tablespoon kirsch*

1. Peel, quarter and core the apples. Cut each quarter into half again.
2. Put the butter, sugar, lemon peel and juice and honey in a large shallow saucepan. Heat gently, stirring, until slightly thickened.
3. Add the apples to the pan and cook gently, turning the pieces frequently, for 10–15 minutes until the apples are just tender when pierced with the tip of a knife. Spoon the juices into a serving container and set aside.
4. Add the kirsch to the apples, heat for 10 seconds, then set alight. Flambé the apples until the flames begin to subside. Spoon the apples, still slightly flaming, on to warmed serving plates. Serve immediately with the juices and flavored whipped cream.

Not suitable for freezing.

COMPOTES

Compotes are mixtures of fruits cooked in sugar syrup, which can be served hot or cold. The syrup may be flavored with spices or with orange and lemon peel, but the fruits, being quite highly flavored themselves, require little or no extra flavoring. Hot compotes make perfect desserts for the winter, not only because they are warming, but also because they are full of vitamins. Chilled compotes will keep well for up to a week in the refrigerator.

Compotes can be made with a single fruit, but it is more interesting to have a mixture. So that the cooked fruits retain their shape as much as is possible, they should be added to the sugar syrup in the order of cooking time—those that need the longest time first, and so on. Small quantities can be made in the microwave but larger quantities cook better in a large saucepan. Always select ripe, but firm fruits. A little liqueur may be added to a compote, just enough to enhance the flavor, not to overpower it.

FOR THE BASIC SUGAR SYRUP

generous 1 cup sugar

1. To make the sugar syrup, put the sugar and 1 cup cold water in a saucepan. Heat very gently until the sugar has completely dissolved.
2. Bring to the boil and boil the syrup for 1 minute.

SPRING COMPOTE

SERVES 6

Spring rhubarb needs careful cooking. It is very delicate and can easily break up.

1 quantity Basic sugar syrup (see above)
¼ cup fresh ginger, peeled and finely shredded
3 pounds rhubarb, cut into 2 inch pieces

1. Make the sugar syrup in a shallow, wide saucepan. Add the ginger and cook gently for 2–3 minutes.
2. Add just enough rhubarb to make a single layer. Cook gently for 5–6 minutes until just tender, turning the pieces frequently. Transfer to a serving dish. Continue cooking the rhubarb in batches.
3. Boil the syrup until reduced and slightly thickened, then pour over the rhubarb. Serve the compote hot or cold, with Orange sabayon sauce (see page 248).

To freeze: cool then pack in a rigid container. Defrost overnight at cool room temperature. Serve cold.

Opposite: SUMMER CURRANT COMPOTE. REDCURRANT HAZELNUT GÂTEAU (PAGE 37).

SUMMER COMPOTE

SERVES 6–8

Serve this compote well chilled on bright, hot, sunny days with Crème Chantilly (see page 248). Or, cheer up a gloomy rainy day by serving it hot.

1 quantity Basic sugar syrup (see left)
1 pound ripe peaches or nectarines, halved, pitted, peeled and cut into thick slices
1 pound ripe apricots, peeled, halved and pitted
1 pound dark cherries, pitted

1. Make the sugar syrup in a large, wide saucepan. Add the peach slices and cook gently for 10–15 minutes until barely tender.
2. Add the apricots and cook for a further 5 minutes until the apricots just begin to soften.
3. Add the cherries and cook just long enough to soften them without losing their color, about 3 minutes.
4. Carefully transfer the fruits and syrup to a serving bowl. Leave to cool, then chill.

To freeze: pack in a rigid container. Defrost overnight at cool room temperature.

SUMMER CURRANT COMPOTE

SERVES 6

Add sugar to taste—with ¼ cup the compote will be quite tart.

¼ cup granulated sugar
1½ cups blackcurrants, stalks removed
generous 3 cups redcurrants, stalks removed
pared peel and juice of 1 medium orange
2 tablespoons honey
2½ cups strawberries, hulled and sliced

1. Dissolve the sugar in ½ cup water in a pan. Boil for 1 minute. (Alternatively, microwave on HIGH for 3 minutes, stirring frequently. Continue to microwave on HIGH for 1 minute.)
2. Add the currants and orange peel and simmer until the fruits are just beginning to soften—about 1 minute only. (If cooking in the microwave, microwave on HIGH for 1–2 minutes or until beginning to soften.)
3. Carefully transfer the fruits and syrup to a serving bowl. Stir in the honey and leave to cool.
4. Mix in the orange juice, cover and chill well.
5. Just before serving, stir the strawberries into the compote. Serve with Baked custard (see page 165).

Not suitable for freezing.

FALL COMPOTE

SERVES 6–8

Select very small pears for this compote. Lemon juice added to the syrup prevents the pears and apples discoloring, and adds a tangy flavor.

1 quantity Basic sugar syrup (see page 23)
juice of 1 lemon
1 pound small ripe, but firm pears
1 pound sweet apples
1 pound purple plums, peeled and pitted

1. Make the sugar syrup in a large saucepan, adding the lemon juice. Thinly peel the pears, cut into half and remove the center core (if only large pears are available, cut the pears into quarters). Add the pears to the syrup and cook very gently for about 10–15 minutes until barely tender.

2. Meanwhile, core the apples. Cut the apples into halves, then cut into slices across the halves.

3. Add the apple slices to the pan and cook for about 5 minutes until the apple slices are just tender. Add the plums and cook for a further 5 minutes.

4. Carefully transfer the fruits and syrup to a serving bowl, taking care not to break up the fruit. Serve hot or cold.

To freeze: cool then pack in a rigid container. Defrost overnight at cool room temperature. Serve cold.

Illustrated on page 31

WINTER COMPOTE

SERVES 6–8

A compote with a bitter sweet flavor, tangy and refreshing.

1 quantity Basic sugar syrup (see page 23)
1 pound kumquats, thickly sliced
1 pound tangerines, peeled and segmented
1½ cups seedless black grapes
1½ cups seedless green grapes
1½ cups cranberries

1. Make the sugar syrup in a wide saucepan. Add the kumquats, cover and cook gently for about 15–20 minutes until barely tender.

2. Add the tangerines and grapes, then cook for a further 5 minutes, gently turning the fruits in the syrup and taking care not to break them up. Add the cranberries and cook the compote for about 5 minutes until softened.

3. Carefully transfer the fruits and syrup to a serving bowl. Serve hot or cold.

To freeze: cool and pack in a rigid container. Defrost at cool room temperature.

STICKY PEAR UPSIDE DOWN PUDDING

SERVES 6–8

A hearty pudding that is quickly put together from kitchen ingredients, yet is hard to resist. Ideal to serve at short notice. The canned pears in natural juice combine perfectly with the rich, dark, spicy sponge.

FOR THE PEAR LAYER
¾ stick butter or margarine
scant 1 cup light brown soft sugar
two 14½ ounce cans of pear halves in natural juice

FOR THE SPONGE
2 cups All Purpose plain flour
1½ cups light brown soft sugar
1 teaspoon soda
pinch of salt
2 teaspoons ginger
½ teaspoon nutmeg
1 tablespoon cinnamon
finely grated peel and juice of 1 large lemon
½ cup molasses
¾ stick butter or margarine
scant 1 cup milk
2 eggs, beaten

1. To make the pear layer, warm the butter and sugar together. Spoon into a 9 cup shallow heatproof dish. Drain the pears and arrange cut side down around the base of the dish.

2. To make the sponge, mix the flour, sugar, soda, salt and spices together in a bowl. Add the finely grated lemon peel, then make a well in the center of the dry ingredients.

3. Warm the molasses and butter together. When evenly blended, pour into the well with the milk and 3 tablespoons lemon juice. Add the eggs and beat well until evenly mixed.

4. Spoon the sponge over the pears. Stand the dish on an edged cookie sheet.

5. Bake in the oven at 400° for about 25 minutes. Reduce the oven temperature to 375° and continue to cook for about a further 50 minutes, covering lightly if necessary. The pudding should be firm to the touch and a cake tester inserted into the center should come out clean.

6. Leave the pudding to stand for about 5 minutes. Run a knife around the edge of the pudding. Invert on to a plate. Serve warm with custard, plain yogurt or light cream.

To freeze: pack and freeze the cooled pudding. Defrost at cool room temperature, then reheat at 375° for about 30 minutes.

DANISH 'PEASANT GIRL IN A VEIL'

SERVES 4

This simple but delicious pudding of stewed apples layered with fried breadcrumbs and sugar is very similar to an apple charlotte. In Denmark, where it is called *bondepige med slør*, it takes its name from the fact that the apple and crumbs are 'veiled' or covered with cream.

$\frac{1}{2}$ stick butter or margarine
3 cups fresh rye or brown breadcrumbs
$\frac{1}{2}$ cup light brown soft sugar
$1\frac{1}{2}$ pounds tart apples
juice of $\frac{1}{2}$ lemon
sugar, to taste
$\frac{1}{2}$ cup heavy or whipping cream
2 squares grated chocolate, to decorate

1. Melt the butter in a skillet. Mix the breadcrumbs and sugar together. Add to the pan and fry until crisp, stirring frequently with a wooden spoon to prevent the crumbs from catching and burning.
2. Peel, core and slice the apples. Put them in a saucepan with 2 tablespoons water, the lemon juice and sugar to taste. Cover and cook gently for 10–15 minutes until they form a purée. (Alternatively, put the apples, lemon juice and sugar in a bowl. Cover and microwave on HIGH for 7–10 minutes until they form a pulp, stirring frequently.) Leave to cool, then taste for sweetness and add more sugar if required.
3. Put alternate layers of the fried crumb mixture and apple purée into a glass serving dish, finishing with a layer of crumbs. Chill for 2–3 hours.
4. Whip the cream until stiff. Pipe over the top of the crumb mixture and decorate with grated chocolate. Serve chilled.

Not suitable for freezing.

ALMOND EVE'S PUDDING

SERVES 4

If liked, add $\frac{1}{3}$ cup white or black raisins to the apple mixture in the base of this delicious family pudding. Grated orange or lemon peel added to the sponge topping also adds extra flavor.

FOR THE FILLING
$1\frac{1}{2}$ pounds tart apples
1 teaspoon cinnamon
$\frac{1}{3}$ cup brownulated sugar
FOR THE TOPPING
1 stick butter, softened
$\frac{2}{3}$ cup brownulated sugar
2 eggs, beaten
1 cup self raising flour
$\frac{1}{4}$ cup ground almonds
$\frac{1}{2}$ teaspoon almond flavoring
2 tablespoons milk
$\frac{1}{4}$ cup slivered almonds
icing sugar, for dredging

1. To make the filling, peel, quarter and core the apples, then slice thickly. Place in a 5 cup heatproof dish. Combine the cinnamon and brownulated sugar and scatter over the apples. Cover tightly with plastic wrap while preparing the topping.
2. To make the topping, cream the butter and sugar together in a bowl until fluffy. Gradually beat in eggs. Fold in the flour, ground almonds, almond flavoring and milk.
3. Spread the mixture over the apples. Place the slivered almonds on top in six squares to form a chequerboard.
4. Bake in the oven at 350° for 50–60 minutes until the apples are tender and the sponge risen and golden brown. Dredge icing sugar between the nut squares. Serve with cream.

Not suitable for freezing.

SPICED APPLE AND PLUM CRUMBLE

SERVES 6

All plums can be cooked, but dessert varieties tend to be more expensive, so it makes good sense to look for cooking plums. Whether you cook with red or yellow plums is entirely a matter of personal choice. Greengages and damsons come from the plum family and can be used in any recipe for plums, although extra sugar may be required.

1 pound plums
1½ pounds tart apples
1 stick butter or margarine
generous ½ cup sugar
1½ teaspoons mixed spice
1½ cups plain Graham flour
⅓ cup blanched hazelnuts, roasted and chopped

1. Using a sharp knife, cut the plums in half, then carefully remove the pits.
2. Peel, quarter, core and slice the apples. Place the apples in a medium saucepan with a quarter of the butter, half of the sugar and about 1 teaspoon of the mixed spice. Cover and cook gently for 15 minutes until the apples begin to soften.
3. Stir in the plums. Transfer the fruit mixture to a 4 cup shallow heatproof dish. Leave to cool for about 30 minutes.
4. Stir the flour and remaining mixed spice well together. Rub in the remaining butter until the mixture resembles fine breadcrumbs. Stir in the rest of the sugar with the hazelnuts. Spoon the crumble over the fruit.
5. Bake in the oven at 350° for about 40 minutes or until the top is golden, crisp and crumbly.

To freeze: cool and freeze in the dish at the end of step 4.

BLUEBERRY OAT CRUMBLE

SERVES 6–8

Originally a wild fruit of the heaths and woodlands of the USA and Canada, blueberries have been grown commercially since the early part of this century. Because of the similarity in name, the blueberry, blackberry and bilberry are often thought to be the same fruit. In fact, they are different varieties of the same family of berries, which also includes whortleberries and huckleberries.

FOR THE FILLING
2 pounds blueberries
3 tablespoons light brown soft sugar
2 tablespoons All Purpose flour
1 tablespoon lemon juice

FOR THE CRUMBLE TOPPING
1 stick butter
generous ½ cup All Purpose flour
½ cup light brown soft sugar
1 cup rolled oats
½ cup pecan or walnut halves, chopped and roasted
nutmeg (optional)

1. To make the filling, mix the blueberries with the sugar, flour and lemon juice in a 5 cup pie plate.
2. To make the crumble topping, rub the butter into the flour in a bowl. Stir in the sugar, oats and nuts. Flavor with nutmeg, if liked. Spoon the crumble mixture on top of the berries and lightly press down.
3. Bake in the oven at 375° for about 30–35 minutes or until golden brown. Serve warm or cold with custard or cream.

To freeze: wrap and freeze in the pie plate before baking. Bake from frozen at 400° for 30 minutes, then at 375° for 40–50 minutes.

Opposite: BLUEBERRY OAT CRUMBLE.

BLACKBERRY AND PEAR COBBLER

SERVES 4

Recipes with the strange sounding title of 'cobbler' are invariably American in origin, although very little is known for certain about the meaning behind the word in culinary terms. Cobblers always have a biscuit dough topping which is stamped into small rounds.

FOR THE FILLING
1 pound blackberries
1 pound ripe tart pears
finely grated peel and juice of 1 lemon
½ teaspoon cinnamon

FOR THE TOPPING
2 cups self raising flour
pinch of salt
½ stick butter or margarine
2 tablespoons superfine sugar
about ½ cup milk, plus extra to glaze

1. To make the filling, pick over the blackberries and wash them. Peel and core the pears, slice thickly.
2. Put the blackberries and pears into a saucepan with the lemon peel and juice and the cinnamon. Poach for 15—20 minutes until the fruit is tender. Cool.
3. To make the topping, place the flour and salt in a bowl. Rub in the butter until the mixture resembles fine breadcrumbs, then stir in the sugar. Gradually add the milk to mix to a fairly soft dough.
4. Roll out the dough on a floured work surface until ½ inch thick. Cut out rounds using a fluted 2 inch cookie cutter.
5. Put the fruit in a pie plate and top with overlapping pastry rounds, leaving a gap in the center.
6. Brush the top of the pastry rounds with milk. Bake in the oven at 425° for 10—15 minutes until the pastry is golden brown. Serve hot.

To freeze: wrap and freeze at the end of step 5. Defrost and cook as above.

LEMON AND YOGURT MOUSSE

SERVES 8

Beautifully smooth, tangy and light, this mousse is delicious served with crisp cookies. If possible, make your own yogurt (page 180) for this recipe.

¼ cup milk
4 eggs, separated
generous ½ cup superfine sugar
2 drops of vanilla
5 teaspoons gelatin
3 cups plain yogurt
juice of 1 lemon
½ cup heavy cream

1. Put the milk in a small saucepan and bring almost to the boil. Beat the egg yolks and 2 tablespoons of the sugar together in a small bowl until pale in color. Gradually add the milk, mixing well. Return to the pan and stir constantly over a low heat until the mixture begins to thicken and just coats the back of a spoon. Do not boil. Pour out the mixture into a large bowl and add the vanilla.
2. Sprinkle the gelatin over 5 tablespoons water in a small bowl and leave to soak for 2—3 minutes. Place the bowl over a pan of simmering water and stir until dissolved. (Alternatively, microwave on HIGH for 30 seconds until dissolved.) Cool slightly and add to the custard. Stir to mix.
3. Whisk in the yogurt and lemon juice, about 3 tablespoons, whisking the mixture until smooth. Leave until cool, beginning to thicken but not set.
4. Whisk the egg whites until stiff but not dry and fold in the remaining sugar. Lightly whip the cream and fold into the yogurt mixture with the whites. Pour into a large glass serving dish. Cover and chill to set—about 3 hours.
5. Remove from the refrigerator about 15 minutes before serving.

Not suitable for freezing.

STRAWBERRY YOGURT MOLD

SERVES 6

A light mousse made in a ring mold always looks pretty filled with fresh fruit, and strawberries are probably the most decorative of all the soft summer berries. The delicately flavored mold has a very light set, just firm enough to turn it out. Substitute buttermilk for the yogurt, if preferred.

3 eggs
scant ¼ cup superfine sugar
finely grated peel and juice of 1 large lemon
1 pound strawberries
4 teaspoons gelatin
½ cup plain yogurt
½ cup strawberry yogurt

1. Whisk the eggs, sugar and lemon peel together in a large bowl, using an electric mixer, until the mixture is pale, thick and creamy and leaves a trail when the whisk is lifted from the bowl.

2. Hull half of the strawberries and place in a blender or food processor with half of the lemon juice. Purée until smooth.

3. Gradually whisk the purée into the mousse mixture, whisking well to keep the bulk.

4. Sprinkle the gelatin over the remaining lemon juice in a small bowl and leave to soak for 2–3 minutes. Place the bowl over a pan of simmering water and stir until dissolved. (Alternatively, microwave on HIGH for 30 seconds or until dissolved.) Leave until cool.

5. Gradually add the dissolved gelatin to the mousse mixture with the plain and strawberry yogurts. Stir carefully but thoroughly to mix. Pour into a greased 6 cup ring mold and chill for 4–5 hours or until set.

6. To serve, dip the mold briefly in hot water, then invert on to a serving plate. Hull most of the remaining strawberries, but leave a few of the green hulls on for decoration. Fill the center of the ring with the fruit. Serve with extra plain yogurt.

Not suitable for freezing.

Below: STRAWBERRY YOGURT MOLD.

PRICKLY PEAR AND LIME MOUSSE

SERVES 6–8

Available from late summer to late fall, prickly pears come mainly from Brazil, Italy and Mexico. Choose those which look firm, fresh and plump. Take great care to avoid the prickles when handling the fruit as they will irritate the skin badly.

6–8 prickly pears, about 1½ pounds
4 eggs, separated
scant ¼ cup superfine sugar
grated peel and juice of 1 lime
1 tablespoon gelatin
½ cup whipping cream

1. Carefully peel the prickly pears. Roughly chop the flesh, place in a food processor or blender and purée until smooth. Rub through a nylon strainer to remove the pips, yielding about 1 cup purée.
2. Whisk the egg yolks, sugar, grated lime peel and juice together in a bowl, using an electric mixer, until thick and mousse-like. Stir in the pear purée.
3. Sprinkle the gelatin over 3 tablespoons water in a small bowl and leave to soak for 2–3 minutes. Place the bowl over a saucepan of simmering water and stir until dissolved. (Alternatively, microwave on HIGH for 30 seconds or until dissolved.)
4. Whip the cream until it just holds its shape. Whisk the egg whites until stiff but not dry.
5. Carefully add the dissolved gelatin to the mousse mixture, stir in the cream, then fold in the egg whites.
6. Pour gently into six to eight individual glass dishes or a large glass serving bowl. Chill until set.

Not suitable for freezing.

MANDARIN AND LYCHEE MOUSSE

SERVES 6

Canned lychees are more widely available than the fresh fruit, and they have a good flavor.

3 eggs, separated
2 egg yolks
scant ½ cup superfine sugar
10½ ounce can mandarin oranges in natural juice
11 ounce can lychees in syrup
1 tablespoon gelatin
½ cup heavy cream

1. Whisk the five egg yolks and sugar in a large bowl standing over a saucepan of gently simmering water until the mixture is thick and holds a ribbon trail.

Remove the bowl from the pan. Leave to cool for 30 minutes, whisking occasionally.
2. Reserve 4 tablespoons of the mandarin juice. Purée half the oranges and the remaining juice in a blender or food processor with the lychees and half the syrup.
3. Sprinkle the gelatin over the reserved mandarin syrup in a small bowl and leave to soak for 2–3 minutes. Place the bowl over a saucepan of simmering water and stir until dissolved. (Alternatively, microwave on HIGH for 30 seconds or until dissolved.) Cool slightly.
4. Stir the mandarin purée into the cooled egg yolk mixture, then stir in the dissolved gelatin until evenly mixed.
5. Whip the cream until standing in soft peaks. Whisk the egg whites until stiff. Fold first the cream, then the egg whites into the mousse until evenly blended. Turn into a glass serving bowl and chill for at least 2 hours until set.
6. When the mousse is set, serve decorated with the reserved mandarin oranges and extra whipped cream.

Not suitable for freezing.

PRUNE AND PORT FOOL

SERVES 4

Because the flavors in this fool are so strong, you can get away with using ready-made custard instead of home-made.

¾ cup pitted prunes, soaked overnight
scant ⅓ cup sugar
4 tablespoons port
finely grated peel and juice of 1 medium orange
½ cup thick custard, cooled
½ cup heavy cream

1. Drain the prunes, then put in a saucepan with the sugar, port, orange peel and juice. Simmer for about 15 minutes until soft. (Alternatively, microwave, covered, on HIGH for 8 minutes or until soft.)
2. Leave to cool slightly, then purée in a blender or food processor. Leave to cool completely.
3. Fold the cooled custard into the puréed prunes. Whip the cream until standing in soft peaks, then fold into the prune custard until evenly blended.
4. Divide the mixture between four individual glasses. Chill for about 2 hours until firm. Serve chilled, with sweet cookies.

To freeze: pour into a rigid container at the end of step 3 and freeze. Defrost in the refrigerator overnight.

Above: FALL COMPOTE *(PAGE 24).*
Below: PRUNE AND PORT FOOL.

PASKHA

This traditional Russian Easter speciality is normally made in a special tall paskha mold, but you can use a clay flower pot instead. The flower pot should have a hole in the bottom, and be scrupulously clean—it is a good idea to buy one especially for making paskha, and keep it with your other kitchen equipment. For the following recipe you will need a 6½ inch wide flower pot that is about 5 inches deep. You will also need some clean white cheesecloth. Make the paskha the day before it is to be served.

1½ sticks sweet butter
finely grated peel of 1 lemon
finely grated peel of 1 orange
generous ¾ cup superfine sugar
2 eggs
1 teaspoon vanilla
4 cups curd cheese
½ cup heavy cream
¼ cup citron peel, chopped
¼ cup candied lemon peel, chopped
¼ cup candied orange peel, chopped
⅔ cup raisins, chopped
½ cup blanched almonds, chopped
½ cup natural color candied cherries, chopped
½ cup candied pineapple, chopped
FOR THE DECORATION
citron peel
candied cherries
candied pineapple
blanched almonds, halved and lightly roasted
fresh violets or primroses (optional)

1. Beat the butter with the lemon and orange peel and the sugar in a bowl until very light and fluffy. Beat in the eggs, one at a time, beating well after each addition. Add the vanilla and curd cheese and beat well together until very smooth.
2. Beat in the cream, then mix in the citron and candied peels, raisins, nuts, cherries and pineapple. Set aside.
3. Place the flower pot in the center of a large square of cheesecloth, then make a diagonal cut to the center of the cloth. Line the flower pot smoothly with the cloth; the cut will enable the cloth to be overlapped for a smoother lining. If there are too many bumps in the cloth, these will mark the paskha and spoil its finished appearance.
4. Fill the flower pot with the paskha mixture, then bring the overhanging cloth up and over the mixture to enclose it completely. Place a small flat plate on top of the paskha, then place some heavy weight, or cans of food, on top of the plate, to compress the mixture. Stand the flower pot on a plate, then refrigerate overnight. (It

is important to stand the pot on a plate as a certain amount of liquid will drain away from the paskha as it is compressed.)
5. To unmold the paskha, open out the cloth on the top, then place a flat serving plate on top of the paskha. Invert the plate and the flower pot together. Remove the flower pot, then very carefully peel away the cheesecloth.
6. Decorate the paskha attractively with strips of citron peel, cherries, pineapple, almonds—and violets and primroses, if liked. Keep the paskha refrigerated until ready to serve.

Not suitable for freezing.

RHUBARB AND ORANGE FOOL

SERVES 6

Serve this fool well chilled with sponge fingers (see page 174) or crisp cookies. Follow the basic recipe to make other fruit fools of your choice.

1 pound rhubarb
grated peel and juice of 1 orange
pinch of cinnamon
2–4 tablespoons sugar
1 cup whipping cream
1 teaspoon orange flower water
shredded orange peel, to decorate

1. Chop the rhubarb into 1 inch pieces, discarding the leaves and the white ends of the stalks.
2. Put the rhubarb, orange peel, juice, cinnamon and sugar into a pan. Cover and cook gently for about 15 minutes.
3. Uncover and boil rapidly for 10 minutes, stirring frequently, until the mixture becomes a thick purée. Leave to cool for 1 hour.
4. When cool, whip the cream until stiff. Fold into the mixture with the orange flower water to taste.
5. Spoon the fool into glasses and chill for 1–2 hours until required. Decorate with orange peel and serve with Sponge fingers (see page 174).

To freeze: pour into a rigid container at the end of step 4. Defrost overnight in the refrigerator.

Opposite: PASKHA.

MEETHE CHAWAL

SERVES 4–6

Meethe Chawal is a sweet Indian rice pudding with almonds, raisins and coconut.

generous 1 cup long grain rice
½ teaspoon salt
generous ½ cup sugar
1 inch cinnamon stick
1 stick ghee or melted butter
seeds of 4 green cardamom pods
¼ teaspoon nutmeg
pinch of saffron
1 cup slivered blanched almonds, roasted
⅔ cup raisins
½ cup sweet shredded coconut

1. Bring a large saucepan of water to the boil. Add the rice and salt and bring back to the boil. Stir once, then simmer, uncovered, for 10 minutes.

2. Meanwhile, put the sugar and cinnamon stick in a separate heavy based pan. Add 1 cup water and heat gently until the sugar has dissolved. Bring to the boil, then boil rapidly for 1 minute. Remove from the heat.

3. Drain the rice. Heat the ghee or butter in a heatproof casserole, add the rice, cardamom and nutmeg and cook gently, stirring, for 1–2 minutes until the rice glistens.

4. Add the sugar syrup (with the cinnamon stick) to the rice and stir gently to mix. Sprinkle in the saffron and stir again. Cover the pan tightly.

5. Bake in the oven at 350° for 40 minutes. Discard the cinnamon stick and cover the casserole tightly again. Leave to stand for 5 minutes, then stir in the nuts, raisins and coconut. Spoon into individual dishes and serve immediately with light cream.

Not suitable for freezing.

Lockshen Pudding

Serves 4

This Jewish recipe was originally made on a Friday and cooked slowly overnight for serving hot on Saturday.

1 cup flat egg noodles (lockshen)
pinch of salt
1 egg
scant $\frac{1}{4}$ cup sugar
$\frac{1}{4}$ teaspoon cinnamon
finely grated peel of $\frac{1}{2}$ lemon
$\frac{1}{3}$ cup raisins
$\frac{1}{2}$ cup chopped almonds (optional)
$\frac{1}{4}$ stick margarine

1. Put the noodles into a pan of rapidly boiling salted water and cook for about 10 minutes until tender.
2. Drain into a strainer and rinse with plenty of hot water to remove excess starch. Drain well.
3. Whisk the egg and sugar together in a bowl. Stir in the cinnamon, lemon peel, raisins and nuts, if using. Stir in the noodles.
4. Melt the margarine in a 2 inch deep, heatproof baking dish until hot but not smoking. Swirl around the dish to coat the sides and pour the excess into the noodle mixture. Stir well and pour the mixture into the baking dish.
5. Bake in the oven at 375° for 45 minutes until set, crisp and brown on top. Serve hot.

Not suitable for freezing.

Steamed Fruit Puddings

Steamed fruit puddings are made by a very gentle method of cooking in a bowl in a steamer or saucepan of boiling water. Follow the rules below and the result will always be soft and moist. These puddings are turned out and often served with a sauce.

General Rules for Steaming

• Half-fill the steamer with water and heat so that it is boiling by the time the pudding is made. If you have no steamer, fill a large saucepan with water to come halfway up the pudding basin. Cover and bring to the boil.
• Grease the ceramic pudding bowl well.
• Cut double wax paper or a piece of foil to cover the pudding bowl and grease well. Put a pleat in the paper or foil to allow the pudding to rise.
• Fill the bowl not more than two-thirds.
• Cover the bowl tightly with paper or foil to prevent steam or water entering. Secure with string and make a string handle to lift the bowl in and out of the pan.
• Keep the water in the steamer boiling rapidly all the time and have a pan of boiling water ready to top it up regularly, or the steamer will boil dry. If using a saucepan, put an old saucer or metal cookie cutter in the base to keep the bowl off the bottom.

Steamed Fruit Pudding

Serves 4

1 pound fruit, prepared and stewed, or drained canned fruit
1 stick butter or margarine
generous $\frac{1}{2}$ cup superfine sugar
2 eggs, beaten
few drops of vanilla
$1\frac{1}{2}$ cups self raising flour
little milk, to mix

1. Half-fill a steamer or large saucepan with water and put it on to boil. Grease a 3 cup ceramic bowl and spoon the fruit into the bottom.
2. Cream the butter and sugar together in a bowl until pale and fluffy. Add the eggs and vanilla, a little at a time, beating well after each addition.
3. Using a metal spoon, fold in half the flour, then fold in the rest, with enough milk to give a dropping consistency.
4. Pour the mixture into the prepared bowl. Cover with greased wax paper or foil and secure with string. Steam for $1\frac{1}{2}$ hours. Serve with custard or cream.

VARIATIONS

Suet Pudding Put 2 tablespoons jelly in the bottom of the bowl. Mix together $1\frac{1}{2}$ cups self raising flour, pinch of salt, scant 1 cup shredded suet, generous $\frac{1}{4}$ cup superfine sugar and $\frac{1}{2}$ cup milk. Cook as above for $1\frac{1}{2}$–2 hours.

Syrup or Jelly Pudding Put 2 tablespoons maple syrup or jelly into the bottom of the bowl instead of the fruit.

Individual Candied Fruit Puddings Add $\frac{2}{3}$ cup candied fruit to the basic mixture. Omit the stewed fruit. Spoon into greased dariole molds and steam as for Steamed castle puddings (see below). *Illustrated opposite.*

Mincemeat Pudding Line the bottom and sides of the bowl with a thin layer of mincemeat and fill with the sponge mixture. When the pudding is cooked, turn it out carefully so that the outside remains completely covered with the mincemeat.

Chocolate Pudding See Steamed chocolate pudding on page 103.

Steamed Castle Puddings Spoon a little jelly in the bottom of greased dariole molds and divide the sponge between them, filling them two-thirds full. Cover each mold with greased foil and secure with string. Steam for 30–45 minutes (depending on size).

Microwave Sponge Pudding Halve the ingredients but use 1 cup flour. Mix to a very soft consistency with 3–4 tablespoons milk. Cover and cook on HIGH for 5–7 minutes or until just moist on the surface. Stand for 5 minutes.

Not suitable for freezing.

COMPOTE OF FRUIT WITH ELDERFLOWER CREAM

SERVES 4

The mixture of fruit, which can include any varieties in season, is here poached in fruit juice rather than the sugary syrup preferred by the Victorians. Elderflowers are beautifully aromatic and grow abundantly in the hedgerows. You can find dry elderflowers in health stores.

2 tablespoons sugar
6 large heads of fresh elderflowers or $\frac{1}{4}$ cup dry elderflowers
generous $\frac{1}{2}$ cup fresh heavy cream
2 pounds mixed fresh fruit, such as gooseberries, rhubarb, pears, strawberries, cherries, prepared
1 cup unsweetened orange or apple juice
1 cinnamon stick
2 strips of lemon peel
clear honey, to taste (optional)

1. To make the elderflower cream, put the sugar and $\frac{1}{2}$ cup water in a saucepan and heat gently until the sugar has dissolved, then boil rapidly until the liquid is reduced by half. Take off the heat and submerge the fresh or dry flowers in the syrup.

2. Leave to infuse for at least 2 hours, then press the syrup through a strainer, discarding the elderflowers. Whip the cream until it just holds its shape, then fold in the elderflower syrup. Chill until ready to serve.

3. Put the fruit, fruit juice, cinnamon and lemon peel in a large saucepan and simmer gently for 3–5 minutes until the fruits are softened, but still retain their shape. Serve the compôte warm or cold with the elderflower cream.

Below: INDIVIDUAL CANDIED FRUIT PUDDINGS.

CHRISTMAS PUDDING

SERVES 8

English plum pudding only took on its connections with Christmas when it was introduced to the Victorians by Prince Albert. Burying a silver coin in the mixture is said to bring good fortune to whoever finds it in their portion. All the family should make a wish while stirring the mixture on Stir Up Sunday, the Sunday before Advent.

1½ cups prunes, pitted and chopped
1 cup currants
1 cup raisins
1 cup white raisins
¼ cup blanched almonds, chopped
finely grated peel and juice of 1 lemon
1 cup All Purpose flour
½ teaspoon nutmeg
½ teaspoon cinnamon
½ teaspoon salt
1½ cups fresh breadcrumbs
generous 1 cup shredded suet
1 cup soft dark brown sugar
2 eggs, beaten
2 tablespoons molasses
½ cup brown ale
½ cup brandy, rum or sherry
5 tablespoons brandy, to flame

1. Grease a 6 cup ceramic bowl.
2. Place the dry fruits, nuts, lemon peel and juice in a large bowl. Mix well.
3. In a separate bowl, sift the flour, nutmeg, cinnamon and salt together. Add the breadcrumbs, suet and sugar and mix.
4. Pour in the beaten egg, molasses and brown ale, and beat well. Stir in the dry fruit mixture until evenly incorporated. Cover with plastic wrap and leave to stand in a cool place for 24 hours.
5. The next day, add the brandy, stirring well. Pack the mixture into the prepared bowl, pressing it down well.
6. Cover with pleated wax paper and foil. Secure with string. Steam for 4–5 hours.
7. Remove the pudding from the pan and leave to cool completely for 1–2 hours. Unwrap the pudding, then rewrap in fresh wax paper and foil.
8. Store in a cool, dry place for at least 1 month (or up to 1 year) before serving.
9. To serve, steam for 2–3 hours. Turn out on to a warmed serving dish and decorate with holly. Serve the pudding with Brandy or rum butter (see page 253), cream or custard.
10. To flame the pudding, warm the brandy gently in a small saucepan, pour over the pudding and light carefully with a match.

To freeze: wrap and freeze after maturing for 1 month.

TO COOK CHRISTMAS PUDDING IN THE MICROWAVE

A Christmas pudding can be cooked in a microwave. However, because the traditional Christmas pudding recipe contains a high proportion of sugar, dry fruits, fat and alcohol, all of which attract microwave energy and quickly reach a high temperature, it means great care must be taken not to overcook and possibly burn the pudding. As it is potentially dangerous, Christmas pudding should be watched during cooking in a microwave.

However, a Christmas pudding can be cooked in only 45 minutes in the microwave instead of 2½ hours by conventional cooking, and you do not need a saucepan of boiling water that has to be continually replenished. If, therefore, you are adapting your favorite Christmas pudding recipe, only add 2 tablespoons of the alcohol suggested and replace the remaining liquid with milk or orange juice. Additional liquid should also be added to keep the pudding moist; allow an extra 1 tablespoon milk for each egg added. A microwaved Christmas pudding should be eaten fairly soon after making. Store for up to 2–3 weeks in a cool place.

TO REHEAT CHRISTMAS PUDDING IN THE MICROWAVE

Remove all the wrappings and bowl from the pudding. Put the pudding on an ovenproof serving plate, cut into the required number of portions and pull apart so that there is a space in the center. Place a small tumbler of water in the center. This introduces steam and helps to keep the pudding moist. Cover with a large upturned bowl. Cook on HIGH for 2–3 minutes, depending on the size of the pudding, or until hot. Remove the cover and glass and reshape the pudding with the hands. Decorate with a sprig of holly and serve.

To reheat an individual portion of Christmas pudding, put on a plate and cook, uncovered, for 1–1½ minutes until hot.

UPSIDE DOWN GUAVA AND ALMOND CAKE

SERVES 4–6

A fragrant sponge suitable for a family lunch or an elegant dinner party. Serve warm to enjoy at its best.

3 tablespoons maple syrup
1 teaspoon lemon juice
2 small ripe guavas, about 12 ounces total weight
1 stick softened butter or margarine
generous ½ cup superfine sugar
2 eggs
2 tablespoons self raising flour
scant 1 cup ground almonds

1. Place a round of non-stick wax paper in the base of a greased 8 inch layer cake pan.

2. Heat the maple syrup and lemon juice together in a pan and pour into the pan.

3. Peel and quarter the guavas and remove the pips. Arrange, rounded side down, on top of the syrup.

4. Beat the butter and sugar together in a bowl until very pale and fluffy. Gradually beat in the eggs, then fold in the flour and ground almonds. Spoon the mixture on top of the guavas and carefully level the surface, without disturbing the guavas.

5. Bake in the oven at 350° for 45–50 minutes or until the sponge is golden, well risen and springs back to the touch; covering lightly if necessary.

6. Cool the sponge in the pan for 3–4 minutes, loosen the edges of the cake with a spatula and turn out on to a serving plate. Serve warm with cream.

Not suitable for freezing.

CRANBERRY AND ORANGE UPSIDE DOWN CAKE

SERVES 8

A moist sponge topped with a layer of tart cranberries. Best served warm.

FOR THE TOPPING
$\frac{1}{4}$ stick butter, melted
4 cups cranberries
scant $\frac{1}{2}$ cup superfine sugar
4 tablespoons cranberry sauce

FOR THE CAKE
2 cups self raising flour
1 teaspoon baking powder
large pinch of salt
1 egg
finely grated peel and juice of 1 large orange
$\frac{1}{4}$ cup milk
1 stick butter or margarine, softened
generous $\frac{1}{2}$ cup sugar

1. Grease a 9 inch round spring-release cake pan.

2. To make the topping, pour the melted butter into the prepared cake pan. Mix the cranberries, sugar and cranberry sauce together. Spoon the cranberry mixture evenly over the base of the cake pan.

3. To make the cake, put all the ingredients into a large bowl and beat until smooth and glossy. Carefully pour over the cranberries and level the surface.

4. Bake in the oven at 350° for about 1 hour or until well risen and firm to the touch. Cover the top with a double sheet of wax paper after 40 minutes to prevent overbrowning.

5. Leave to cool in the pan for 5 minutes, then turn the cake out on to a serving plate. Serve while warm with Fruit ice cream (see page 217) or whipped cream.

Not suitable for freezing.

Illustrated on page 13

REDCURRANT HAZELNUT GÂTEAU

SERVES 8–10

Cardamom adds a fragrant lemon taste to this light sponge. The hazelnuts are roasted first to bring out their flavor. This elegant summer dessert will impress dinner party guests.

FOR THE SPONGE
$\frac{1}{4}$ cup hazelnuts
6 green cardamom pods
2 eggs
$\frac{2}{3}$ cup superfine sugar
$\frac{1}{2}$ cup All Purpose flour

FOR THE FILLING
3 cups redcurrants, stalks removed
1 tablespoon arrowroot
1 tablespoon lemon juice
$\frac{1}{2}$ cup heavy cream
4 tablespoons plain yogurt
icing sugar, for dusting

1. Grease an 8 inch layer cake pan and line the base with wax paper. Dust with sugar and flour.

2. To make the sponge, first roast the hazelnuts under the broiler until well browned. Rub off the skins. Cool, then coarsely grind.

3. Split open the cardamom pods and remove the seeds. Crush to a fine powder.

4. Using an electric whisk, beat the eggs, 6 tablespoons of the sugar and the ground cardamom together in a bowl until really thick. When the whisk is lifted the mixture should be thick enough to leave a trail.

5. Lightly fold in the flour and ground hazelnuts. Spoon the mixture into the prepared pan.

6. Bake in the oven at 350° for about 25 minutes or until well risen but browned. Leave to cool in the pan for 10 minutes then turn out on to a wire rack to finish cooling.

7. Meanwhile to make the filling, place the redcurrants in a small pan with the remaining sugar and $\frac{1}{2}$ cup water. Heat gently until the fruit softens and the sugar dissolves.

8. Mix the arrowroot to a smooth paste with a little water. Stir into the fruit, then bring to the boil, stirring all the time. Boil for 1 minute. Add the lemon juice, then cool, cover and chill.

9. To complete the gâteau, cut the sponge into two layers. Whip the cream until it just holds its shape and stir in the yogurt. Sandwich the sponge layers with the cream and fruit. Chill until required. Dust with icing sugar before serving.

To freeze: wrap and freeze the cakes at the end of step 6. Defrost at cool room temperature, then finish as above.

Illustrated on page 22.

5. Quickly lattice the pastry strips over the fruit mixture. Brush with beaten egg and dust with sugar. Bake at 400° for about 20 minutes, or until golden brown and crisp.

BLUEBERRY BUCKLE

SERVES 12

Serve this satisfying dessert with tangy crème fraîche or plain yogurt.

FOR THE CAKE
$1\frac{1}{2}$ *pounds blueberries*
3 cups plus 2 tablespoons self raising flour
1 teaspoon baking powder
$\frac{1}{2}$ *stick butter or margarine*
$\frac{2}{3}$ *cup superfine sugar*
1 egg
1 cup milk
almond flavoring

FOR THE TOPPING
$\frac{1}{2}$ *stick butter or margarine*
$\frac{1}{2}$ *cup All Purpose flour*
scant $\frac{1}{3}$ cup superfine sugar

1. Grease a 9 inch round baking dish.
2. To make the cake, toss the blueberries in the 2 tablespoons flour and set aside.
3. Cream the butter and sugar in a bowl until pale and fluffy. Beat in the egg, then gradually add the milk, almond flavoring to taste and the remaining flour. Stir in the blueberries. Pour into the prepared dish.
4. To make the topping, rub the butter into the flour until the mixture resembles fine breadcrumbs. Stir in the sugar. Sprinkle over the cake mixture.
5. Bake in the oven at 375° for $1-1\frac{1}{4}$ hours or until a cake tester inserted into the center comes out clean. Leave to cool for 15 minutes, then serve warm.

To freeze: wrap and freeze after cooling. Defrost at cool room temperature. Reheat, covered with foil, at 400° for 30 minutes, removing the foil for the last 5 minutes.

PANADE

SERVES 6–8

The *boulangeries* of Provençe, France, provide wonderful fruit tarts but there are local specialities to make at home too. *Panade* is unusual: apples and pears are grated, cooked together with orange juice, then enclosed in pastry or dough. The origins of this recipe are not hard to trace, with so many fruit trees covering the valleys.

$1\frac{1}{2}$ *sticks butter or margarine*
2 cups All Purpose flour
large pinch cinnamon
$1\frac{1}{2}$ *pounds sweet apples*
$1\frac{1}{2}$ *pounds ripe pears*
grated peel and juice of 1 large orange
beaten egg and sugar, for glazing

1. Rub 1 stick butter into the flour and cinnamon until the mixture resembles fine breadcrumbs. Add enough chilled water, about 6 tablespoons, to bind to a soft paste. Wrap in plastic wrap and refrigerate for 10 minutes.
2. On a lightly floured surface, roll the dough out thinly and line a $9\frac{1}{2}$ inch loose-based fluted pie plate. Re-roll the excess pastry and cut into $\frac{1}{2}$ inch wide strips. Cover and refrigerate until required. Bake the pastry blind in the oven at 400° for about 20 minutes.
3. Meanwhile, melt the remaining butter in a large non-stick skillet. Stir in the peeled, cored and grated apples and pears, the grated orange peel and 3 tablespoons orange juice.
4. Cook over a high heat, stirring constantly, until all excess moisture has evaporated and the mixture is quite dry. Spoon into the warm pastry case.

Above: PANADE.

RASPBERRY AND WALNUT SHORTBREAD

SERVES 8

Two of Scotland's most celebrated foods—shortbread and raspberries—come together in this recipe to make a truly mouthwatering dessert that tastes even better than it looks. The walnuts are ground and added to the shortbread mixture for a subtle nutty flavor.

1 cup walnut pieces
1 stick butter
scant $\frac{1}{2}$ cup superfine sugar
1$\frac{1}{2}$ cups All Purpose flour
1 pound raspberries, hulled
$\frac{1}{2}$ cup icing sugar
2 tablespoons raspberry-flavored liqueur or kirsch (optional)
1 cup whipping cream

1. Draw three 8 inch circles on non-stick wax paper. Place the circles on baking sheets.
2. Grind the walnuts finely in a blender or food processor.
3. Cream the butter and sugar together in a bowl until pale and fluffy. Beat in the walnuts and flour until a dough is formed. Divide the dough into three shortbread portions.
4. Put a portion of shortbread dough in the center of each paper circle and press out with the heel of the hand until the dough is the same size as the circle.
5. Cut one of the circles into eight triangles with a sharp knife and ease them slightly apart. Refrigerate the circles and triangles for 30 minutes.
6. Bake in the oven at 375° for 15–20 minutes, changing over the sheets to ensure the shortbread browns evenly. Leave to cool and harden for 10 minutes on the paper, then transfer to wire racks to cool completely.
7. Meanwhile, reserve a third of the raspberries for decoration. Put the rest in a bowl with the icing sugar and liqueur, if using. Crush the raspberries with a fork, then leave them to macerate while the pastry rounds are cooling.
8. Assemble the shortbread just before serving, to ensure that the pastry remains crisp. Whip the cream until thick, then fold in the crushed raspberries and juice. Stand one round of pastry on a flat serving plate and spread with half of the cream mixture. Top with the remaining round of pastry, then the remaining cream mixture.
9. Arrange the triangles of pastry on top of the cream, wedging them in at an angle. Scatter the reserved whole raspberries in between. Serve the shortbread as soon as possible.

To freeze: wrap the cooled shortbread at the end of step 6. Defrost at cool room temperature, then finish as above.

Illustrated on page 20

APPLE AND BLACKBERRY CHARLOTTE

SERVES 4

A charlotte mold is a large round mold with sloping sides and is used for making the classic Charlotte Russe (see page 170) as well as a hot charlotte like this. A deep round cake pan works just as well if you do not have the special pan.

1 pound tart apples
1 pound blackberries
grated peel and juice of $\frac{1}{2}$ lemon
$\frac{1}{4}$ teaspoon cinnamon
1 cup sugar
2 tablespoons bread or cake crumbs
6 large bread slices
$\frac{1}{2}$ stick butter or margarine, melted

1. Grease a 5 cup charlotte mold or a 6 inch round cake pan.
2. Peel, core and thickly slice the apples. Put in a saucepan with the blackberries, lemon peel and juice and cinnamon and cook gently for 10 minutes until the apples have softened slightly. Add the sugar and crumbs.
3. Cut the crusts off the bread. Trim one piece to a round the same size as the base of the pan, dip it into the melted butter and fit into the pan. Dip the remaining slices of bread in the butter and arrange closely around the side of the pan, reserving one piece for the top.
4. Spoon in the stewed fruit mixture and cover with the remaining slice of bread, trimmed to fit the top of the mold.
5. Bake in the oven at 375° for about 1 hour. Turn out and serve with custard.

To freeze: wrap and freeze at the end of step 5.

CRISP AND LIGHT PASTRIES

Perfect pâtisserie to rival any store-bought creation is
easy to create in your own kitchen following our recipes.
Rich and gooey Profiteroles, Linzertorte and Strawberry
shortcake make unforgettable dinner party treats. Along
with all those much loved family pies, tarts and fruit
dumplings, here you will find a splendid pastry for every
occasion.

Despite the mystique attached to making pastry, the only secrets to success are patience, practice and care. Unless making choux or filo (strüdel) pastry, the golden rule is keep everything cool—kitchen, work surface, utensils, ingredients and yourself.

The perfect pastry is 'short'—light, crumbly and crisp, but not hard. The amount of fat and water added to the flour and the way the pastry is handled all govern the shortness. Even pastries with a little fat in them only require a little water. The more water you add, the harder and tougher the pastry will be. A very soft, easy to roll pastry will probably have too much water in it. It will shrink badly in the oven and have a tough, hard texture. Always add water a little at a time, remembering that the amount needed can vary from day to day depending on the absorbency of the flour and the humidity in your kitchen.

When rolling out pastry, dust the work surface and the rolling pin, never the pastry, with as little flour as possible. Roll the dough lightly and evenly in one direction only. Always roll away from you, rotating the pastry frequently to keep an even shape. Use light but firm strokes. Overrolled pastry will shrink dramatically when baked.

Baking Blind
Baking blind is the term used to describe the cooking of pastry cases without any filling. The pastry may be partially prebaked to be cooked for a further period when filled, or completely cooked if the filling requires no further cooking.

1. Make the pastry and line the pie plate or tarts. Chill for 30 minutes to 'rest' the pastry.
2. Cut out a piece of wax paper or foil larger than the pastry case. Remove the pastry case from the refrigerator and prick the base.
3. Lay the paper or foil in the pastry case and fill with baking beans.
4. For partially prebaked cases, bake in the oven at 400° for 10—15 minutes until the pastry is just 'set'. Remove the paper and beans, then bake for a further 5 minutes until lightly colored. Pastry cases which need complete baking should be returned to the oven for a further 15 minutes or until pale golden brown.

Pastry cases which have been baked blind will keep for several days in an airtight container or may be frozen.

Shortcrust Pastry Quantity Guide for Tarts and Pies

Dish size	Pastry (flour amount)
6 inch plain or fluted pie ring	1 cup
7 inch plain or fluted pie ring	1¼ cups
8 inch plain or fluted pie ring	1½ cups
9 inch plain or fluted pie ring	1¾ cups
2½ inch tarts	2 cups (pastry top)
3 inch tarts	2 cups
3 cup pie plate	1½ cups (pastry top only)
4 cup pie plate	2 cups (pastry top)
8 inch pie plate	2¼ cups (line and top)

APRICOT GLAZE

Apricot glaze is used for glazing pastries to make them look more attractive. The addition of a little liqueur gives extra flavor.

12 ounce jar apricot conserve
1—2 tablespoons liqueur; kirsch, brandy, orange or almond-flavored liqueur (optional)

1. Put the conserve into a small saucepan and heat gently, stirring all the time, until melted.
2. Press through a nylon strainer into another small, clean saucepan. Add the liqueur, or a little water, then bring to the boil, stirring. The glaze should always be at boiling point when used to ensure that it sets well.
3. Keep made up apricot glaze in a jar in the refrigerator, ready to be heated when required for glazing.

SHORTCRUST PASTRY
MAKES 8 OUNCES PASTRY

This plain short pastry is probably the most widely used of all pastries. For shortcrust pastry, the proportion of flour to fat is 2:1, or twice the quantity. Therefore, for a recipe using quantities of shortcrust pastry other than 8 ounces, simply use half the quantity of fat to the flour weight specified.

2 cups All Purpose flour
pinch of salt
½ stick butter or margarine, chilled and diced
4 tablespoons lard, chilled and diced

1. Mix the flour and salt together in a bowl. Add the fat to the flour.
2. Using your fingertips, rub the fat lightly into the flour until the mixture resembles fine breadcrumbs.
3. Add 3—4 tablespoons chilled water, sprinkling it evenly over the surface. (Uneven addition may cause blistering when the pastry is cooked.)
4. Stir in with a round-bladed knife until the mixture begins to stick together in large lumps. With one hand, collect the dough mixture together to form a ball.
5. Knead lightly for a few seconds to give a firm, smooth dough. Do not overhandle the dough.
6. To roll out, sprinkle a very little flour on a working surface and the rolling pin (not on the pastry) and roll out the dough evenly in one direction only, turning it occasionally. The usual thickness is ⅛ inch. Do not pull or stretch the pastry.
7. The pastry can be baked straight away, but it is better if allowed to 'rest' for about 30 minutes in the plate or dish, covered in foil or plastic wrap, in the refrigerator.
8. Bake in the oven at 400—425°, except where otherwise specified, until lightly browned (see individual recipes).

VARIATIONS

Wholewheat pastry Follow the recipe and method for Shortcrust pastry but use Graham flour instead of white. You may need a little extra water due to the absorbency of Graham flour.

Nut pastry Follow the recipe and method for Shortcrust pastry but stir in $\frac{1}{4}$ cup very finely chopped, shelled walnuts, cashew nuts, hazelnuts or almonds before adding the water.

To freeze: wrap tightly and freeze. Defrost at cool room temperature or overnight in the refrigerator.

SHORTCRUST PASTRY MADE IN A FOOD PROCESSOR

MAKES 8 OUNCES PASTRY

A food processor makes shortcrust pastry very quickly and gives good results. It is most important not to overmix the dough as a food processor works in seconds not minutes. For even 'rubbing in', turn the machine on in short bursts rather than letting it run continuously. Make sure you know the capacity of your food processor and never overload the processor bowl. If making a large quantity of pastry, make it in two batches.

2 cups All Purpose flour
pinch of salt
$\frac{1}{2}$ stick butter or margarine, chilled and diced
4 tablespoons lard, chilled and diced

1. Mix the flour and salt together in the bowl of the food processor.
2. Add the fat to the flour. Mix for a few seconds until the mixture resembles fine breadcrumbs.
3. Add 3–4 tablespoons chilled water and switch on until the mixture forms a smooth dough. Roll out and use as for shortcrust pastry.

Freeze as shortcrust pastry.

SWEET PASTRY

MAKES 4 OUNCES PASTRY

Sweet pastry is made by the same rubbing-in method as shortcrust, but the liquid used is beaten egg instead of water. It is usually sweetened with superfine sugar which improves the flavor and is ideal for pies, small tarts and other sweet pastries. Quick and easy to prepare, sweet pastry benefits from being chilled for at least 30 minutes before use.

1 cup All Purpose flour
pinch of salt
$\frac{3}{4}$ stick butter or margarine and lard, chilled and diced
1 teaspoon superfine sugar
1 egg, beaten

1. Mix the flour and salt together in a bowl. Rub the fat into the flour as for shortcrust pastry, until the mixture resembles fine breadcrumbs. Stir in the sugar.
2. Add the egg, stirring with a round-bladed knife until the ingredients begin to stick together in large lumps.
3. With one hand, collect the mixture together and knead lightly for a few seconds to give a firm, smooth dough. Roll out as for shortcrust pastry.
4. Bake in the oven at 400°, unless otherwise stated, until lightly browned.

Freeze as shortcrust pastry.

PÂTE SUCRÉE

MAKES 4 OUNCES PASTRY

This French, rich, sweet, short pastry is the best choice for Continental pâtisserie. Pâte sucrée is thin, crisp yet melting in texture. It keeps its shape, shrinks very little and does not spread during baking. Pâte sucrée is fairly quick and easy to make. Although it can be made in a bowl, the classic way to make this pastry is on a flat, cold surface such as marble.

1 cup All Purpose flour
pinch of salt
$\frac{1}{4}$ cup superfine sugar
$\frac{1}{2}$ stick butter (at room temperature)
2 egg yolks

1. Sift the flour and salt on to a work surface. Make a well in the center and add the sugar, butter and yolks.
2. Using the fingertips of one hand, pinch and work the sugar, butter and egg yolks together until well blended.
3. Gradually work in all the flour to bind the mixture together. Knead lightly until smooth.
4. Wrap the pastry in foil or plastic wrap and leave to 'rest' in the refrigerator or a cool place for about 30 minutes, or overnight if possible.
5. Bake in the oven at 375°, unless otherwise stated, until lightly browned.

Freeze as shortcrust pastry.

Previous Page: LAVENDER-SCENTED TARTS *(PAGE 59).*

SUETCRUST PASTRY

MAKES 8 OUNCES PASTRY

This pastry may be used for sweet bowl puddings, roly-poly puddings and dumplings. It can be steamed, boiled or baked; the first two methods are the most satisfactory, as baked suetcrust pastry is inclined to be hard. Suetcrust pastry is quick and easy to make, and should be light and spongy in texture—the correct mixing, quick light handling and long, slow cooking will achieve this. For a lighter texture or if using Graham flour, replace $\frac{1}{4}$ cup of the flour with 1 cup fresh breadcrumbs.

2 cups self raising flour
$\frac{1}{2}$ teaspoon salt
1 cup shredded suet

1. Mix the flour, salt and suet together in a bowl.
2. Using a round-bladed knife, stir in enough chilled water, about $\frac{1}{2}$ cup, to give a light, elastic dough. Knead very lightly until smooth.
3. Roll out to $\frac{1}{4}$ inch thick and use as required.
4. Steaming or boiling bowl and roly-poly puddings takes about 2–4 hours, depending on filling and size. Roly-poly puddings can also be wrapped in foil and baked in the oven at 400° for about 45 minutes, unless otherwise stated. Dumplings cooked in simmering liquid take about 25 minutes.

Freeze as shortcrust pastry.

FLAKY PASTRY

This pastry can be used instead of puff pastry where a great rise is not needed. The fat should be of about the same consistency as the dough with which it is to be combined, which is why it is worked on a plate beforehand. This quantity is equivalent to one 13 ounce packet.

2 cups All Purpose flour
pinch of salt
$1\frac{1}{2}$ sticks butter or a mixture of butter and lard
a squeeze of lemon juice

1. Mix the flour and salt together in a bowl. Soften the fat by working it with a knife on a plate, then divide into four equal portions.
2. Add one quarter of the fat to the flour and rub it in until the mixture resembles fine breadcrumbs.
3. Stirring with a round-bladed knife, add a squeeze of lemon juice and about 8 tablespoons chilled water or sufficient to make a soft, elastic dough. Turn the dough on to a lightly floured work surface and knead until smooth. Roll out into an oblong three times as long as it is wide.
4. Using a round-bladed knife, dot a second quarter of the fat over the top two thirds of the pastry in flakes, so that it looks like buttons on a card.

5. Fold the bottom third of the pastry up and the top third down, then turn it so that the folded edges are at the sides.
6. Seal the edges of the pastry by pressing with a rolling pin. Wrap the pastry and leave in the refrigerator to 'rest' for 15 minutes. Re-roll as before and repeat twice more until the remaining fat has been used up.
7. Wrap the pastry loosely and leave to 'rest' in the refrigerator for at least 30 minutes before using.
8. Roll out on a lightly floured work surface to $\frac{1}{8}$ inch thick and use as required. Leave to rest in the refrigerator for 30 minutes before baking. Brush with beaten egg before baking to give the characteristic glaze.
9. Bake in the oven at 400°, unless otherwise stated.

Freeze as shortcrust pastry.

CHOUX PASTRY

This light, crisp-textured pastry is used for making sweet and savory eclairs, cream puffs, airgrettes and gougère. As long as the recipe instructions are strictly adhered to, choux pastry will always give good results. Always collect the ingredients together before starting to make choux pastry as all the flour needs to be added quickly as soon as the mixture has come to the boil. Raw choux paste is too soft and sticky to be rolled out and is, therefore, piped or spooned on to a dampened cookie sheet for baking. During baking, the moisture in the dough turns to steam and puffs up the mixture leaving the center hollow. Thorough cooking is important; if insufficiently cooked, the choux may collapse when taken from the oven and there will be uncooked pastry in the center to scoop out.
When the cooked choux has cooled and dried out, it can be filled with whipped cream or a savory filling. Choux pastry can also be deep fried—pipe or spoon it directly into hot oil.

$\frac{1}{3}$ cup All Purpose flour
$\frac{1}{2}$ stick butter or margarine
2 eggs, lightly beaten

1. Sift the flour on to a plate or piece of paper. Put the butter and $\frac{1}{2}$ cup water in a saucepan. Heat gently until the butter has melted, then bring to the boil. Remove the pan from the heat. Tip the flour at once into the hot liquid. Beat thoroughly with a wooden spoon.
2. Continue beating the mixture over the heat until smooth and forms a ball in the center of the pan (take care not to overbeat or the mixture will become fatty). Remove from the heat and leave the mixture to cool for 1–2 minutes.
3. Beat in the eggs, a little at a time, adding only just enough to give a piping consistency.
4. It is important to beat the mixture vigorously at this stage to trap in as much air as possible. A hand held electric mixer is ideal for this purpose. Continue beating until the mixture develops an obvious sheen. Use as required.

5. Bake in the oven at 400°. Immediately after the choux pastry is removed from the oven, it should be pierced to allow steam to escape.

To freeze: freeze cooked choux pastry in a rigid container. Defrost at cool room temperature. Refresh in a hot oven.

PIPING CHOUX PASTRY

1. To fill a pastry tube, usually fitted with a plain $\frac{1}{2}$ inch tip, place it in a tall jug and turn back the open end over the jug rim. Spoon the pastry mixture into the bag and squeeze it down to eliminate air bubbles.
2. When making eclairs, it may help to mark evenly spaced lines on the cookie sheet with the end of a wooden spoon as a guide for piping.
3. Hold the pastry tube in one hand and, with the thumb and one finger of your other hand on the tip to guide it, press out the pastry. When the required length is reached, cut off the paste with a wet knife. Choux puffs and profiteroles can be piped or spooned into mounds.

the refrigerator for 30 minutes before baking. Brush with beaten egg before baking.
9. Bake in the oven at 425°, for about 15 minutes on its own or longer if filled, unless otherwise stated.

Freeze as shortcrust pastry.

MILLE-FEUILLES

Roll out $\frac{1}{4}$ quantity Puff pastry or a $7\frac{1}{2}$ ounce packet frozen puff pastry, defrosted, into a rectangle measuring 10×9 inches and place on a dampened cookie sheet. Prick all over. Bake as above for 10 minutes until golden brown. Cool, then trim the edges. Cut in half lengthways and cut each half across into six slices. Spread each half with raspberry jelly then whipped cream. Sandwich together. Spread the tops with white glacé frosting, reserving 2 tablespoons. Color the reserved frosting pink, then pipe fine lines of pink glacé frosting across each pastry. Draw a cake tester through the length of the Mille-feuilles to make a 'feather' pattern. Leave to set. Serves 6.

PUFF PASTRY

The richest of all the pastries, puff requires patience, practice and very light handling. Whenever possible it should be made the day before use. It is not practical to make in a quantity with less than 4 cups flour. This quantity is equivalent to two 13 ounce packets.

4 cups strong All Purpose flour
pinch of salt
4 sticks butter or margarine, chilled
1 tablespoon lemon juice

1. Mix the flour and salt together in a bowl. Cut off $\frac{1}{2}$ stick of the butter and flatten the remaining butter with a rolling pin to a slab $\frac{3}{4}$ inch thick.
2. Cut the $\frac{1}{2}$ stick butter into small pieces, add to the flour and rub in. Using a round-bladed knife, stir in the lemon juice and about 1 cup chilled water or sufficient to make a soft, elastic dough.
3. Quickly knead the dough until smooth and shape into a round. Cut through half the depth in the shape of a cross. Open out to form a star.
4. Roll out, keeping the center four times as thick as the flaps. Place the slab of butter in the center of the dough and fold the flaps envelope-style.
5. Press gently with a rolling pin and roll out into a rectangle measuring about 16×8 inches.
6. Fold the bottom third up and the top third down, keeping the edges straight. Seal the edges.
7. Wrap the pastry in wax paper and leave to 'rest' in the refrigerator for 30 minutes. Put the pastry on a lightly floured work surface with the folded edges to the sides, then repeat the rolling, folding and resting sequence five times.
8. Shape the pastry as required, then leave to 'rest' in

ROUGH PUFF PASTRY

Similar in texture to flaky pastry, rough puff can be used instead of flaky, except when even rising and appearance are particularly important. Rough puff is quicker and easier to make than puff or flaky pastry. This quantity is equivalent to one 13 ounce packet.

2 cups All Purpose flour
pinch of salt
$\frac{3}{4}$ stick butter or margarine, chilled
6 tablespoons lard, chilled
lemon juice

1. Mix the flour and salt together in a bowl. Cut the butter and lard into $\frac{3}{4}$ inch cubes. Stir into the flour, without breaking up the pieces.
2. Add a squeeze of lemon juice and about $\frac{1}{2}$ cup chilled water or sufficient to mix to a faily stiff dough, using a rounded-bladed knife.
3. On a lightly floured work surface, roll out into an oblong three times as long as it is wide. Fold the bottom third up and the top third down, then turn the pastry so that the folded edges are at the sides. Seal the ends of the pastry with a rolling pin. Wrap the pastry in wax and 'rest' in refrigerator for 15 minutes.
4. Repeat this rolling and folding process three more times, turning the dough so that the folded edge is on the left-hand side each time. Wrap and 'rest' for 30 minutes.
5. Roll out the pastry to $\frac{1}{8}$ inch thick and use as required. Leave to 'rest' in the refrigerator for 30 minutes before baking. Brush with beaten egg before baking to give the characteristic glaze.
6. Bake in the oven at 425°, unless otherwise stated.

Freeze as shortcrust pastry.

FILO OR STRÜDEL PASTRY

MAKES 8 OUNCES PASTRY

Filo is a pastry of water-like thinness from the Middle East which is used for both savory and sweet pastries, such as Baklava. It is identical to strüdel pastry which originated in Europe and is used for the popular Apfel strüdel. Filo or strüdel pastry is fairly difficult and time-consuming to make. Unlike most pastries, it requires warm ingredients and, instead of light handling, it has to be kneaded and beaten. The dough is kneaded vigorously to enable the gluten in the flour to develop strength so the pastry can be stretched into a very thin, resilient sheet. For the same reason, strong All Purpose flour is used as it yields more gluten to help produce an elastic dough. The thin sheet is either spread with a filling and rolled or folded, or it is cut into rectangles and stacked with a filling in between. Ready-made filo or strüdel pastry is available in sheets from continental shops and delicatessens.

1 cup strong All Purpose flour
½ teaspoon salt
1 egg, lightly beaten
2 tablespoons vegetable oil
¼ teaspoon lemon juice
¼ stick butter, melted

1. Mix the flour and salt together in a large bowl. Make a well in the center and pour in the egg, oil and lemon juice. Stirring with a fork, gradually add 5 tablespoons lukewarm water or sufficient to make a soft, sticky dough.
2. Work the dough in the bowl until it leaves the sides. Turn out on to a lightly floured work surface and knead for 15 minutes. The dough should feel smooth.
3. Form it into a ball, place on a cloth and cover with a warmed bowl. Leave to 'rest' in a warm place for 30 minutes.
4. Lightly flour a clean cotton cloth. Place the ball of dough on the cloth and roll out into a rectangle about ⅛ inch thick, lifting and turning to prevent it sticking to the cloth.
5. Brush the top of the dough with little melted butter. Gently stretch the dough by carefully lifting it on the backs of the hands and fingertips, and pulling it from the center to the outside, trying to keep it in a rectangle.
6. Continue lifting and stretching the dough until it becomes paper thin and the rectangle measures no less than 30 × 20 inches. Trim off uneven thick edges with scissors or a sharp knife.

7. Leave the dough on the cloth to dry and 'rest' for about 15 minutes before lifting off carefully.
8. Bake in the oven at 375°, unless otherwise stated, until lightly browned.

Freeze as shortcrust pastry.

PEACH PIE

SERVES 6

Nectarines work equally well. Choose firm, but ripe fruit.

FOR THE PASTRY
1 cup All Purpose flour
½ cup walnuts, finely chopped
1 stick softened butter or margarine, cut into pieces
scant ½ cup superfine sugar
2 egg yolks

FOR THE FILLING
2 pounds peaches
1 egg white, for glazing
superfine sugar, for dredging

1. To make the pastry, place the flour on a work surface and sprinkle the walnuts over the top. Make a well in the center and add the butter, sugar, egg yolks and 2 tablespoons water.
2. Using the fingertips of one hand only, work the well ingredients together until evenly blended. Using a spatula, gradually draw in the flour, then knead lightly until just smooth.
3. Roll out two thirds of the pastry on a floured work surface and use to line a 9 inch loose-based fluted pie plate. Chill for 30 minutes.
4. To make the filling, quarter the peaches and ease away from the pit. Peel off the skins carefully and divide each quarter in two lengthways.
5. Arrange the peaches in the pastry case. Roll out the remaining pastry and use to cover the pie, sealing well. Make a small hole in the center to let steam escape.
6. Bake in the oven at 400° for about 20–25 minutes or until just beginning to brown.
7. Brush the top of the pie with lightly beaten egg white and dredge with sugar. Return to the oven for a further 10 minutes or until well browned and crisp. Cool for 15 minutes in the plate before removing. Serve while still slightly warm, with cream.

Not suitable for freezing.

PAPAYA PIE

SERVES 8

Choose papayas that are firm yet ripe. If too soft, they will be difficult to slice evenly.

FOR THE PASTRY

1¼ cups All Purpose flour
teaspoon cinnamon
1¼ sticks softened butter
⅓ cup superfine sugar
2 egg yolks
grated peel and juice of 1 large orange

FOR THE FILLING

2 medium ripe papayas
1 egg white, lightly beaten, for glazing
superfine sugar, for dredging
1 cup heavy or whipping cream

1. To make the pastry, sift the flour and cinnamon on to a work surface. Make a well in the center and add the butter, cut in small pieces, sugar, egg yolks and grated orange peel with 3 tablespoons juice (reserve the remaining juice).

2. Using the fingertips of one hand only, work the well ingredients together until evenly blended. Using a spatula, gradually draw in the flour, then knead lightly until just smooth. Wrap and chill for about 20 minutes.

3. Roll out two-thirds of the pastry on a floured work surface and use to line a 9½ inch loose-based fluted pie plate.

4. To make the filling, peel the papayas, halve, scoop out the pips and thinly slice the flesh. Arrange in the pastry case.

5. Roll out the remaining pastry and use to cover the pie, sealing well.

6. Bake in the oven at 350° for about 25 minutes or until just set but not browned.

7. Brush the top of the pie with egg white and dredge with sugar. Return to the oven for a further 20–25 minutes until well browned. Serve warm.

8. Lightly whip the cream. Stir in about 3 tablespoons of the remaining orange juice. Serve with the pie.

Not suitable for freezing.

Above: PAPAYA PIE.

47

PECAN PIE

SERVES 8–10

Do not overcook or it will not have the sticky qualities
essential for a good pecan pie. It works equally well
with walnuts.

7 ounces Shortcrust pastry (see page 42)

FOR THE FILLING
3 eggs
1⅓ cups dark brown soft sugar
⅔ cup maple syrup
large pinch of salt
1 teaspoon vanilla
½ stick butter, melted
scant 1 cup pecans

1. Roll out the pastry and use to line a 9 inch fluted pie
plate. Chill for 30 minutes. Bake blind in the oven at
400° for 15 minutes.
2. To make the filling, put all of the remaining ingredients, except the pecans, into a bowl and beat
together until smooth. Stir in the pecans. Pour the pecan
mixture into the pastry case.
3. Bake in the oven at 350° for 1 hour or until just set.
Serve warm or cold with cream or vanilla ice cream.

Not suitable for freezing.

PUMPKIN PIE

SERVES 4–6

Increase or decrease the spices according to your own
taste.

1 quantity Shortcrust pastry (see page 42)

FOR THE FILLING
1 pound fresh pumpkin
2 eggs
generous ½ cup superfine sugar
4 tablespoons milk
pinch of nutmeg
pinch of ginger
2 teaspoons cinnamon

1. Roll out the pastry on a floured work surface and use
to line an 8 inch deep pie plate. Trim and decorate the
edges. Chill for about 30 minutes.
2. To make the filling, cut the pumpkin into pieces,
remove any seeds and soft inside part and cut off the
outside skin.
3. Steam the pieces of pumpkin between two plates
over a pan of boiling water for 15–20 minutes until
tender. Drain thoroughly, then mash well with a fork or
purée in a blender or food processor.

4. Beat the eggs and sugar together in a bowl. Add the
pumpkin purée, the milk and spices. Blend well and pour
into the pastry case.
5. Bake in the oven at 425° for 15 minutes, then reduce
the oven temperature to 350° and bake for a further 30
minutes or until the filling is set. Serve this pie warm,
with whipped cream.

Not suitable for freezing.

ANGOSTURA PIE

SERVES 6–8

Normally associated with pink gin and hangovers,
Angostura bitters is surprisingly good when it is
sweetened and mixed with cream—as it is in this
creamy pie.

1½ quantity Pâte sucrée (see page 43)

FOR THE FILLING
1 tablespoon gelatin
2 eggs, separated
generous ¼ cup superfine sugar
1½ tablespoons Angostura bitters
1 cup heavy cream

FOR THE DECORATION
½ cup heavy cream
1 tablespoon icing sugar, sifted
14–16 pistachios, peeled

1. Roll out the pastry on a lightly floured work surface
and use to line a deep 8 inch pie plate. Trim and
decorate the edges. Prick the pastry all over with a fork.
Chill the pastry in the refrigerator for at least 30
minutes.
2. Bake blind in the oven at 425° for 20–25 minutes
until the pastry is cooked. Leave to cool.
3. To make the filling, sprinkle the gelatin over 3
tablespoons water in a small bowl and leave to soak for
2–3 minutes. Place the bowl over a pan of simmering
water and stir until dissolved. (Alternatively, microwave
on HIGH for 30 seconds or until dissolved.)
4. Whisk the egg yolks and sugar together in a bowl
until very thick, then whisk in the Angostura bitters.
5. Whip the cream until it will hold soft peaks. Whisk
the egg whites in a bowl until quite foamy, but not too
stiff.
6. Whisk the dissolved gelatin into the Angostura
mixture, then carefully fold in the cream and egg whites.
Immediately pour the mixture into the pastry case. Chill
until set.
7. To make the decoration, whip the cream with the
icing sugar until thick enough to pipe, then fill a pastry-
tube fitted with a large star tip. Pipe rosettes or stars of
cream on top of the pie, then decorate with pistachios.
Chill until ready to serve.

Not suitable for freezing.

ALL SEASONS FRUIT SALAD PIE

SERVES 6

For convenience, use a packet of dry mixed fruit, or mix your own.

---

1 quantity Rough puff pastry (see page 45)

FOR THE FILLING

1 pound dry mixed fruits, such as prunes, pears, peaches, apricots, apple rings, soaked overnight

scant ½ cup sugar

beaten egg white, for glazing

sugar, for dredging

2 tablespoons orange-flavored liqueur

½ cup heavy cream

---

1. To make the filling, drain the dry fruit, reserving 6 tablespoons of the liquid. Layer the fruit in a 4 cup pie plate with the sugar and the reserved liquid. Place a pie funnel in the center.

2. Roll out the pastry and use to cover the pie. Glaze with egg white and dredge with sugar.

3. Bake in the oven at 425° for 25 minutes. Cover with foil, reduce the oven temperature to 375° and bake for about 20 minutes.

4. Pour the liqueur, then the cream through the pie funnel to serve.

Not suitable for freezing.

OLD ENGLISH APPLE PIE

SERVES 6

A traditional apple pie flavored with brown sugar, nutmeg, cinnamon and orange peel.

1½ quantity Shortcrust pastry (see page 42)

FOR THE FILLING

1½ pounds tart apples

finely grated peel and juice of ½ lemon

scant ⅓ cup sugar

⅓ cup soft dark brown sugar

1 tablespoon All Purpose flour

pinch of nutmeg

¼ teaspoon cinnamon

finely grated peel and juice of ½ orange

⅓ cup white raisins

¼ stick butter or margarine

sugar, for dredging

---

1. Roll out two thirds of the pastry on a floured work surface and use to line a 9 inch pie plate. Chill for 30

minutes with the remaining dough, wrapped in plastic wrap.

2. Meanwhile to make the filling, peel and core the apples, then slice them thickly into a bowl of cold water to which the lemon juice has been added.

3. Mix the sugars, flour, nutmeg, cinnamon, lemon and orange peel together and sprinkle a little of this on to the pastry lining.

4. Cover the base of the pastry lining with half of the sliced apples, then sprinkle with half of the white raisins and half of the remaining sugar mixture. Repeat, using all the apples, raisins and sugar. Sprinkle the fruit with the orange juice and dot with the butter.

5. Roll out the remaining pastry and use to cover the pie, sealing the edges well. Slash the top twice to let steam escape.

6. Use the pastry trimmings to make decorations for the pie. Brush the top of the pie with water and place on the decorations. Dredge with sugar.

7. Bake in the oven at 375° for 35–40 minutes until the fruit is tender and the top is golden brown. Serve warm, with custard or cream.

To freeze: wrap and freeze at the end of step 7 and defrost at room temperature. Reheat in a hot oven if required. Alternatively, freeze the uncooked pie. Bake from frozen at 425° for about 1 hour.

FRENCH APPLE TART

SERVES 8

Because it is attributed to the apple growing region of France, this tart is sometimes called Normandy Apple Tart. This recipe, which is just one of many versions, uses two types of apples, cooked in different ways, each one contrasting with the other. If you do not have apple brandy, use ordinary brandy.

double quantity Pâte sucrée (see page 43)

FOR THE FILLING
2 pounds tart apples
scant 1 cup sugar
$\frac{1}{3}$ cup raisins
4 tablespoons apple brandy
4–5 large sweet apples
scant $\frac{1}{3}$ cup sugar
$\frac{1}{2}$ quantity Apricot glaze (see page 42)

1. To make the filling, peel, quarter, core and slice the apples. Put into a large saucepan with the sugar and 2 tablespoons water. Cover and cook gently for about 20 minutes until the apples become soft and fluffy.
2. Pour the cooked apples into a nylon strainer placed over a bowl. Leave to drain and cool. (The apple juice will not be needed.)
3. Put the raisins into a small saucepan with the apple brandy and cook gently for 2–3 minutes to soften the raisins. Leave to cool.
4. Roll out the pastry on a lightly floured work surface to a round, 1 inch larger than a 10 inch fluted pie plate. Line the plate with the pastry, pressing it well into the flutes. Trim the edges.
5. Beat the cooked apples until fairly smooth, then fold in the raisins and apple brandy. Spread the apple mixture evenly over the base of the pastry case.
6. Peel and core the apples. Cut each apple in half, then cut each half into thin slices. Arrange the apple slices in concentric circles on top of the cooked apple mixture. Sprinkle the apple slices with the sugar.
7. Bake in the oven at 425° for 30–35 minutes until the pastry is cooked and the apple slices are tender and very lightly browned.
8. Heat the apricot glaze until boiling. Immediately the flan is removed from the oven, brush the apricot glaze evenly over the apple slices. Leave the tart to cool to room temperature before serving. Serve with lightly whipped cream.

To freeze: freeze the tart before glazing. Defrost at cool room temperature, then reheat and glaze.

FRUIT AND CRÈME PÂTISSIÈRE PIE

SERVES 8–10

A delicious rich, sweet pastry enclosing a filling bursting with fruit and creamy pastry cream.

FOR THE PASTRY
$1\frac{1}{4}$ cups All Purpose flour
finely grated peel of $\frac{1}{2}$ lemon
3 tablespoons icing sugar, sifted
pinch of salt
1 egg
2 egg yolks
$1\frac{3}{4}$ sticks butter, cut into small pieces
milk, for glazing

FOR THE FILLING
1 pound mixed fruit, such as cherries, blueberries, loganberries or blackberries
2 tablespoons rum
1 cup Crème pâtissière (see page 248)
icing sugar, for dusting

1. Grease and line a $9\frac{1}{2}$ inch layer cake pan.
2. To make the pastry, mix together the flour, lemon peel, icing sugar and salt in a bowl. Make a well in the center. Beat the egg and egg yolks together and pour into the well. Add the butter. Using your fingertips, gradually work the eggs and butter into the flour.
3. Turn the pastry on to a floured work surface and knead lightly until smooth. Shape into a ball, wrap and chill for 30 minutes.
4. Take two-thirds of the dough and spread it over the base and the sides of the prepared pan. Make sure that there are no holes or the filling will leak out.
5. To make the filling, put the fruit in a single layer in the pastry case. Stir the rum into the crème patissière and spread on top of the fruit. Fold the pastry sides down over the filling. Brush the pastry with milk.
6. Roll out the remaining pastry and use to cover the pie. Seal the edges.
7. Bake in the oven at 375° for 30 minutes, then reduce the oven temperature to 325° and cook for 30–45 minutes until golden brown and shrinking away from the edges. Leave to cool in the pan. When cold, carefully turn out and dust with icing sugar.

Not suitable for freezing.

TARTE TATIN

SERVES 8

Correctly called Tarte des Demoiselles Tatin in French, this famous upside-down apple tart is named after the sisters Tatin, hoteliers in the nineteenth century who originated the recipe.

FOR THE PASTRY

1 stick butter or margarine
1½ cups All Purpose flour
1 tablespoon superfine sugar
1 egg yolk

FOR THE FILLING

¼ stick butter or margarine
scant ⅓ cup superfine sugar
1 pound crisp sweet apples

1. To make the pastry, rub the butter into the flour in a bowl until the mixture resembles fine breadcrumbs. Add the sugar. Blend the egg yolk with 1 tablespoon water and stir into the mixture. Knead the dough lightly. Chill while making the filling.

2. To make the filling, melt the butter in a saucepan and add the sugar. Heat until caramelized and golden brown. Remove from the heat and pour into an 8 inch round layer cake pan.

3. Peel, core and halve the apples. Slice into ½ inch pieces. Pack them tightly to fill the bottom of the pan, leaving no gaps.

4. Roll out the pastry on a floured work surface to a round slightly larger than the pan. Place on top of the apples and tuck in around the edges of the pan. Chill for 30 minutes. Place the pan on a cookie sheet.

5. Bake in the oven at 400° for 30–35 minutes until the pastry is golden. Turn out, apple side uppermost, on to a warmed serving dish. Serve hot, with crème frâiche or sour cream.

Not suitable for freezing.

Below: TARTE TATIN.

DEEP-DISH APPLE TART

SERVES 8

A pretty pie covered with a top of interlocking pastry leaves.

1½ quantity sweet pastry (see page 43)

FOR THE FILLING
3 pounds tart apples
3 cloves
½ stick butter
1 teaspoon mixed spice
1 cinnamon stick
scant ½ cup superfine sugar
beaten egg, for glazing
slivered almonds
brownulated sugar
icing sugar, for dusting

1. Roll out the pastry and use to line a deep 8½ inch loose-based fluted pie plate. Chill the pastry trimmings, wrapped in plastic wrap.
2. To make the filling, peel, quarter, core and thickly slice the apples. Put half of them in a medium saucepan. Add the cloves, butter, mixed spice, cinnamon and sugar. Cook, stirring, over a high heat until the apples are soft. Off the heat, remove the cloves and cinnamon stick, then add the remaining apples. Leave to cool slightly.
3. Spoon the apple mixture into the pastry case. Make pastry leaves from the trimmings. Arrange attractively interlocking over the apple filling and brush the pastry lightly with beaten egg. Sprinkle with slivered almonds and brownulated sugar.
4. Bake in the oven at 350° for about 35 minutes or until golden brown and crisp. Leave to cool for 10 minutes before removing from the plate. Serve warm dusted with icing sugar.

Not suitable for freezing.

APRICOT AND CARDAMOM TART

SERVES 6

Soaking the apricots with cardamoms and bay leaves gives them a delicious aromatic flavor.

¾ cup no-soak dry apricots
6 green cardamom pods, split
2 bay leaves
1½ quantity Pâte sucrée (see page 43)
½ cup light cream
1 egg
1 egg yolk
2 tablespoons superfine sugar
4 tablespoons apricot jelly

1. Place the apricots, cardamoms and bay leaves in a medium bowl. Completely cover with cold water and leave to soak overnight in the refrigerator.
2. Roll out the pastry on a lightly floured work surface and use to line a 13½ × 4½ inch loose-based fluted tranche pan. Chill for 10–15 minutes. Place on a flat cookie sheet.
3. Bake blind in the oven at 375° for about 20 minutes.
4. Drain the apricots, discard the bay leaves and cardamoms. Cut the apricots in half and pat dry with kitchen paper.
5. Whisk the cream, eggs and sugar together. Arrange the apricots, cut-side down, in the pastry case. Pour over the cream mixture.
6. Reduce the oven temperature to 350° and bake for 35 minutes or until just set. Brown under the broiler. Cool before removing the pan.
7. Melt the apricot jelly with 1 tablespoon water over a gentle heat in a pan. Bring to the boil. Brush evenly over the warm tart. Serve warm or cold.

Not suitable for freezing.

Above left: APRICOT AND CARDAMOM TART. Above right: GLAZED NUT TART (PAGE 56). Below: DEEP-DISH APPLE TART.

LINZERTORTE

SERVES 12–16

Linzertorte, another Austrian speciality, is really more of a jelly tart than a gâteau. However one classifies Linzertorte, it is a delicious and quickly made cake. The pastry acquires its distinctive coloring from the fact that the almonds are ground with their skins on. Linzertorte is best eaten when it has cooled to room temperature, but is still excellent cold.

FOR THE PASTRY

1 cup All Purpose flour
scant 2 cups unblanched almonds, finely ground
pinch of salt
1 teaspoon cinnamon
1 cup icing sugar, sifted
finely grated peel of 1 lemon
2 sticks sweet butter, at room temperature
2 egg yolks

FOR THE FILLING

1½ cups raspberry conserve

FOR THE GLAZE

1 small egg, beaten with 1 tablespoon milk
1 teaspoon superfine sugar
¼ cup slivered almonds, for sprinkling (optional)
icing sugar, for dusting

1. Place a square of foil on a cookie sheet, then place an 11 inch, 1¼ inch deep, tart ring in the center. Butter the ring, then bring the foil up smoothly around the side of the ring to seal the bottom edge and prevent the pastry seeping out at the beginning of baking.
2. To make the pastry, mix the flour, almonds, salt, cinnamon, icing sugar and lemon peel together in a bowl. Cut the butter into pieces and add to the mixture with the egg yolks. Work all the ingredients together until they form a smooth ball of pastry. Wrap in plastic wrap and chill for about 40 minutes until the pastry is firm.
3. Roll out just a little more than half of the pastry on a lightly floured work surface to a round 1 inch larger than the prepared tart ring. Line the ring with the pastry, pressing it smoothly around the side. Trim the pastry level with the top of the tart ring.
4. Add the pastry trimmings to the remaining pastry and roll out to an oblong about 11 × 6 inches, the same thickness as the pastry in the tart ring. Trim the edges neatly, then cut into 10 long strips, about ½ inch wide.
5. Spread the raspberry conserve evenly over the base of the pastry in the tart ring. Lay the pastry strips flat, on top of the jelly (the sides of the pastry will be above them) in a lattice pattern, cutting them to fit exactly. Loosen the sides of the pastry from the tart ring with a small spatula, then bring them down over the pastry strips to form a neat border.

6. To make the glaze, lightly whisk the egg, milk and sugar together, then brush evenly over the pastry. Sprinkle the torte with slivered almonds, if wished.
7. Bake in the oven at 400° for 10 minutes, then reduce the oven temperature to 350° and continue cooking for 35 minutes until the pastry is golden brown. Leave to cool on the cookie sheet without removing the tart ring.
8. When the pastry begins to firm, run a spatula carefully around the sides to loosen the tart ring—but do not remove the ring until the torte has cooled to room temperature. Remove the tart ring, dust the icing sugar over the torte and transfer to a doily-lined plate.

To freeze: pack carefully and freeze the cooled torte. To defrost, unwrap and defrost at room temperature.

RICH PEAR SPONGE TART

SERVES 12

Make sure you use ripe even-sized pears or the appearance of the finished tart will be spoilt.

1¼ quantity Shortcrust pastry (see page 42)

FOR THE FILLING

1¼ sticks butter or margarine
⅔ cup superfine sugar
few drops of almond flavoring
3 eggs
½ cup self raising flour
¼ cup cornstarch
1 teaspoon baking powder
1 cup ground almonds
2 tablespoons milk
3 small ripe, even-sized pears
icing sugar, for dusting

1. Grease a 9½ inch round spring-release cake pan.
2. Roll out the pastry and use to line the pan. Chill.
3. To make the filling, cream the butter and sugar together in a bowl until pale and fluffy. Beat in a few drops of almond flavoring, then add the eggs, one at a time. Fold in the flour, cornstarch, baking powder and ground almonds, then fold in the milk. Spoon the mixture into the pastry case and level the surface.
4. Peel, core and halve the pears. Make a series of parallel cuts across the width of each pear half, but do not cut right through. Arrange the pear halves, rounded sides up, on top of the filling.
5. Bake in the oven at 375° for 1¼ hours or until a tester inserted into the center comes out clean. Cool in the pan for 15 minutes, then carefully remove the sides of the pan. Serve warm or cold, dusted with icing sugar.

Not suitable for freezing.

Opposite: RICH PEAR SPONGE TART.

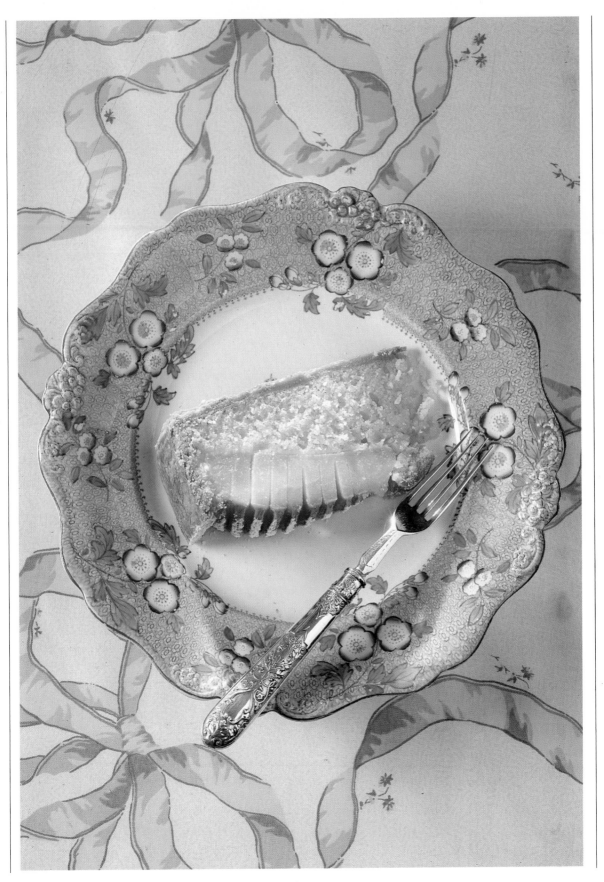

Strawberry Tarts with Spun Sugar

SERVES 8–10

This pretty tart is decorated with a nest of spun sugar; it is not difficult to make but requires plenty of time.

1½ quantity Pâte sucrée (see page 43)
½ quantity Choux pastry (see page 44)

FOR THE FILLING
1 cup blanched almonds
generous ½ cup superfine sugar
2 cups heavy cream
1 pound strawberries, hulled

FOR THE SPUN SUGAR
generous ½ cup sugar
3 tablespoons water
1½ teaspoons liquid glucose

1. Roll out the pâte sucrée on an upturned cookie sheet to an 11 inch round. Prick the pastry well with a fork. Chill.

2. Put the choux pastry into a pastry tube fitted with a ½ inch plain tip. Pipe a single ring of choux pastry round the edge of the pastry base, piping it ¼ inch in from the edge.

3. Bake in the oven at 400° for 25–30 minutes or until the choux pastry is well risen and golden brown. Remove from the oven and pierce the choux pastry in several places to allow the steam to escape. Return to the oven for 2–3 minutes to dry out completely. Leave to cool on a wire rack.

4. To make the filling, put the almonds and sugar into a small, heavy-based saucepan and heat gently until the sugar dissolves and turns a rich caramel color. Immediately pour on to an oiled cookie sheet and allow to cool and set hard. Grind the nut mixture in an electric grinder, or crush finely with a rolling pin. Whisk the cream until it just holds soft peaks, then gently fold in the praline.

5. Place the pastry case on a large flat serving plate and fill with the praline cream. Cut the strawberries in half, or slices, and arrange them neatly on top of the cream.

6. To make the spun sugar, lightly oil a rolling pin. Cover the work surface with newspaper, and also cover the floor immediately below. Cover the newspaper on the work surface with wax paper.

7. Put the sugar, water and liquid glucose into a heavy-based saucepan and heat gently until every granule of sugar dissolves, brushing down the sides of the pan with a little hot water. Boil the sugar syrup to a temperature of 320°. Immediately plunge the base of the pan into cold water to prevent further cooking.

8. Dip two forks, held together, into the syrup, then hold them up high until a fine thread starts to fall. Gently spin the sugar threads around the rolling pin until a good quantity of threads accumulate. Remove from the rolling pin and set aside. Repeat until all the syrup has been used.

9. Pile the sugar nest on top of the strawberry tarts and serve within 1 hour.

To freeze: wrap and freeze the tart case. Defrost at cool room temperature, then finish as above.

Glazed Nut Tart

SERVES 6–8

A light, crisp tart full to bursting with mixed nuts.

1 quantity Pâte sucrée (see page 43)

FOR THE FILLING
½ cup hazelnuts
¼ cup pistachios
1 egg
2 tablespoons superfine sugar
¼ stick butter, melted
grated peel and juice of 1 lemon
pinch of nutmeg
4 tablespoons corn syrup
1 tablespoon All Purpose flour
¾ cup walnut pieces
¾ cup Brazil nuts
½ cup pecans

1. Roll out the pastry and use to line an 8½ inch loose-based fluted pie plate. Chill for 15 minutes.

2. Bake blind in the oven at 400° for 10–12 minutes. Remove the beans and paper, then reduce the oven temperature to 350° and bake for a further 10 minutes until pale golden.

3. Meanwhile to make the filling, brown the hazelnuts under a hot broiler. Place in a clean cloth and rub well to remove the skins. Dip the shelled pistachios in boiling water for 1 minute. Drain and remove the skins.

4. Using an electric whisk, beat the egg and sugar together in a bowl until very thick and pale— about 5 minutes. Quickly stir in the melted butter, lemon peel, nutmeg and 2 tablespoons of the syrup. Fold in the flour and finally all the nuts.

5. Spoon the nut mixture into the pastry case. Bake in the oven at 350° for about 35 minutes or until golden brown and firm to the touch. Leave to cool for 10–15 minutes.

6. Heat the remaining syrup and 2 tablespoons lemon juice together in a pan. Boil for 2–3 minutes until syrupy. Brush over the warm flan. Leave in the dish for 10–15 minutes before removing to a wire rack to cool. Serve warm or cold.

Not suitable for freezing.

Illustrated on page 53

ENGLISH TREACLE TART

SERVES 4–6

Here is a traditional English recipe using golden syrup available in good food stores. If it is not easily obtainable you can substitute it with light molasses or corn syrup. You may wonder why a recipe for treacle tart contains golden syrup rather than treacle. The explanation is quite simple. Treacle is the syrup which is left in the sugar refining process when the sugar has been crystalized. In the seventeenth century, when West Indian sugar cane was first refined to make sugar, treacle was unrefined and recipes for treacle tart such as this one would have used black treacle rather than syrup. It was not until the late nineteenth century that treacle itself was refined to make the golden syrup. As tastes changed, recipes which had originally used treacle began to specify syrup instead.

$\frac{3}{4}$ quantity Shortcrust pastry (see page 42)

FOR THE FILLING
1 cup golden syrup, light molasses or corn syrup
$\frac{1}{4}$ cup butter or margarine
finely grated peel and juice of 1 lemon
2 cups fresh white breadcrumbs
little beaten egg or milk, for glazing

1. Roll out the pastry on a floured work surface and use to line an 8 inch loose-based pie plate. Reserve the pastry trimmings. Chill while making the filling.
2. To make the filling, warm the syrup in a heavy-based pan with the butter and lemon peel and juice.
3. Sprinkle the breadcrumbs evenly over the base of the pastry case, then slowly pour in the melted syrup.
4. Make strips from the reserved pastry trimmings and place these over the tart in a lattice pattern, brushing the ends with water to stick them to the pastry case. Brush with a little beaten egg or milk.
5. Bake in the oven at 375° for about 25–30 minutes until the filling is just set. Serve warm with whipped cream.

Not suitable for freezing.

FIG AND ALMOND TART

SERVES 4–6

Depending on the juiciness of the figs, the ground almond and Farina filling can be quite dry and crumbly, or moist: either way, it's delicious!

FOR THE PASTRY
$\frac{1}{3}$ cup All Purpose flour
$\frac{1}{2}$ cup ground almonds
3 tablespoons superfine sugar
1 stick butter or margarine, softened
1 egg yolk
1–2 drops of vanilla

FOR THE FILLING
6–8 ripe figs
2 tablespoons brandy
2 tablespoons ground almonds
2 tablespoons Farina
2 tablespoons soft brown sugar
3 tablespoons apricot jelly
1 tablespoon lemon juice

1. To make the pastry, place the flour on a work surface or pastry board and make a large well in the center. Sift the ground almonds on to the flour.
2. In the well, place the sugar, butter, egg yolk and vanilla. Using the fingertips of one hand only, pinch and work these ingredients together until evenly blended. Gradually draw in the flour and ground almonds, using a spatula, then form the mixture, with your hand, into a smooth, pliable dough. Wrap and chill well for at least 30 minutes.
3. Meanwhile to make the filling, peel the figs, slice thinly and place them in layers in a dish. Pour over the brandy and leave to soak.
4. Roll out the pastry and use to line a 7 inch fluted loose based pie plate. Prick the base.
5. Bake blind in the oven at 375° for about 10–15 minutes or until dry and beginning to color.
6. Mix the ground almonds, Farina and brown sugar together. Spoon evenly over the base of the tart. Arrange the figs on top. Return to the oven for 15–20 minutes.
7. Meanwhile, strain the jelly into a small pan. Add the lemon juice and heat until the jelly has melted. Brush over the baked tart to glaze. Leave to cool slightly before serving with light cream or Greek yogurt.

Not suitable for freezing.

LAVENDER-SCENTED TARTS

SERVES 2

Lavender sugar gives the pastry a delicious flavor and it is really simple to make. Place 2 teaspoons dry lavender blossom in a screw-top jar with 2 tablespoons superfine sugar. Shake well and leave overnight. Strain and discard the lavender.

FOR THE PASTRY
$\frac{1}{3}$ cup butter
scant 1 cup All Purpose flour
1 teaspoon lavender sugar (see above)
1 egg

FOR THE FILLING
1 tablespoon plus 2 teaspoons lavender sugar
1 egg
$\frac{1}{4}$ cup light cream
selection of seasonal fruits
$\frac{1}{8}$ cup dry vermouth
1 teaspoon gelatin

1. To make the pastry, rub the butter into the flour in a bowl until the mixture resembles breadcrumbs. Stir in the sugar and egg. Knead lightly to form a smooth dough. Wrap in plastic wrap and chill for 10 minutes.
2. Roll out the pastry thinly on a lightly floured work surface and use to line two shallow, fluted pie plates, about $3\frac{1}{2}$ inch in diameter. Chill for 20 minutes.
3. Bake blind in the oven at 400° for about 20 minutes. Reduce the oven temperature to 300°.
4. To make the filling, whisk 1 tablespoon of the sugar, the egg and cream together. Pour into the pastry cases and bake for 20 minutes or until lightly set. Leave to cool completely.
5. Arrange a selection of fruits, some whole, some sliced, over the surface of the tarts.
6. In a small bowl, stir the remaining sugar into the vermouth and $\frac{1}{4}$ cup water. Sprinkle the gelatin over the liquid and leave to soak for 2–3 minutes. Place the bowl over a saucepan of simmering water and stir until dissolved. Cool slightly, then spoon evenly over the fruits to cover. Chill until set, about 5 minutes.

To freeze: wrap and freeze the baked tart cases. Unwrap and defrost at cool room temperature.

Illustrated on pages 40–41

CARAMELIZED APPLE WAFER

SERVES 6

Do not worry if the tops of the apple slices or the pastry edges look very dark—this is how it should be.

8 ounces frozen puff pastry, defrosted
6 small green apples, total weight about 1–1½ pounds
$\frac{3}{4}$ stick butter or margarine, melted
4 tablespoons brownulated sugar

1. Cut the pastry into two equal pieces. Roll out each half very thinly on a lightly floured work surface to a rectangle measuring about $8 \times 4\frac{1}{2}$ inches. Trim the edges. Place on a cookie sheet.
2. Peel, halve and core the apples. Thinly slice the apple halves but not quite through to the base. The apples should still keep their shape.
3. Evenly space six halves flat side down on each pastry base. Cut each pastry base into three.
4. Brush the apple with the butter and sprinkle over the sugar.
5. Bake in the oven at 475° for about 20 minutes or until the pastry is risen and golden. The apples should be quite soft and caramelized. Serve immediately with sour cream, Greek yogurt or crème frâiche.

Not suitable for freezing.

Opposite: CARAMELIZED APPLE WAFER.

APFEL STRÜDEL

SERVES 6

Although an apple filling has become synonymous with strüdel, it is equally good filled with fresh cherries or pears.

1 quantity Strüdel pastry (see page 46)

FOR THE FILLING
2 pounds tart apples, peeled, cored and roughly chopped
finely grated peel and juice of 1 lemon
⅓ cup white raisins
½ cup almonds, chopped
scant ½ cup superfine sugar
1 teaspoon cinnamon
⅓ cup butter, melted
1 cup ground almonds
icing sugar, for dredging

1. Grease a cookie sheet. Leave the dough to 'rest' in a warm place for 1 hour.
2. Spread a clean cotton cloth on a large surface and sprinkle lightly with flour. Place the dough on the cloth and roll out into a rectangle about ⅛ inch thick, lifting and turning it to prevent it sticking to the cloth.
3. Gently stretch the dough, working from the center to the outside and using the backs of the hand until it is paper-thin. Trim the edges to form a rectangle measuring about 27 × 20 inches. Leave the strüdel dough on the cloth to dry and 'rest' at room temperature for about 15 minutes before filling and rolling.
4. Meanwhile to make the filling, mix the apples, lemon peel and juice, raisins, chopped almonds, sugar and cinnamon together.
5. Position the dough with one of the long sides towards you, brush with half the melted butter and sprinkle with the ground almonds. Spread the apple mixture over the dough, leaving a 2 inch border all round the edge.
6. Fold the pastry edges over the apple mixture, towards the center. Lift the corners of the cloth nearest to you over the pastry, causing the strüdel to roll up, but stop after each turn in order to pat it into shape and to keep the roll even. Form the roll into a horseshoe shape. Brush with the rest of the melted butter and slide it on to the prepared cookie sheet.
7. Bake in the oven at 375° for about 40 minutes or until golden brown. Dredge thickly with icing sugar. Serve warm or cold.

To freeze: wrap and freeze the cold strüdel. Defrost at cool room temperature. Dredge with icing sugar and serve cold.

GALATABOUREGO

SERVES 12

This Cypriot dessert is similar to the Greek Baklava, but with a creamy custard filling.

5 sheets of filo or strüdel pastry
¾ cup butter, melted

FOR THE FILLING
2 cups milk
scant ½ cup superfine sugar
¾ cup Farina
finely grated peel of 1 orange
1 stick butter
4 eggs
½ cup heavy cream

FOR THE SYRUP
1¾ cups superfine sugar
juice of 1 orange
2 tablespoons orange blossom water

1. To make the filling, put the milk, sugar and Farina in a saucepan and heat gently, stirring all the time, until the sugar dissolves. Increase the heat, bring to the boil and cook until thickened. (Alternatively, put all of the ingredients in a large bowl and microwave on HIGH for 10–12 minutes or until boiling and thickened, stirring every minute.) Leave to cool slightly.
2. Stir in the orange peel, butter, a knob at a time, the eggs and cream. Cover the surface with a piece of wax paper to prevent a skin forming and cool.
3. When the filling is cold, fold one sheet of filo pastry in half and trim to fit a roasting pan, measuring about 11 × 8 inches. Brush with a little melted butter. Repeat with two more sheets of pastry.
4. Pour the custard filling on top of the pastry. Top with one folded sheet of pastry, brush with butter, then top with the remaining folded sheet of pastry. Brush the top generously with butter and mark the pastry into 12 squares with a sharp knife.
5. Bake in the oven at 375° for 45–50 minutes or until golden brown.
6. Meanwhile to make the syrup, put the sugar, scant 1 cup water and the orange juice in a pan. Heat gently until the sugar has dissolved, then simmer for 10 minutes. (Alternatively, put the ingredients in a large bowl and microwave on HIGH for 8 minutes, stirring occasionally.) Stir in the orange blossom water.
7. Pour the hot syrup evenly over the hot Galatabourego. Cool. Chill before serving cut into squares.

Not suitable for freezing.

PAPAYA WONTONS WITH GINGER AND HONEY

SERVES 6

In Chinese cookery, wontons are usually filled with a savory mixture. Here we adapt the recipe to use a sweet filling of papaya and lime.

FOR THE PASTRY
1 cup All Purpose flour
large pinch of salt
1 egg

FOR THE FILLING
1 ripe papaya
finely grated peel of 1 lime

FOR THE DIP
5 tablespoons clear honey
juice of 2 limes
1 teaspoon finely chopped candied ginger
oil, for deep frying

1. To make the pastry, mix the flour and salt together in a bowl. Make a well in the center, then add the egg. Beat well to make a smooth dough. Knead for about 5 minutes until elastic. Cover with a damp cloth and leave to 'rest' for 30 minutes.

2. Meanwhile to make the filling, halve the papaya and scoop out the pips. Cut the flesh into twenty-four small chunks, then remove the skin. Mix with the lime peel.

3. Cut the pastry in half. Roll out one half on a lightly floured work surface until paper thin. Cut into twelve 3 inch squares. Cover with a damp cloth. Repeat with the remaining pastry.

4. Place a piece of papaya on a piece of pastry. Wet the edges of the pastry with water, then fold diagonally in half to enclose the filling. Repeat with the remaining pastry and papaya.

5. To make the dip, mix the honey with the lime juice and ginger. Transfer to a small bowl or individual bowls for dipping.

6. Heat the oil in a deep fat fryer to 375°. Fry the wontons in batches for about 4 minutes or until golden brown. Drain on kitchen paper and keep warm while frying the remainder. Serve with the ginger and honey dip.

Not suitable for freezing.

BAKLAVA

MAKES 20 SQUARES

If you have difficulty in obtaining filo pastry, you can replace it with a 13 ounce packet bought puff pastry. Cut into six equal pieces and roll out very thinly to a $9\frac{1}{2} \times 7$ inch rectangle. Layer the pastry with the walnut mixture as below, using only $\frac{1}{2}$ stick melted butter. Bake and finish as below.

1 cup walnuts, ground
$\frac{1}{4}$ cup light brown soft sugar
$\frac{1}{2}$ teaspoon cinnamon
1 pound packet filo or strüdel pastry
$1\frac{1}{4}$ sticks butter, melted
$\frac{1}{2}$ cup clear honey, warmed

1. Grease a $9\frac{1}{2} \times 7$ inch roasting pan.

2. Mix the walnuts, sugar and cinnamon together in a bowl. Halve each sheet of pastry to measure a 10 inch square.

3. Fit one sheet of pastry into the bottom of the prepared pan, allowing it to come up the sides, and brush with melted butter. Repeat with five more pastry sheets. Sprinkle with $\frac{1}{4}$ cup of the nut mixture.

4. Repeat step 3 four more times to produce five layers of walnut mixture. Top with the remaining pastry and trim the sheets to fit the pan. Mark the surface of the pastry into 20 squares with the tip of a sharp knife.

5. Bake in the oven at 425° for 15 minutes. Reduce the oven temperature to 350° and bake for a further 10–15 minutes until golden brown.

6. Meanwhile, warm the honey in a saucepan over a low heat. Spoon over the cooked Baklava and leave to cool in the pan for 1–2 hours. Cut out the marked squares.

Not suitable for freezing.

TANGERINE COOKIES WITH APRICOT SAUCE

SERVES 6

These make a convenient dinner party dessert because both the cookies and filling can be made a day or two ahead. Store the cookies in an airtight container, and apricot sauce in a covered container in the refrigerator.

FOR THE COOKIES

$\frac{3}{4}$ cup All Purpose flour
pinch of salt
2 egg whites, very lightly whisked
scant $\frac{3}{4}$ cup icing sugar, sieved
generous $\frac{1}{2}$ stick sweet butter, melted
icing sugar, for dusting

FOR THE FILLING

generous $\frac{1}{4}$ cup milk
$\frac{1}{2}$ teaspoon cornstarch
1 egg yolk
1–2 tablespoons superfine sugar
drop of vanilla
2 teaspoons brandy
2 tablespoons ground almonds
$\frac{1}{2}$ cup heavy cream, whipped
6–9 tangerines, peeled, pips removed and segmented

FOR THE APRICOT SAUCE

generous $\frac{1}{3}$ cup sugar
$1\frac{1}{3}$ cups dry apricots, soaked overnight
squeeze of lemon juice

1. Line two cookie sheets with greased wax paper.
2. To make the cookies, mix the flour, salt, egg whites and icing sugar together in a bowl. Stir in the melted butter. Spoon the mixture in 12 equal rounds, spaced a little way apart on the prepared cookie sheets.
3. Bake in the oven at 350° for about 10 minutes until a light golden color. Leave to cool on a wire rack.
4. To make the filling, heat the milk to boiling point in a pan. Blend the cornstarch with the egg yolk, then stir in the hot milk. Pour into a clean pan and cook over a low heat, stirring constantly until the sauce thickens. Remove from the heat and stir in the sugar, vanilla, brandy and ground almonds.
5. Cover the surface of the filling closely with plastic wrap and leave to cool. When cold, fold in the whipped cream.
6. To make the sauce, dissolve the sugar in about 4 tablespoons water in a pan. Add the drained apricots and lemon juice, then cover and simmer until soft.
7. Purée the sauce in a blender or food processor, or press through a strainer. Boil down further if the purée is too liquid, then leave to cool. Chill.

8. To assemble the dessert, place six of the cookies on six cold plates. Cover with the filling, then top with tangerine segments. Place the remaining cookies on top and dust with icing sugar.
9. A decorative pattern can be created in the icing sugar by placing a red hot skewer briefly on it a number of times. Brush any surplus icing sugar from the plates.
10. Spoon the apricot sauce around the cookies.

To freeze: pack the cooled cookies and sauce separately. Defrost at cool room temperature.

BAKEWELL PUDDING

SERVES 6

A buttery mixture, flavored with ground almonds and baked in a light, flaky pastry case, is the basis of this traditional British recipe, also known as Bakewell tart.

$7\frac{1}{2}$ ounce packet frozen puff pastry, defrosted, or $\frac{1}{4}$ quantity Puff or $\frac{1}{2}$ quantity Flaky pastry (see pages 45 and 44)
4 tablespoons strawberry or raspberry jelly

FOR THE FILLING

generous 1 cup ground almonds
generous $\frac{1}{2}$ cup superfine sugar
$\frac{1}{2}$ stick butter
3 eggs, beaten
$\frac{1}{4}$ teaspoon almond flavoring

1. Roll out the pastry on a floured work surface and use to line a 3 cup shallow pie plate.
2. 'Knock up' the edge of the pastry with the back of a knife and mark the rim with the prongs of a fork. Spread the jelly over the base. Chill while making the filling.
3. To make the filling, beat the almonds, sugar, butter, eggs and almond flavoring together in a bowl. Pour the filling over the jelly and spread evenly.
4. Bake in the oven at 400° for 30 minutes or until the filling is set. Serve warm or cold with cream or custard.

To freeze: wrap and freeze the cooled baked pudding. Defrost at cool room temperature. Serve cold.

Opposite: TANGERINE COOKIES WITH APRICOT SAUCE.

CITRUS CURD TARTS

SERVES 6

Pretty individual tarts filled with a three citrus curd.
Serve warm or cold.

double quantity Pâte sucrée (see page 43)

FOR THE FILLING
finely grated peel and juice of 2 limes
finely grated peel and juice of 1 lemon
finely grated peel and juice of 1 orange
3 eggs, beaten
generous 1 cup superfine sugar
¾ stick butter, diced

1. Roll out the pastry on a lightly floured work surface and use to line six 4 inch fluted tart cases. Cover and chill while making the curd filling.
2. To make the filling, put all the ingredients in the top of a double boiler or in a bowl standing over a pan of simmering water. Stir until the sugar has dissolved. Continue to cook over a low heat for about 20 minutes, stirring all the time, until the curd thickens. (Alternatively, put all of the ingredients in a large bowl and microwave on HIGH for 6–8 minutes until thickened, whisking every minute.)
3. Remove the curd from the heat and continue whisking for 3–4 minutes until the curd is very thick. Cover the surface with a piece of wax paper and leave to cool while baking the pastry cases.
4. Place the tart cases on a cookie sheet. Bake blind in the oven at 400° for 10–15 minutes until set. Remove the paper and beans, then bake for a further 5–10 minutes until pale golden brown.
5. Fill the warm pastry cases with the warm curd and serve warm. Alternatively, cool both the curd and pastry cases before filling and serve cold.

To freeze: pack and freeze the empty pastry cases. Defrost at cool room temperature, then finish as above.

PROFITEROLES

SERVES 4

If you do not wish to use a pastry tube to fill the puffs with cream, the choux puffs can be split in half, then sandwiched with the cream.

1 quantity Choux pastry (see page 44)

FOR THE CHOCOLATE SAUCE AND FILLING
4 squares semi sweet chocolate
⅛ stick butter or margarine
2 tablespoons corn syrup
2–3 drops of vanilla
½ cup heavy cream
icing sugar, for dusting

1. Put the choux pastry in a pastry tube fitted with a ½ inch plain tip. Pipe about 20 small round shapes on two damp cookie sheets.
2. Bake in the oven at 425° for about 20–25 minutes until well risen and golden brown. Reduce the oven temperature to 350°. Remove the choux puffs from the oven and make a hole in the side of each bun with a skewer or knife. Return to the oven for 5 minutes to dry out completely. Leave to cool on a wire rack.
3. For the chocolate sauce, melt the chocolate, butter, 2 tablespoons water, the syrup and vanilla in a small saucepan over a very low heat. Stir well until smooth and well blended.
4. Whip the cream until it just holds its shape. Spoon into a pastry tube, fitted with a medium plain tip and use to fill the choux puffs through the hole in the sides.
5. Dust with icing sugar and serve with the chocolate sauce spooned over or served separately.

To freeze: pack the choux puffs and chocolate sauce in separate rigid containers and freeze. Defrost at cool room temperature, then finish as above.

VARIATION

Chocolate eclairs Make the choux paste as page 44, then pipe 2½ inch long strips on damp cookie sheets. Bake as above and cool on a wire rack. Fill with cream and dip the tops in melted chocolate or frosting made with a scant 1 cup icing sugar and 2 teaspoons cocoa blended with a little hot water.

Opposite: PROFITEROLES.

CROQUEMBOUCHE

SERVES 25–30

The Croquembouche is a traditional French wedding cake, made up of lots of choux puffs piled into a pyramid. The puffs are filled with crème pâtissière and coated in caramel. It may also be decorated with spun sugar (see page 56).

treble quantity Choux pastry (see page 44)
1 quantity Pâte sucrée (see page 43)
quadruple quantity Easy crème pâtissière (see page 248) or 3 cups heavy cream, 1 cup light cream and 6 tablespoons superfine sugar
5 cups sugar
FOR THE DECORATION
crystalized rose petals
crystalized violets

1. Dampen three cookie sheets with water.

2. Put the choux pastry into a pastry tube fitted with a medium plain tip and pipe about sixty $\frac{3}{4}$ inch puffs on to the cookie sheets.

3. Bake in the oven at 400° for 20–25 minutes until well risen and golden brown. Make a small slit in the side of each puff to release the steam, then transfer to a wire rack and leave to cool for 30 minutes.

4. Roll out the pâte sucrée on a lightly floured work surface to an $8\frac{1}{2}$ inch round. Place on a cookie sheet, crimp the edge and prick all over with a fork.

5. Bake in the oven at 350° for 20 minutes until light golden brown. Cool for 30 minutes on a wire rack then transfer to a cake stand; use a highly ornamental one for a very special occasion.

6. Fill each choux puff with a little crème pâtissière. Or whip the heavy and light cream together until stiff, fold in the superfine sugar and use to fill the puffs.

7. To make the caramel, put one third of the sugar with 2 cups water into a heavy based saucepan. Heat gently to dissolve the sugar and then bring to the boil and boil to 290–310° on a sugar thermometer or until the mixture reaches the hard crack stage. Remove from the heat and place the pan on a mat so it is tilted.

8. Dip one side of the filled choux puffs into the caramel. Arrange around the edge of the pâte sucrée base, sticking the edges together.

9. Fill the center with more caramel choux puffs. When the first layer is completed, make another on top. Continue in this way, building up into a cone shape and packing the puffs loosely. Make more caramel as necessary, using a second third of the sugar and 1 cup water.

10. When the cone is completed, make up more caramel using the remaining sugar and water and drizzle over the Croquembouche. Decorate with crystalized rose petals and violets.

To freeze: pack the choux puffs in an airtight container at the end of step 3. Wrap and pack the pâte sucrée base separately. Defrost at cool room temperature, then finish as above.

PARIS-BREST

SERVES 8–10

This speciality of Paris is a large choux ring, split and filled with praline-flavored cream. It could also be filled with crème Chantilly and fresh fruits, such as strawberries and raspberries. The top is strewn with slivered almonds, giving it a very attractive appearance.

double quantity Choux pastry (see page 44)
$\frac{1}{4}$ cup slivered almonds, blanched
FOR THE FILLING
1 cup unblanched almonds
generous $\frac{1}{2}$ cup superfine sugar
8 lady fingers
3–4 tablespoons orange-flavored liqueur
2 cups heavy cream
icing sugar, for dusting

1. Line a large cookie sheet with non-stick wax paper, then draw an 8 inch circle on the paper, using a plate as a guide.

2. Put the choux pastry into a large pastry tube fitted with a large star tip. Following the drawn circle, pipe two rings of choux closely together on the cookie sheet, then pipe two more rings on the top. Scatter the slivered almonds evenly over the top.

3. Bake in the oven at 425° for 40–45 minutes until well risen and crispy. Remove the choux ring from the oven and pierce it in several places to allow the steam to escape. Return to the oven for 5–10 minutes to dry out completely. Transfer the choux ring to a wire rack and allow to cool for a few minutes.

4. Slice horizontally into two, cutting evenly around the center. Separate the two halves, then scoop out any uncooked pastry from the center. Leave to cool completely.

5. To make the filling, put the unblanched almonds and sugar into a heavy-based saucepan and heat very gently until the sugar dissolves and turns a rich caramel color—do not let it become too dark as this will make the praline bitter. Pour the nuts on to a lightly oiled cookie sheet and leave to cool. Finely crush or grind.

6. Cut the lady fingers in half and lay them in a shallow dish. Sprinkle the liqueur over them, cover and leave to stand until the fingers have absorbed the liqueur.

7. Whip the cream until it just holds its shape, then carefully fold in the praline.

8. Place the bottom half of the choux ring on a plate and fill with half the praline cream. Break up the soaked fingers with a fork, then spoon over the praline cream. Spread the remaining praline cream evenly on top of the fingers. Replace the top of the choux ring, then dust lightly with icing sugar. Chill until ready to serve.

To freeze: wrap and freeze at the end of step 4. Defrost at cool room temperature, then finish as above.

PITHIVIERS

SERVES 8

This decorative puff pastry cake is a speciality of Pithiviers, a town just south of Paris. It is filled with a rum-flavored almond cream, and the top is scored in a distinctive spiral pattern.

---

13 ounce packet puff pastry or ½ quantity Puff pastry (see page 45)

FOR THE FILLING

½ stick sweet butter

1 cup icing sugar, sieved

2 egg yolks

2 tablespoons rum

1 cup ground almonds

FOR THE GLAZE

1 egg

2 teaspoons icing sugar, sifted

---

1. Cut the pastry into two equal pieces. Roll out each piece on a lightly floured work surface to a square, a little larger than 10 inches. Cut a 10 inch round from each piece of pastry, using a large plate or saucepan top as a guide. Place one of the rounds on a cookie sheet.
2. To make the filling, beat the butter until very soft in a bowl. Beat in the icing sugar, egg yolks and rum. Mix in the ground almonds until well combined.
3. Spread the almond filling in the center of the pastry round on the cookie sheet, leaving a border of about 1 inch all round.
4. Brush the pastry border with a little cold water, then place the second pastry round on top to enclose the filling. Press the edges firmly together to seal. Chill for at least 30 minutes.
5. To make the glaze, lightly beat the egg and icing sugar together.
6. Lightly flake the edge of the pastry by tapping it gently with a small knife, then decorate the edge by fluting it all the way round with the back of a knife.
7. Brush the top of the pastry with beaten egg glaze—do not allow the glaze to run down the side of the pastry as this will prevent it rising evenly. Using a small sharp knife, mark the top of the pastry with long curved lines, scoring about halfway through the pastry, starting at the center of the pastry and ending at the edge. The lines should be about ¼ inch apart and should look like a spiral pattern when finished. Make a small hole in the center to allow the steam to escape.
8. Bake in the oven at 450° for about 20–25 minutes until well risen and golden brown. Leave to cool on the cookie sheet. Serve at room temperature.

Not suitable for freezing.

RELIGIEUSE

SERVES 12

These two-tiered choux puffs acquired their name from the fact that they look like nuns. These are filled with a coffee-flavored crème pâtissière, and iced with a coffee frosting. They may also be filled with cream and coated with chocolate frosting, if preferred.

---

double quantity Choux pastry (see page 44)

1½ quantity Crème pâtissière (see page 248) with 1 tablespoon coffee granules added to the milk when making the custard

---

½ quantity Crème Chantilly (see page 248)

FOR THE ICING

2 cups icing sugar, sieved

1 teaspoon coffee granules

---

1. Line several cookie sheets with non-stick wax paper.
2. Put the choux pastry into a pastry tube fitted with a ½ inch plain nozzle. Pipe 12 puffs, 2 inches in diameter, on to the prepared cookie sheets, spacing them well apart. Then pipe another 12 smaller puffs, about 1½ inches in diameter.
3. Bake the puffs, with the small ones placed below the larger ones, at 425° for about 35 minutes until well risen, golden brown and crisp. Remove the puffs from the oven and pierce underneath to allow the steam to escape. Return to the oven for 5 minutes to dry out completely. Transfer to a wire rack to cool.
4. Put the coffee-flavored crème pâtissière into a pastry tube fitted with a ¼ inch plain tip. Fill all the puffs with the crème pâtissière, piping it in through the hole made in the bottom. Place the puffs, spaced well apart, on a wire rack. Place the rack over a tray or large plate.
5. To make the frosting, put the icing sugar into a bowl and make a well in the center. Dissolve the coffee granules in 3 tablespoons boiling water, then add to the icing sugar and mix together to form a smooth, shiny icing that will coat the back of the spoon.
6. Spoon the frosting evenly over each choux puff, then leave until completely set before fitting together.
7. Whip the crème Chantilly until thick enough to pipe, then fill a pastry tube fitted with a large star tip. Pipe a rosette on top of each large choux puff, then carefully place the smaller puffs on top of the cream, pressing gently into the cream to secure.

To freeze: pack and freeze the cooled puffs. Defrost at cool room temperature, then finish as above.

PISTACHIO AND HAZELNUT GALETTE

SERVES 12

This simple cake is made with two rounds of pistachio and hazelnut pastry, filled with an orange liqueur-flavored cream, mangoes and mandarin segments.

FOR THE PASTRY
1¾ cups All Purpose flour
pinch of salt
½ cup icing sugar
¾ cup pistachios peeled and ground fairly finely
½ cup hazelnuts, peeled, roasted, and ground fairly finely
1¾ sticks sweet butter, cut into pieces

FOR THE FILLING
2 cups heavy cream
finely grated peel of 1 orange
2 tablespoons orange-flavored liqueur
1 tablespoon icing sugar, sieved
1 large ripe mango
15 ounce can mandarin segments
icing sugar, for sifting
chopped pistachios, for sprinkling

1. To make the pastry, sift the flour, salt and icing sugar into a bowl, add the nuts and mix well together. Rub the butter into the flour and nut mixture, working the ingredients together gently until they form a ball.
2. Cut the pastry into two equal pieces. Roll out each piece on a lightly floured surface to a round a little smaller than 10 inches.
3. Place each pastry round in a 10 inch fluted pie plate, then press the pastry gently over the base of the plates until it fits exactly. Smooth the pastry with the back of a spoon, but do not stretch it. Prick with a fork.
4. Bake blind in the oven at 350° for 30–35 minutes until the pastry is cooked and very lightly browned (if you have only one pie plate, bake the pastry rounds one at a time, keeping the one not being baked refrigerated until needed.)
5. Remove the cooked pastry rounds from the oven and immediately cut one of the rounds into 12 triangle-shaped pieces. Leave to cool slightly, then transfer to wire racks to cool completely.
6. To make the filling, whip the cream with the orange peel, liqueur and icing sugar until it will hold soft peaks.
7. Peel the mango, then cut the flesh from the pit in long thin slices. Drain the mandarin segments well, putting about 12 of the best ones aside for decoration.
8. Carefully place the whole pastry round on a large plate. Spread a generous layer of cream over the pastry, then arrange the mango slices and mandarin segments evenly over the cream.
9. Whip the remaining cream until thick enough to pipe and fill a pastry tube fitted with a large star tip. Pipe 12 large rosettes on top of the fruits, about 1 inch in from the edge.

10. Arrange the triangle-shaped pieces of pastry on top of the galette, placing them at an angle, each one supported by a rosette of cream. Sieve the icing sugar lightly over the galette. Decorate the galette with the remaining cream and reserved mandarin orange segments, then sprinkle over the nuts.

To freeze: wrap and freeze the unfilled pastry. Defrost at cool room temperature, then finish as above.

CENCI

MAKES 50

The Italians eat Cenci at any time of day, whenever they feel like a snack or something sweet to nibble. However, they make a delicious dessert served warm with Fruit purée sauce using raspberries (see page 244) or stewed fruit.

2¾ cups All Purpose flour
2 eggs, beaten
3 tablespoons rum
4 tablespoons superfine sugar
1 teaspoon baking powder
pinch of salt
oil, for deep frying
icing or superfine sugar, for sprinkling

1. Sieve 2¼ cups of the flour into a bowl. Make a well in the center and add the eggs, rum, sugar, baking powder and salt. Mix the ingredients well together with a fork until they form a dough.
2. Sprinkle a work surface with some of the remaining flour. Turn out the dough on to the floured surface and gather into a ball with your fingers. Knead until smooth. Cut the dough into quarters. Roll out one quarter of the dough until almost paper thin, adding more flour to the work surface as necessary.
3. Cut into strips about 6 inches long and 1 inch wide. Tie the strips into loose knots. Repeat rolling, cutting and tying with the remaining three quarters of dough.
4. Heat the oil in a deep-fat fryer to 375°. Fry four or five pastry twists for 1–2 minutes until golden. Drain on kitchen paper while frying the remainder. Sift icing sugar over the twists while hot. Serve warm or cold.

To freeze: pack the cooled Cenci in a rigid container. Defrost at cool room temperature. Dust with icing sugar.

Illustrated on page 149

Opposite: PISTACHIO AND HAZELNUT GALETTE.

APPLE AND HAZELNUT LAYER

SERVES 8

¾ *cup hazelnuts, shelled*
¾ *stick butter*
3 tablespoons superfine sugar
generous 1 cup All Purpose flour
pinch of salt
1 pound apples, peeled, cored and sliced
1 tablespoon apricot jelly or marmalade
grated peel of 1 lemon
1 tablespoon candied fruit, chopped
2 tablespoons raisins
2 tablespoons white raisins
icing sugar, whipped cream and hazelnuts, to decorate

1. Cut out two 8 inch circles of wax paper. Grease two cookie sheets.

2. Reserve 8 nuts and finely chop the remainder. Cream the butter and sugar until pale and fluffy. Stir in the flour, salt and chopped nuts, then form into a ball and chill for 30 minutes.

3. Put the apple in a saucepan with the jelly and lemon peel and cook over a low heat for 5 minutes, until soft. Add the candied fruit and dry fruit and simmer for 5 minutes.

4. Divide the pastry in half, place on the sheets of wax paper and roll out into two circles. Transfer to the prepared cookie sheets.

5. Bake in the oven at 375° for 7–10 minutes, until light brown. Cut one circle into 8 triangles while warm. Leave to cool.

6. Just before serving, place the complete circle on a serving plate and cover with the apple mixture. Arrange the triangles on top. Dust with icing sugar, pipe cream on top and decorate the apple layer with hazelnuts.

To freeze: pack and freeze the pastry rounds and the filling separately. Defrost at cool room temperature, then finish as above.

GÂTEAU SAINT-HONORÉ

SERVES 12

This gâteau is named after Saint-Honoré, who was a Bishop of Amiens and is considered the patron saint of bakers. It is a wonderful gâteau, that combines two types of pastry, pâte sucrée and choux, to form a case that may be filled with an endless variety of fillings. This recipe uses the traditional crème Saint-Honoré, topped with a chocolate-flavored cream.

1½ quantity Pâte sucrée (see page 43)
double quantity Choux pastry (see page 44)

FOR THE CRÈME SAINT-HONORÉ
double quantity Crème pâtissière (see page 248)
1 tablespoon gelatin
2 tablespoons orange-flavored liqueur

FOR THE CARAMEL
generous 1 cup sugar

FOR THE TOPPING
3 squares semi sweet chocolate, broken into small pieces
1 cup heavy cream
chopped pistachios for sprinkling

1. Line a large cookie sheet with non-stick wax paper.

2. Roll out the pâte sucrée on a flat, or upturned, cookie sheet to a round a little larger than 11 inches in diameter. Using a pie plate or saucepan top as a guide, cut the pastry into an 11 inch round. Remove the trimmings, then prick the pastry all over with a fork. Chill for 30 minutes.

3. Put the choux pastry into a pastry tube fitted with a ½ inch plain tip. Pipe a single ring of choux pastry around the edge of the pâte sucrée, about ¼ inch in from the edge.

4. Bake in the oven at 400° for 25–30 minutes until the choux pastry is well risen, golden brown and crisp. Remove from the oven and pierce the choux ring at intervals to allow the steam to escape. Return to the oven for 2–3 minutes to dry out completely. Transfer to a wire rack to cool.

5. Pipe the remaining choux in whirls, about 1½ inches in diameter, on the prepared cookie sheet, spacing them well apart (only 14–15 puffs are needed for the gâteau but it is best to make extra buns because all those used have to be perfect).

6. Bake in the oven at 425° for 25–30 minutes until well risen, golden brown and crisp. Remove from the oven and pierce each puff underneath to allow the steam to escape. Return to the oven for about 5 minutes to dry out completely. Transfer to a wire rack to cool.

7. To make the crème Saint-Honoré, prepare the crème pâtissière to the stage where the custard is cooled, ready for adding the egg whites and cream.

8. Sprinkle the gelatin over 3 tablespoons water in a small bowl and leave to soak for 2–3 minutes. Place the bowl over a saucepan of simmering water and stir until

dissolved. (Alternatively, microwave on HIGH for 30 seconds or until dissolved.)

9. Whisk the egg whites until stiff, then fold into the cooled custard. Whip the cream, adding the liqueur, until it just holds its shape, then quickly whisk in the dissolved gelatin. Fold the cream into the custard. Keep at room temperature while completing the gâteau.

10. Spoon some of the crème Saint-Honoré into a pastry tube fitted with a ¼ inch plain tip, and fill 14–15 of the best choux puffs, piping it in through the hole made in the bottom. Scrape any cream from the base of the puffs with a small spatula. Put the puffs aside while making the caramel.

11. To make the caramel, put the sugar into a saucepan with ⅓ cup water. Heat gently until the sugar has dissolved, brushing down the sides of the pan with the hot water from time to time. Bring the syrup to the boil and boil until it turns a golden caramel color. Immediately, plunge the base of the pan into cold water to prevent the caramel darkening further. Place the pan in a large bowl and fill the bowl to halfway up the side of the pan with boiling water—this will keep the caramel fluid.

12. Place the pâte sucrée base on a plate. Take one of the choux puffs and dip the base in the caramel, then place it on the choux ring, holding it in position for a few seconds to secure. Continue with the remaining puffs, placing them close together. Spoon the remaining caramel over each puff to coat evenly. Spoon the remaining crème Saint-Honoré into the choux case. Chill while making the topping.

13. For the topping, put the chocolate into a small bowl with 3 tablespoons water. Stand the bowl over a pan of simmering water then heat until the chocolate melts, stirring frequently until smooth. Remove from the heat and leave to cool. Whip the cream until thick but not buttery, then carefully fold in the cooled chocolate.

14. Put the chocolate cream into a pastry tube fitted with a medium star tip and pipe the cream decoratively over the top of the crème Saint-Honoré. Sprinkle with pistachios and serve. If not serving immediately, keep in a cool place—the gâteau will stand quite well for 1–2 hours.

To freeze: pack and freeze the choux puffs and the base separately. Defrost at cool room temperature, then finish as above.

Opposite: GÂTEAU SAINT-HONORÉ.

STRAWBERRY SHORTCAKES

SERVES 6

Any other soft fruits such as raspberries, loganberries, blackberries, bilberries or redcurrants can be used as an alternative filling for these delicious shortcakes. Peeled and roughly chopped peaches and nectarines would also be delicious. The tart flavor of berries or currants can be counteracted by adding a little more sugar.

FOR THE SHORTCAKE

2½ cups self raising flour
1½ teaspoons baking powder
good pinch of salt
¾ stick butter, cut into pieces
scant ⅓ cup superfine sugar
1 egg, beaten
few drops of vanilla
5–6 tablespoons milk

FOR THE FILLING

1 pound strawberries, 6 set aside, the remainder hulled
2 tablespoons orange-flavored liqueur
2 tablespoons icing sugar
1 cup heavy or whipping cream
3 tablespoons redcurrant jelly

1. Grease and flour a cookie sheet.
2. To make the shortcake, sift the flour, baking powder and salt into a bowl. Rub in the butter until the mixture resembles breadcrumbs. Stir in the sugar.
3. Make a well in the center of the dry ingredients and add the egg, vanilla and milk. Using a spatula, cut through the dry ingredients until evenly blended, then quickly and lightly bring the mixture together using the fingertips of one hand.
4. Gently knead the dough on a lightly floured work surface until just smooth. Roll out to a thickness of ½ inch and cut out six 3½ inch fluted rounds.
5. Gather up the scraps, knead lightly and roll out again. Place the rounds on the prepared cookie sheet. Brush the tops of the rounds with milk—do not let it trickle down the sides.
6. Bake in the oven at 450° for about 11 minutes or until the shortcakes are well risen and golden brown. Remove from the oven and keep warm.
7. To make the filling, thickly slice half the strawberries. Put into a bowl and add the liqueur. Sieve in 1 tablespoon of the icing sugar.
8. With a fork, lightly crush the remaining strawberries and sift in the rest of the icing sugar. Whip the cream until it just holds its shape and stir in the crushed strawberries.
9. Cut the shortcakes in half while still warm. Carefully

run the point of a sharp knife from the side of the shortcake into the center. Rotate the shortcake and saw with the sharp knife until the cake is cut in two.
10. Spoon half the cream on to the shortcake bases and cover with the sliced strawberries. Spoon over the remaining cream and replace the shortcake tops.
11. Put the redcurrant jelly into a small pan and heat gently until liquid. (Alternatively, place in a small bowl and microwave on HIGH for 1–2 minutes.) Leave to cool for 5–10 minutes, then brush over the shortcakes. Decorate with whole strawberries.

To freeze: wrap and freeze the cooled shortbread at the end of step 6. Defrost at cool room temperature. Warm in a hot oven for 5 minutes, then finish as above.

ROLY-POLY WITH HOT JELLY SAUCE

SERVES 4

If you prefer a baked roly-poly, wrap in foil and bake at 400° for 45 minutes. (1 hour if cooking from frozen.)

¾ quantity Suetcrust pastry (see page 44)
6 tablespoons red jelly
little milk, for brushing

FOR THE SAUCE

3 tablespoons red jelly
finely grated peel of 1 orange
2 teaspoons arrowroot
½ cup fresh orange juice

1. Roll out the pastry on a floured work surface to a 10 × 8 inch oblong. Spread the 6 tablespoons jelly over the pastry to ¼ inch of the edges. Brush the edges with milk.
2. Roll up the pastry evenly like a jelly roll, starting from one short side.
3. Place the roll, seam side down, on a sheet of greased foil measuring at least 12 × 9 inches. Wrap the foil loosely around the roll to allow room for expansion during cooking. Seal well.
4. Place the roly-poly in the top of a steamer over a pan of boiling water and steam for 1½–2 hours, topping up the water as necessary.
5. Just before serving, make the sauce. Put the jelly and orange peel in a heavy-based saucepan. Mix the arrowroot to a paste with a little of the orange juice, then stir the remaining orange juice into the pan. Heat gently until the jelly has melted, then stir in the arrowroot paste and bring to the boil. Simmer until thickened, stirring constantly.
6. Unwrap the roly-poly and place on a warmed serving plate. Pour over the hot jelly sauce and serve immediately.

To freeze: wrap the roly-poly at the end of step 3. Steam from frozen, allowing an extra 30 minutes.

Opposite: ROLY-POLY WITH HOT JELLY SAUCE.

Sussex Pond Pudding

SERVES 6

An old-fashioned recipe from the south of England, Sussex pond pudding takes its name from the fact that during cooking the whole lemon inside bursts, and the resulting juice combines with the other ingredients of butter and sugar to produce a delicious pool or 'pond' of lemon sauce. Be sure to prick the fruit thoroughly all over with a skewer before placing it inside the suet-crust pastry case, otherwise the lemon will remain whole and spoil the finished effect.

1½ quantity Suetcrust pastry (see page 44)
½ stick butter, cut into pieces
⅔ cup brownulated sugar
1 large lemon

1. Roll out two-thirds of the pastry on a floured work surface to a circle, 1 inch larger all round than the top of a 5 cup ceramic bowl. Use to line the bowl.
2. Put half of the butter into the center with half of the sugar. Prick the lemon all over with a skewer. Put the whole lemon on top of the butter and sugar. Add the remaining butter and sugar.
3. Roll out the remaining pastry and use to cover the pudding. Dampen the edges and seal the top. Cover with wax and foil. Secure with string.
4. Place over a pan of boiling water and steam for about 4 hours, topping up the water as necessary.
5. Remove the foil and paper and turn out on to a warmed serving dish. During cooking the lemon inside the pudding bursts and produces a delicious lemon sauce. Each serving should have a piece of the lemon, which will be much softened by the cooking.

Not suitable for freezing.

Pear and Apple Dumplings

SERVES 4

Delicious, lightly cooked pears or apples, filled with apple brandy-soaked fruit and encased in crisp pastry. If preferred, the dumplings can be filled with a more everyday mixture of cinnamon, sugar and butter.

1 quantity Suetcrust pastry (see page 44) or 1 quantity Rough puff pastry (see page 45) or a 13 ounce packet, defrosted
beaten egg, for glazing
FOR THE FILLING
⅓ cup white raisins
2 tablespoons apple brandy
4 ripe, firm pears or sweet apples

1. For the filling, put the raisins and apple brandy in a small bowl and leave to soak for 30 minutes.
2. Peel the fruit, leaving the stalks on the pears. Remove the cores from the bottom and fill with the soaked raisins. Reserve any remaining apple brandy.
3. Divide the pastry into four. Roll out each piece on a lightly floured work surface to a 7 inch square if making pear dumplings or a 6 inch square if making apple dumplings. Cut each square into a large cross. Cut leaves from the pastry trimmings.
4. Brush the fruit with any remaining apple brandy, then place a fruit on the center of each pastry cross. Bring the edges of the pastry together to completely enclose the fruit.
5. Brush the edges with beaten egg and seal together. Brush the pastry leaves with beaten egg and stick on to the dumplings to decorate. Transfer the dumplings to a cookie sheet, then brush with beaten egg to glaze.
6. Bake in the oven at 400° for 25 minutes until golden brown. Serve warm with whipped cream flavored with a little apple brandy and icing sugar.

Not suitable for freezing.

Pear and Ginger Roll

SERVES 6

1 quantity Suetcrust pastry (see page 44)
FOR THE FILLING
1 pound firm, but ripe pears, peeled, cored and sliced
⅓ cup white raisins
½ teaspoon ginger
⅓ cup brownulated sugar
icing sugar, for dusting

1. Roll out the pastry on a lightly floured work surface to an 11 × 9 inch rectangle.
2. Mix the pears with the raisins, ginger and sugar.
3. Spread evenly over the pastry to within ½ inch of the edges. Turn in the edges to contain the filling and brush them lightly with water. Roll up the pastry from the longest side, like a jelly roll.
4. Place the roll, seam side down, on a large sheet of greased foil Wrap the foil loosely around the roll to allow room for expansion during cooking. Seal well.
5. Place the roll in the top of a steamer over a pan of boiling water and steam for about 1½ hours, topping up the water as necessary.
6. Lift the roll carefully from the saucepan. Allow it to stand for a minute or two, then unwrap and place on a hot serving dish. Dredge with sugar and serve with Walnut Rum Sauce (see page 247).

Not suitable for freezing.

Opposite: PEAR AND APPLE DUMPLINGS.

COMPLETE BOOK OF DESSERTS

74

CHOCOLATE CREATIONS

Wonderfully wicked, sinfully rich, these chocolate
desserts take your eye and tempt your palate. Such very
special melt-in-the-mouth concoctions are pure
pleasure—resist them if you can.

Passionate chocolate lovers know that there is nothing quite like the rich, dark, smooth sensation of chocolate. It is rarely out of favor or fashion; it is still the most luxurious and versatile of ingredients when you want to produce a sensational dessert. The following recipes will take you from a simple but delicious Chocolate lime mousse to the most wonderful Squidgy chocolate mousse cake.

A variety of chocolate has been used in the recipes: semi sweet, milk, white and cocoa. As each one has different cooking properties, it is not really advisable to substitute one for another, unless stated.

Melting Chocolate

Many of the recipes require melted chocolate and it is important to do this gently. Stand the bowl containing the chocolate over a saucepan of just simmering water and stir until the chocolate becomes smooth and creamy. Extra care should be taken when melting white chocolate because it has a tendency to separate on heating. Stir it all the time to ensure that one area does not get particularly hot. Alternatively, melt plain or white chocolate in the microwave on LOW, stirring frequently.

If chocolate is overheated, it will become very granular and can easily scorch. Overheated chocolate can sometimes be rectified by adding a small knob of blended white vegetable fat.

Decorating with Chocolate

Chocolate flavor cake covering is useful for scrolls and curls because it is more pliable, but the flavor is not so good. Grated chocolate makes a useful last minute decoration.

Handle chocolate decorations as little as possible since body heat will melt them and leave fingerprints on the surface.

Chocolate caraque   Melt at least 4 squares chocolate in a bowl over a pan of simmering water. Pour it in a thin layer on to a marble slab or cold cookie sheet and leave to set until it no longer sticks to your hand when you touch it. Holding a large knife with both hands, push the blade across the surface of the chocolate to roll pieces off in long curls. Adjust the angle of the blade to get the best curls.

Chocolate shapes   Make a sheet of chocolate as above and cut into neat triangles, squares or shapes with a sharp knife, or stamp out circles with a small round cutter.

Leaves   Using a small paintbrush, thinly spread melted chocolate on the undersides of clean, dry, undamaged rose leaves. Leave to set. Gently peel off leaves.

Chocolate curls   Using a potato peeler, pare thin curls from the edge of a thick block of chocolate.

Lacy chocolate shapes   Drizzle melted chocolate in irregular shapes on to a sheet of foil. Chill until set. Peel off carefully to use.

Chocolate caraque, shapes, leaves and curls can be stored in an airtight container in the refrigerator or frozen.

CHOCOLATE FUDGE CAKE

SERVES 12–14

This gooey, triple-layered chocolate cake is best cut with a large, sharp, wetted knife.

FOR THE CAKE
2½ cups All Purpose flour
3 tablespoons cocoa
1¼ teaspoons baking powder
½ teaspoon soda
large pinch of salt
4 squares semi sweet chocolate
1¼ sticks butter
1½ cups light brown soft sugar
2 eggs, beaten
½ cup plain yogurt
½ teaspoon vanilla

FOR THE FUDGE FROSTING
3½ cups icing sugar
1 cup cocoa
1 stick butter
6 tablespoons milk

1. Grease three 7 inch layer cake pans, line the bases with wax paper and grease the paper.
2. To make the cake, sift the flour, cocoa, baking powder, soda and salt together.
3. Break the chocolate into small pieces. Place in a heatproof bowl over a pan of simmering water and heat gently until the chocolate melts. (Alternatively, microwave on LOW for 4–5 minutes or until melted, stirring occasionally.) Leave to cool for 30 minutes.
4. Cream the butter and brown sugar together in a bowl until light and fluffy. Beat in the eggs, then fold in the chocolate, the sifted ingredients, yogurt and vanilla. Turn the mixture into the prepared pans and level the surface.
5. Bake in the oven at 375° for 25–30 minutes until risen and firm to the touch. Turn out on to a wire rack and leave to cool.
6. To make the fudge frosting, sieve the icing sugar and cocoa together. Put into a heavy-based saucepan with the butter and milk. Heat gently until the butter has melted, then beat until smooth. Remove from the heat.
7. Use some of the fudge frosting to sandwich the three cakes together. Cover the sides and top of the cake with the remaining frosting.

To freeze: open freeze until firm, then place in a rigid container or wrap in foil.

Previous Page: DARK CHOCOLATE TRUFFLE CAKE (PAGE 87).
Opposite: CHOCOLATE ROULADE.

CHOCOLATE ROULADE

SERVES 8–10

Do not worry if the roulade cracks as you roll it, the cracks are part of its charm.

FOR THE ROULADE

4 squares semi sweet chocolate
4 eggs, separated
generous ½ cup superfine sugar

FOR THE FILLING

½ cup heavy cream
1 tablespoon icing sugar
½ cup Greek yogurt
few drops of rose water (optional)
2 cups raspberries

FOR THE DECORATION

icing sugar, for dusting
½ cup heavy cream
½ cup raspberries, hulled
few small rose, geranium or mint leaves

1. Grease a 9 × 13 inch jelly roll pan, line with wax paper and grease the paper.
2. To make the roulade, break the chocolate into small pieces. Place in a heatproof bowl standing over a pan of simmering water and heat gently until the chocolate melts. (Alternatively, microwave on LOW for 4–5 minutes or until melted, stirring occasionally.)
3. Whisk the egg yolks and sugar together in a bowl until very thick and pale in color. Beat in the chocolate. Whisk the egg whites until stiff, then fold carefully into the chocolate mixture. Pour the mixture into the prepared pan and spread out evenly.
4. Bake in the oven at 350° for 20–25 minutes until well risen and firm to the touch.
5. While the roulade is cooking, lay a piece of wax paper on a flat work surface and sprinkle generously with superfine sugar. When the roulade is cooked, turn it out on to the paper. Carefully peel off the lining paper. Cover the roulade with a warm, damp cloth and leave to cool.
6. To make the filling, whip the cream with the icing sugar until it forms soft peaks. Fold in the yogurt with a few drops of rose water. Spread the cream over the roulade. Sprinkle with the raspberries. Starting from one of the narrow ends, carefully roll it up, using the paper to help. Transfer the roulade to a serving plate and dust generously with icing sugar.
7. To make the decoration, whip the remaining cream until it forms soft peaks and spoon into a pastry tube fitted with a star tip. Pipe the cream down the center of the roulade and the sides. Decorate with raspberries and rose, geranium or mint leaves.

To freeze: roll the cooled roulade with the paper inside it, then overwrap. Defrost at cool room temperature, then finish as above.

DEVIL'S FOOD CAKE

SERVES 16–18

This authentic version makes a cake of huge
proportions in true American style!

FOR THE CAKES

3½ cups All Purpose flour
1 tablespoon soda
pinch of salt
1 cup cocoa
1 cup plus 3 tablespoons milk
2 teaspoons vanilla
1¼ sticks butter or margarine
2¾ cups dark brown soft sugar
4 eggs

FOR THE FROSTING AND DECORATION

3 cups superfine sugar
3 egg whites
2 squares semi sweet chocolate (optional)

1. Grease three 8½ inch layer cake pans and line the bases with wax paper.
2. To make the cakes, sift the flour, soda and salt together. Mix the cocoa, milk and vanilla together until smooth.
3. Using an electric hand-held mixer, cream the butter in a bowl until pale and fluffy, then gradually beat in the sugar. Add the eggs, one at a time, beating very thoroughly after each addition. Beat in the flour and cocoa mixtures alternately. Divide the mixture between the prepared pans.
4. Bake in the oven at 350° for about 35 minutes until firm to the touch. Turn out on to a wire rack and cool.
5. To make the frosting, put the sugar and ½ cup plus 2 tablespoons water in a heavy-based saucepan and heat gently until the sugar has dissolved. When completely dissolved, boil rapidly to 240°—use a sugar thermometer to check the temperature.
6. Meanwhile, whisk the egg whites until stiff in a large deep bowl. Allow the bubbles to settle, then slowly pour the hot syrup on to the egg whites, whisking constantly. When all the sugar syrup is added, continue whisking until the mixture stands in peaks and just starts to become matt around the edges. The frosting sets quickly, so work rapidly.
7. Sandwich the three cakes together with a little of the frosting. Spread the remaining frosting over the top and sides of the cake with a spatula. Pull the frosting up into peaks all over. Leave the cake on a wire rack for 30 minutes to allow the frosting to set slightly.
8. Break the chocolate into small pieces. Place in a heatproof bowl standing over a pan of simmering water and heat gently until the chocolate melts. (Alternatively, microwave on LOW for 2–3 minutes or until melted, stirring occasionally.) Spoon the chocolate

into a wax paper pastry tube and drizzle over the top of the cake. Leave to set completely.

To freeze: wrap and freeze at the end of step 4. Defrost, then finish as before.

CINNAMON CHOCOLATE TORTE

SERVES 6–8

Most supermarkets and delicatessens sell French, Swiss or Belgian chocolate that is suitable for baking—they are not oversweet and have excellent melting properties. For this cake, do not use the chocolate or chips labeled 'cooking chocolate'—their flavor could ruin the finished cake.

FOR THE CAKE

6 squares semi sweet chocolate
1½ sticks butter
1 cup superfine sugar
5 eggs, separated
1 cup All Purpose flour
3 teaspoons cinnamon
1 cup ground almonds

FOR THE FILLING

6 tablespoons apricot jelly
2 tablespoons lemon juice
1 cup whipping cream, whipped
icing sugar, for dusting

1. Grease and line two 7½ inch layer cake pans.
2. To make the cake, first break the chocolate into small pieces. Place in a heatproof bowl with 3 tablespoons water. Stand the bowl over a pan of simmering water and heat gently until the chocolate melts. (Alternatively, microwave on LOW for 6 minutes or until melted, stirring occasionally.) Leave to cool.
3. Cream the butter and sugar together in a bowl until light. Beat in the egg yolks. Add the cooled chocolate, mixing well.
4. Whisk the egg whites. Sift the flour with 2 teaspoons of the cinnamon and fold into the creamed mixture with the ground almonds and egg whites. Spoon the mixture into the prepared pans.
5. Bake in the oven at 375° for 35–40 minutes or until a tester inserted into the center comes out clean. Turn out the cake on to a wire rack and leave to cool for about 2 hours. Cut each cake into two layers.
6. To make the filling, put the apricot jelly in a small pan with the lemon juice and remaining cinnamon, then heat gently. Cool and spread on the cakes. Layer up with cream and dust the top with icing sugar just before serving.

To freeze: wrap and freeze at the end of step 5. Defrost, unwrapped, at cool room temperature.

SQUIDGY CHOCOLATE MOUSSE CAKE

SERVES 8

This delicious combination of rich chocolate sponge and soft, squidgy chocolate mousse topping is perfect for a dinner party dessert.

1 pound semi sweet chocolate
3 tablespoons orange-flavored liqueur
9 eggs, 5 of them separated
$\frac{3}{4}$ cup superfine sugar
1 stick sweet butter, softened

FOR THE DECORATION
blanched julienne strips of orange peel
grated chocolate

1. Grease an 8 inch spring-release cake pan, line with wax paper and grease the paper.
2. Break 8 squares of the chocolate into small pieces. Place in a heatproof bowl standing over a pan of simmering water and heat gently until the chocolate melts. (Alternatively, microwave on LOW for 4–5 minutes or until melted, stirring occasionally.) Stir in 1 tablespoon of the liqueur, then remove from the heat.
3. Using an electric mixer, whisk 5 egg yolks and the sugar together in a bowl until thick and creamy. Beat in the butter, a little at a time, until smooth. Beat in the melted chocolate until smooth.
4. Whisk the 5 egg whites until stiff, then fold into the chocolate mixture. Turn into the prepared pan.
5. Bake in the oven at 350° for 40 minutes until risen and firm. Leave the cake to cool in the pan for 1 hour.
6. To make the top layer, melt the remaining chocolate as before, then stir in the remaining liqueur. Remove from the heat and cool for 1–2 minutes. Separate the remaining eggs and beat the egg yolks into the chocolate mixture. Whisk the egg whites until stiff, then fold into the chocolate mixture.
7. Press the crust down on the baked cake with your fingers and pour the top layer over it. Chill overnight.
8. The next day, remove the cake carefully from the pan and put on to a serving plate. Arrange strips of orange peel around the outside edge and decorate with grated chocolate.

To freeze: wrap and freeze at the end of step 7. Defrost overnight at cool room temperature, then finish as above.

CHOCOLATE COFFEE REFRIGERATOR SLICE

SERVES 6

This luxurious chilled entertaining dessert requires no cooking.

2 tablespoons instant coffee granules
3 tablespoons brandy
4 squares semi sweet chocolate
scant $\frac{1}{2}$ cup icing sugar
1 stick sweet butter, softened
2 egg yolks
1 cup whipping cream
$\frac{1}{2}$ cup chopped almonds, roasted
about 30 lady fingers
coffee beans, to decorate

1. Grease an $8\frac{1}{2} \times 4\frac{1}{2}$ inch top measurement loaf pan and line the base with wax paper. Grease the paper.
2. Make up the coffee granules with 1 cup boiling water and stir in the brandy. Set aside to cool for 15 minutes.
3. Break the chocolate into small pieces. Place in a heatproof bowl with 1 tablespoon water. Stand the bowl over a pan of simmering water and heat gently until the chocolate melts. (Alternatively microwave on LOW for 4–5 minutes or until melted, stirring occasionally.) Remove from the heat and leave to cool for about 5 minutes.
4. Sift the icing sugar into a bowl. Add the butter and beat together until pale and fluffy. Add the egg yolks, beating well.
5. Lightly whip the cream and chill half of it. Stir the remaining cream, the cooled chocolate and the nuts into the butter and egg yolk mixture.
6. Line the bottom of the prepared pan with lady fingers, cutting to fit if necessary. Spoon over one third of the coffee and brandy mixture.
7. Layer the chocolate mixture and lady fingers in the pan, soaking each layer with coffee and ending with soaked lady fingers. Weight down lightly and chill for 3–4 hours until set.
8. Turn out, remove the paper and decorate with the reserved whipped cream and the coffee beans.

To freeze: turn out and open freeze until firm. Wrap and freeze. Defrost overnight in the refrigerator.

CHOCOLATE BOX GÂTEAU

SERVES 9

The sides of this cake are covered with neat home-made squares of chocolate. If you do not have time to make them yourself, buy ready made chocolate squares from good candy stores or delicatessens.

FOR THE SPONGE
3 eggs
generous $\frac{1}{3}$ cup superfine sugar
$\frac{3}{4}$ cup All Purpose flour
2 tablespoons cocoa

FOR THE FILLING AND DECORATION
5 squares semi sweet chocolate
1 cup heavy cream
$1\frac{1}{2}$ pounds tangerines, peeled and segmented
1 quantity Apricot glaze (see page 42)

1. Grease and flour a 7 inch square cake pan, then line the base with wax paper.
2. To make the sponge, using an electric mixer, whisk the eggs and sugar together in a bowl until very thick and pale, and the mixture leaves a trail when the whisk is lifted. Sieve the flour and cocoa over the mixture, then fold in using a large metal spoon. Transfer to the prepared pan.
3. Bake in the oven at 375° for 30–35 minutes or until firm to the touch and shrunken from the sides of the pan. Turn out and cool on a wire rack.
4. Break the chocolate into small pieces. Place in a heatproof bowl standing over a pan of simmering water and heat gently until the chocolate melts. (Alternatively, microwave on LOW for 4–5 minutes or until melted.)
5. Meanwhile, spread a sheet of foil on a cookie sheet and mark an $8\frac{1}{2}$ inch square. Spread the chocolate evenly over the square marked on the foil. Leave until set. When set, trim the edges and cut into 24 squares, measuring about 2 inches.
6. Whip the cream until it just holds its shape. Cut the cake in half horizontally, then sandwich together with a little of the cream and a few of the tangerines.
7. Arrange the rest of the fruit evenly all over the top of the cake and brush with warm apricot glaze.
8. Spread a little of the remaining cream round the sides of the cake. Press on the chocolate squares, overlapping each one slightly. Spoon the remaining cream into a pastry tube fitted with a star tip and pipe around the top of the cake.

To freeze: wrap and freeze at the end of step 3. Defrost at cool room temperature, then finish as above.

Left: CHOCOLATE AND LIME MOUSSE (PAGE 98).
Right: CHOCOLATE BOX GÂTEAU.

BLACK FOREST GÂTEAU

SERVES 10

This famous and much loved cake from Germany is perfect for any grand occasion, or as a dessert for a dinner party. The cherries should really be fresh morello cherries, but as these are not always easy to come by, canned cherries are used instead. When fresh morello cherries are available, poach them in a sugar syrup and carefully remove their pits before using in the gâteau.

FOR THE CAKE

1 stick butter
6 eggs
generous 1 cup superfine sugar
¾ cup All Purpose flour
scant ½ cup cocoa
½ teaspoon vanilla

FOR THE FILLING AND DECORATION

two 15 ounce cans pitted black cherries, drained and syrup reserved
4 tablespoons kirsch
2 cups whipping cream
4 ounces Chocolate caraque (see page 78)
1 teaspoon arrowroot

1. Grease a deep 9 inch round cake pan and line the base with wax paper.
2. To make the cake, put the butter into a bowl, place over a pan of warm water and beat until really soft but not melted.
3. Whisk the eggs and sugar together in a large bowl standing over a pan of simmering water until pale and creamy, and thick enough to leave a trail on the surface when the whisk is lifted. Remove from the heat and whisk until cool.
4. Sift the flour and cocoa together, then lightly fold into the mixture with a metal spoon. Fold in the vanilla essence and softened butter. Turn the mixture into the prepared pan and tilt the pan to spread the mixture evenly.
5. Bake in the oven at 350° for about 40 minutes until well risen, firm to the touch and beginning to shrink away from the sides of the pan. Turn out of the pan on to a wire rack, covered with wax paper, and leave to cool for 30 minutes. Cut the cake into three horizontally.
6. Place one layer on a flat plate. To make the filling, mix 5 tablespoons of the cherry syrup and the kirsch together. Spoon 3 tablespoons over the cake layer.
7. Whip the cream until it just holds its shape, then spread a little thinly over the soaked sponge. Reserve a quarter of the cherries for decoration and scatter half the remainder over the cream.
8. Repeat the layers of sponge, syrup, cream and cherries. Top with the third cake round and spoon over the remaining kirsch-flavored syrup.
9. Spread a thin layer of the remaining cream around the sides of the cake, reserving a third to decorate. Press on the chocolate caraque, reserving a few to decorate the top.
10. Spoon the remaining cream into a pastry tube fitted with a large star tip and pipe whirls of cream around the edge of the cake. Top each whirl with a chocolate curl.
11. Fill the center with the reserved cherries. Blend the arrowroot with 3 tablespoons cherry syrup. Place in a small saucepan, bring to the boil and boil, stirring, for a few minutes until the mixture is clear. Brush the glaze over the cherries.

To freeze: wrap the cooled cake at the end of step 5. Defrost, unwrapped, at room temperature, then finish as above.

CHOCOLATE AND CHESTNUT GÂTEAU

SERVES 12

Thin layers of chocolate sponge are sandwiched together with a rich, gooey chestnut cream. The easiest way to cut the cake into four is to use a large knife with a long, sharp blade. Lay the cake flat on a board, then slice through horizontally. When sandwiching the pieces back together, make sure they are replaced in their original position, or you may end up with a lop-sided cake. Try to obtain unsweetened chestnut paste for best results.

9 inch chocolate Genoese (see page 124)
15 ounce can natural chestnut paste
1 cup heavy cream
2 tablespoons brandy
canned whole chestnuts, drained
grated chocolate
icing sugar, for dusting

1. To make the filling, break the chocolate into small pieces. Place in a heatproof bowl standing over a pan of simmering water and heat gently until the chocolate melts. (Alternatively, microwave on LOW for 4 minutes or until melted, stirring occasionally.) Pour the chocolate into a food processor with the chestnut paste, cream and brandy and blend until smooth. Leave to cool and thicken slightly.
2. Carefully slice the cake into four horizontally and sandwich together with a little of the chestnut cream. Cover the top and sides with the remaining cream and mark in a decorative pattern with a spatula. Decorate with chestnuts dipped in grated chocolate, semi sweet chocolate preferably. Dust the gâteau lightly with a little icing sugar.

To freeze: wrap and freeze before decorating. Defrost, then finish as above.

WHISKY MOCHA PIE

SERVES 6–8

This pie is made with a coffee-flavored bavarois mixture and topped with whisky cream.

1 quantity Shortcrust pastry (see page 42)

FOR THE FILLING
3 squares semi sweet chocolate
2 teaspoons gelatin
$\frac{1}{2}$ cup milk
1 tablespoon instant coffee granules
3 egg yolks
1 tablespoon superfine sugar
$\frac{1}{2}$ cup heavy cream

FOR THE TOPPING
scant cup heavy cream
1–2 tablespoons whisky
1 tablespoon superfine sugar
Chocolate caraque (see page 78), to decorate

1. Roll out the pastry on a lightly floured work surface and use to line a 9 inch fluted pie plate. Trim the edges, then prick with a fork. Chill for 30 minutes.

2. Bake blind in the oven at 425° for 20–25 minutes until the pastry is cooked and very lightly browned. Leave to cool.

3. To make the filling, break the chocolate into small pieces. Place in a heatproof bowl standing over a pan of simmering water and heat until the chocolate melts. Stir until smooth. (Alternatively, microwave on LOW for 3–4 minutes or until melted, stirring occasionally.)

4. Remove the pastry case from the pie plate and place it, upside down, on a sheet of wax paper. Using a pastry brush, brush half of the melted chocolate evenly all over the pastry case. Leave in a cool place until the chocolate sets. Turn the pastry over and brush the inside with the remaining chocolate and leave to set.

5. Sprinkle the gelatin over 2 tablespoons water in a small bowl and leave to soak for 2–3 minutes. Place the bowl over a pan of simmering water and stir until dissolved. (Alternatively, microwave on HIGH for 30 seconds or until dissolved.)

6. Put the milk and coffee granules into a small saucepan. Heat gently until the coffee dissolves completely and the milk comes almost to the boil. Very lightly whisk the egg yolks and sugar together in a bowl. Pour in the coffee-flavored milk and mix well.

7. Place the bowl over a pan of hot water and cook the custard, stirring continuously, until thick enough to coat the back of the spoon. (Alternatively, microwave the custard on HIGH for 2–2½ minutes, stirring every 30 seconds.)

8. As soon as the custard thickens, strain it through a nylon strainer into a clean bowl. Stir in the dissolved gelatin. Leave the custard to cool, stirring frequently to prevent a skin forming.

9. Whip the cream until it will just hold soft peaks, then gently fold into the coffee custard. Place the chocolate coated pastry on a flat serving plate, fill with the coffee cream mixture. Chill until set.

10. To make the topping, whip the cream with the whisky and sugar until it will just hold soft peaks. Spread an even layer of cream over the top of the pastry. Whip the remaining cream until thick enough to pipe and fill a pastry tube fitted with a medium star tip. Pipe whirls of cream around the top of the pastry, then decorate with chocolate caraque. Chill.

To freeze: freeze at the end of step 9. Defrost in the refrigerator overnight, then finish as above.

FROZEN CHOCOLATE RUM AND RAISIN CAKE

SERVES 12

A delicious, mousse-like ice cream cake with a crisp, dark chocolate base. Serve with cream.

FOR THE FILLING
$\frac{1}{3}$ cup raisins
4 tablespoons dark rum
generous $\frac{1}{3}$ cup superfine sugar
3 egg yolks
6 squares semi sweet chocolate
1 cup heavy cream

FOR THE COOKIE CRUST
1 stick butter or margarine, melted
8 squares chocolate cookies, crushed

1. Put the raisins and rum in a small bowl and leave to soak for several hours or overnight.

2. To make the cookie crust, mix the butter and cookies together. Press into the base of an 8 inch spring-release cake pan. Chill for 30 minutes or overnight.

3. To make the filling, put the sugar and 5 tablespoons water in a small saucepan and heat gently until dissolved. When the sugar is completely dissolved, increase the heat and boil the mixture rapidly for 4 minutes to make a syrup.

4. Meanwhile, lightly whisk the egg yolks with any excess rum from the soaked raisins. Gradually pour the sugar syrup on to the egg yolks, whisking all the time.

5. Break the chocolate into small pieces. Place in a heatproof bowl standing over a pan of simmering water and heat gently until the chocolate melts. (Alternatively, microwave on LOW for 4–5 minutes or until melted, stirring occasionally.) Stir into the egg yolk mixture. Leave to cool.

6. When cold, whip the cream until stiff, then fold into the chocolate mixture. Fold in the raisins. Pour the mixture into the pan on top of the cookie base.

7. Cover tightly with plastic wrap and foil, then freeze for at least 3–4 hours or until firm. Remove from the freezer for 5 minutes before serving. Serve cut into wedges.

Opposite: WHISKY MOCHA PIE.

CHOCOLATE MACAROON LOG

SERVES 10

To make the hazelnut flavor more pronounced in this recipe, substitute ground, unblanched hazelnuts for the almonds when making the macaroons and omit the almond flavoring.

FOR THE MACAROONS
3 small egg whites
2 cups ground almonds
1½ cups superfine sugar
1½ teaspoons almond flavoring

FOR THE FILLING AND DECORATION
1 cup hazelnuts
4 squares semi sweet chocolate
1 cup heavy cream
3 tablespoons almond-flavored liqueur

FOR THE DECORATION
icing sugar, for dusting
cocoa, for dusting
Chocolate leaves (see page 78)
hazelnuts

1. To make the macaroons, line two cookie sheets with non-stick wax paper. Whisk the egg whites in a bowl until stiff, then fold in the ground almonds, sugar and almond flavoring.
2. Spoon the mixture into a pastry tube fitted with a ½ inch plain tip and pipe 30 small rounds on to the prepared cookie sheets, allowing room between each for the mixture to spread.
3. Bake in the oven at 350° for about 20 minutes. Transfer to a wire rack to cool for 20 minutes.
4. To make the filling, spread the nuts out on a cookie sheet. Brown in the oven at 400° for 5–10 minutes. Tip on to a cloth and rub off the skins. Chop finely.
5. Break the chocolate into small pieces. Place in a heatproof bowl standing over a pan of simmering water and heat gently until the chocolate melts. (Alternatively, microwave on LOW for 4–5 minutes or until melted, stirring occasionally.) Leave to cool for 5 minutes.
6. Whip the cream until it holds its shape. Gradually beat in the cooled chocolate, nuts and liqueur.
7. Use some of the chocolate cream to sandwich the macaroons together. Place them side by side on a serving plate to form a double log. Spread chocolate cream on top and add a further layer of macaroons. Spread the remaining chocolate cream over the top and sides. Chill overnight.
8. To serve, dust with icing sugar and cocoa, then decorate with chocolate leaves and whole hazelnuts.

Not suitable for freezing.

CHOCOLATE CINNAMON PIE

SERVES 6–8

When sliced, this pie reveals its layers of creamy chocolate and cinnamon custard.

1 quantity Shortcrust pastry (see page 42)

FOR THE FILLING
1 cup milk
1 vanilla pod
1 tablespoon gelatin
3 eggs, separated
generous 1 cup superfine sugar
2 squares semi sweet or milk chocolate
1 teaspoon cinnamon

FOR THE DECORATION
Chocolate curls (see page 78)
icing sugar, for dusting

1. Roll out the pastry and use to line a deep 9½ inch fluted pie ring.
2. Bake blind in the oven at 400° for 20–25 minutes or until golden brown and cooked through. Leave to cool.
3. To make the filling, place the milk and vanilla pod in a small saucepan and bring to the boil. Cover and leave to infuse for about 30 minutes.
4. Sprinkle the gelatin over 3 tablespoons water in a small bowl and leave to soak for 2–3 minutes. Place the bowl over a pan of simmering water and stir until dissolved. (Alternatively microwave on HIGH for 30 seconds or until dissolved.)
5. Whisk the egg yolks and three-quarters of the sugar together in a bowl until very pale and thick. Remove the vanilla pod from the milk. Return the milk to the boil and pour on to the egg mixture, whisking.
6. Return the mixture to the pan and heat gently until it thickens enough to coat the back of a wooden spoon. Do not boil.
7. Remove from the heat, add the dissolved gelatin and stir.
8. Divide the mixture between two bowls. Break the chocolate into one bowl and stir until melted. Cool until beginning to set. Whisk the cinnamon into the other bowl. Cool until beginning to set.
9. Whisk the egg whites until stiff but not dry. Add the remaining sugar and whisk again until stiff. Fold half the meringue mixture into each custard.
10. Pour half the chocolate custard into the pastry case. Freeze for a few minutes to set. Add the cinnamon custard and freeze quickly to set. Finish with the remaining chocolate mixture. Decorate with chocolate curls and dust with icing sugar. Chill until ready to serve.

To freeze: pack and freeze. Defrost overnight in the refrigerator. (The pastry will be slightly softer but still acceptable.)

DARK CHOCOLATE TRUFFLE CAKE

SERVES 24

A very rich chocolate cake with a brandy truffle filling.
If you have time, make extra filling, chill until firm
enough to shape, then roll into small truffle balls. Roll
in cocoa and use to decorate the top of the cake.

FOR THE CAKE

8 squares semi sweet chocolate
1 stick butter
1¾ cups superfine sugar
½ teaspoon vanilla
2 eggs, separated
½ cup sour cream
3 cups self raising flour
1 teaspoon soda

FOR THE FILLING

12 squares semi sweet chocolate
1½ sticks butter
5 tablespoons brandy

FOR THE FROSTING

7 squares semi sweet chocolate
scant 1 cup heavy cream

1. Grease a 10 inch spring-release cake pan and line the
base with wax paper.
2. To make the cake, break the chocolate into small
pieces. Place in a large heatproof bowl with the butter
and ½ cup water. Stand the bowl over a pan of
simmering water and heat gently until the chocolate
melts. (Alternatively, microwave on HIGH for 2–3
minutes or until melted, stirring occasionally.) Beat in
the sugar and vanilla, then leave to cool.
3. Beat in the egg yolks, then fold in the sour cream,
flour and soda. Whisk the egg whites until stiff, then
fold into the mixture. Pour the mixture into the
prepared pan.
4. Bake in the oven at 350° for 1 hour or until risen and
just firm to the touch. Turn out on to a wire rack and
leave to cool.
5. To make the filling, break the chocolate into small
pieces. Place in a large heatproof bowl with the butter.
Stand the bowl over a pan of simmering water and heat
gently until the chocolate melts, stirring. (Alternatively,
microwave on HIGH for 2–3 minutes or until the
chocolate melts, stirring occasionally.) Stir in 3 tablespoons of the brandy. Leave until slightly thickened.
6. Cut the cake into two layers and sprinkle the
remaining brandy on each cut half. Place the top half in
the base of the pan, cut side up. Pour in the truffle filling.
Place the second half of sponge on top. Chill until set.
7. When the cake is set, unmold and stand on a wire
rack placed over a cookie sheet.
8. To make the frosting, break the chocolate into
pieces. Place in a large heatproof bowl with the cream.

Stand the bowl over a pan of simmering water and heat
gently until the chocolate melts. (Alternatively,
microwave on LOW for 3–4 minutes or until melted,
stirring occasionally.)
9. Cool until the frosting coats the back of a spoon.
Pour the frosting over the cake, using a spatula to cover
the sides. Leave until set.

*To freeze: wrap and freeze at the end of step 6. Defrost in the
refrigerator overnight, then finish as above.*

Illustrated on pages 76–77

CHOCOLATE FUDGE SAUCE CAKE

SERVES 8–10

A sticky rich chocolate cake with its own delicious
sauce topping. Serve with ice cream or chilled whipped
cream.

FOR THE CAKE

1½ cups self raising flour
½ teaspoon baking powder
pinch of salt
2 tablespoons cocoa
¾ cup dark brown soft sugar
scant 1 cup milk
¼ stick butter or margarine, melted
½ teaspoon vanilla
½ cup walnuts, almonds or pecan nuts, chopped

FOR THE SAUCE

¾ cup dark brown soft sugar
½ teaspoon instant coffee powder
2 tablespoons cocoa

1. Grease a 7 inch square cake pan.
2. To make the cake, put all the ingredients, except the
nuts, in a bowl and beat until smooth and glossy. Stir in
the nuts. Pour the mixture into the prepared pan and
level the surface.
3. To make the sauce, put all the ingredients and ½ cup
water in a saucepan. Heat gently until the sugar
dissolves, stirring all the time, then increase the heat and
bring to a rapid boil. Carefully pour over the cake
mixture.
4. Bake in the oven at 350° for 35–40 minutes or until
the cake is risen and firm to the touch. Leave to cool in
the pan.
5. When the cake is cold, turn it out on to a serving
plate. Some of the fudge topping will be left in the pan,
simply scrape it out with a spatula and spread on top of
the cake. Serve the cake cut into squares, on its own or
with vanilla ice cream.

*To freeze: pack in a rigid container. Defrost overnight at cool
room temperature.*

EXCEEDINGLY GOOEY CHOCOLATE BROWNIES

MAKES 24 SQUARES

As the name suggests, this makes very rich, gooey brownies.

1¼ pounds semi sweet chocolate
2 sticks butter, cut into pieces
3 eggs
2 tablespoons freshly made strong coffee
generous 1 cup superfine sugar
¾ cup self raising flour
½ teaspoon salt
1½ cups walnut halves, chopped
1 teaspoon vanilla

1. Grease and line a baking pan measuring 8½ × 11½ inches across the top and 7½ × 10½ inches across the base.
2. Using a very sharp knife, roughly chop ½ pound of the chocolate. Break the remaining chocolate into small pieces. Place in a heatproof bowl with the butter. Stand the bowl over a pan of simmering water and heat gently until the chocolate melts, stirring. (Alternatively, microwave on LOW for 10 minutes or until melted, stirring occasionally.) Leave to cool.
3. Mix the eggs, coffee and sugar together in a bowl, then gradually beat in the chocolate mixture. Fold in the flour, salt, walnuts, vanilla and chopped chocolate. Pour the mixture into the prepared pan.
4. Bake in the oven at 375° for 45 minutes or until just firm to the touch in the center. Leave to cool in the pan.
5. When the cake is completely cold, turn out on to a board and trim the edges. Cut into 24 squares. Serve on their own or with Cinnamon or Chocolate flake ice cream (see page 217).

To freeze: pack and freeze the cooled brownies, interleaved with wax paper. Defrost at cool room temperature.

HAZELNUT AND CHOCOLATE GÂTEAU

SERVES 14

Chocolate and hazelnut spread is sold in tubs in good grocery stores and delicatessens.

FOR THE CAKE
2 sticks butter
1½ cups light brown soft sugar
4 eggs, separated
1 cup self raising flour
pinch of salt
1⅓ cups ground hazelnuts
4 squares semi sweet chocolate, finely grated

FOR THE FILLING
2 cups heavy cream
10 tablespoons chocolate and hazelnut spread
½ cup hazelnuts, roasted and finely chopped

FOR THE DECORATION
cocoa, sifted
whole hazelnuts

1. Grease and line a 9 inch round spring-release cake pan.
2. To make the cake, cream the butter and sugar together in a bowl until pale and fluffy. Beat in the egg yolks, one at a time, then fold in the flour and salt. Stir in the hazelnuts and chocolate. Whisk the egg whites until stiff and fold into the cake mixture. Pour the mixture into the prepared pan.
3. Bake in the oven at 325° for 1–1¼ hours or until a tester inserted into the center comes out clean. Leave to cool in the pan.
4. To make the filling, whip the cream until it holds its shape. Mix with the chocolate and hazelnut spread.
5. Cut the cake into three layers and sandwich together with some of the hazelnut cream. Spread more cream around the sides of the cake and coat in the nuts.
6. Spread more of the hazelnut cream over the top of the cake. Spoon the remaining hazelnut cream into a pastry tube fitted with a large star tip and pipe around the edge of the cake. Decorate with a little cocoa and whole hazelnuts.

To freeze: omit the hazelnut and cocoa decoration. Open freeze until firm then wrap. Defrost at cool room temperature or overnight in the refrigerator. Complete the decoration.

Above: EXCEEDINGLY GOOEY CHOCOLATE BROWNIES.
Below: MISSISSIPPI MUD PIE (PAGE 92).

RIGO JACSI

MAKES 24 SQUARES

Absolute temptation! These rich squares of chocolate gâteau, classic in their make-up of chocolate flavored Genoese and ganache, were named after a gypsy violinist, who was said to have broken the heart of many a princess.

½ quantity chocolate Genoese (see page 124)

FOR THE GANACHE
15 squares semi sweet chocolate
2 cups heavy cream
3 tablespoons brandy

FOR THE FROSTING
4 squares semi sweet chocolate
2 tablespoons brandy
1 cup icing sugar, sifted

1. Grease a 9 × 13 inch jelly roll pan and line the base with wax paper. Spread the cake mixture evenly in the prepared pan.
2. Bake in the oven at 350° for 20–25 minutes until well risen, firm to the touch and beginning to shrink away from the sides of the pan. Leave to cool in the pan.
3. To make the ganache, break the chocolate into small pieces. Place the chocolate and cream in a large saucepan and heat gently, stirring, until the chocolate melts and blends smoothly with the cream. Do not boil. (Alternatively, put the ingredients in a bowl and microwave on LOW for 8–10 minutes or until melted. Do not allow the mixture to boil.)
4. Pour the ganache into a bowl if necessary and leave to cool, but not set hard, stirring the cream frequently to prevent a skin forming. When cold, whip the ganache with the brandy until very light and fluffy, taking care not to overwhip.
5. Cut the chocolate sponge into two layers. Place one piece on a flat board or cookie sheet. Cut a length of card, or several thicknesses of foil, long enough to fit around the sponge cake, and about 3 inches deep. Fit the card snugly around the sponge, forming square corners as you do so, and secure with tape. Alternatively, place the sponge cake in a deep square cake pan, placing it against two sides of the pan, then form a false 'wall' for the other side, with several thicknesses of foil.
6. Spoon the whipped ganache on top of the layer of chocolate sponge to a depth of about 2 inches and spread evenly. Place the second layer of sponge on top. Chill for at least 1 hour.
7. To make the frosting, break the chocolate into small pieces. Place in a small saucepan with 1 tablespoon water, the brandy and icing sugar. Stir over a gentle heat until the chocolate melts and blends with the icing sugar to make a smooth frosting. (Alternatively, put the ingredients in a bowl and microwave on LOW for 5 minutes or until melted, stirring frequently.) Spread the chocolate frosting over the top layer and leave to set.
8. Carefully remove the 'wall' from around the cake. Cut the gâteau into twenty-four 1½ inch squares, using a sharp knife dipped in hot water and dried each time before cutting. Chill until 20–30 minutes before serving.

To freeze: open freeze the completed cakes. Defrost overnight in the refrigerator.

CAPPUCINO CAKE

SERVES 16–18

A dark chocolate and coffee cake with a frothy cream and cocoa topping, reminiscent of a good cappucino. Use freshly made coffee, not instant.

FOR THE CAKE
8 squares semi sweet chocolate
1 tablespoon instant coffee granules
2 sticks butter or margarine
1½ cups dark brown soft sugar
5 eggs
scant 2 cups ground almonds
scant 1 cup cornstarch
2 tablespoons strong coffee, cooled
2 tablespoons dark rum

FOR THE TOPPING
1 cup whipping cream
1 tablespoon dark rum
cocoa

1. Grease a 9 inch round spring-release cake pan and line the base with wax paper.
2. To make the cake, break the chocolate into small pieces. Place in a heatproof bowl with the instant coffee. Stand the bowl over a pan of simmering water and heat gently until the chocolate melts, stirring. (Alternatively, microwave on LOW for 6–7 minutes or until melted.)
3. Cream the butter and sugar together in a bowl until pale and fluffy. Beat in the eggs, one at a time, beating well after each addition. Fold in the almonds, cornstarch and chocolate. Pour the mixture into the prepared pan and level the surface.
4. Bake in the oven at 350° for 1 hour 15–20 minutes or until risen and just firm to the touch. Cover the cake with wax paper to prevent it becoming too brown, if necessary. Leave the cake to cool in the pan.
5. When cold, prick the cake all over with a fine tester. Mix the coffee and rum together, then pour evenly over the cake. Leave for at least 30 minutes.
6. To make the topping, whip the cream with the rum until it just holds its shape. Remove the cake from the pan and transfer to a serving plate. Spoon the cream on top and spread evenly with a spatula. Sift a little cocoa over the cream to decorate.

To freeze: wrap and freeze at the end of step 5. Defrost at cool room temperature, then finish as above.

WHITE CHOCOLATE GÂTEAU

SERVES 18–20

This rich gâteau, covered in a mass of white chocolate curls, is delicious enough to be served as an alternative wedding cake. If doing so, place the cake on a large cake stand and surround with fresh flowers.

9 inch Genoese cake (see page 124)

FOR THE FILLING
6 squares semi sweet chocolate
2 tablespoons brandy
2 eggs, separated
1 cup heavy cream
1 teaspoon gelatin

FOR THE DECORATION
10 squares white chocolate
$\frac{1}{2}$ cup heavy cream
icing sugar, for dusting

1. To make the filling, break the chocolate into small pieces. Place in a heatproof bowl standing over a pan of simmering water and heat gently until the chocolate melts. (Alternatively, microwave on LOW for 5–7 minutes or until melted, stirring occasionally.) Remove from the heat and stir in the brandy and egg yolks. Whip the cream until it just stands in soft peaks, then fold into the chocolate mixture.

2. Sprinkle the gelatin over 1 tablespoon water in a small bowl and leave to soak for 2–3 minutes. Place the bowl over a pan of simmering water and stir until dissolved. (Alternatively, microwave on HIGH for 30 seconds or until dissolved.) Cool, then stir into the chocolate mixture. Whisk the egg whites until stiff, then fold in.

3. Cut the cake into two layers. Put one piece of sponge back in the pan. Pour the mousse filling on top. Put the second piece of sponge on top. Leave to set.

4. While the filling is setting, make the decoration. Melt the white chocolate as in step 1. Spread out thinly on a marble slab or a clean, smooth work surface. Leave until set. When the chocolate is set, push a clean stripping knife (see Note below) across the chocolate at an angle of about 25 degrees to roll off large thick chocolate curls. Chill until ready for decorating.

5. When the mousse is set, whip the cream until it holds its shape. Ease the cake out of the pan and cover with the cream. Cover completely with the chocolate curls and dust lightly with a little icing sugar.

Note: A stripping knife is a decorator's tool used for scraping off wallpaper! It has a sharp flexible blade and is ideal for making large chocolate curls. Buy one and keep it specifically for this purpose.

Not suitable for freezing.

Above: WHITE CHOCOLATE GÂTEAU.

CHOCOLATE CUSTARD PIE

SERVES 8

1 quantity Shortcrust pastry (see page 42)

FOR THE FILLING
generous ½ cup sugar
½ cup All Purpose flour
pinch of salt
1¼ cups milk
2 squares semi sweet chocolate
3 egg yolks
⅓ stick butter or margarine
1 teaspoon vanilla
1 cup heavy or whipping cream
Chocolate curls (see page 78) or grated chocolate, to decorate

1. Roll out the pastry on a lightly floured work surface and use to line a 9 inch loose-based fluted pie plate or ring placed on a cookie sheet. Crimp the edges of the pastry and chill for 30 minutes. Prick the base of the pastry case.
2. Bake blind in the oven at 400° for 10–15 minutes until set. Remove the paper and beans and bake for a further 5–10 minutes until lightly colored. Leave to cool.
3. To make the filling, mix the sugar, flour and salt in a large saucepan and stir in the milk.
4. Break the chocolate into small pieces and add to the pan. Heat gently until the chocolate has melted, stirring continuously.
5. Whisk until the chocolate and milk are blended, then increase the heat and cook for about 10 minutes, stirring constantly. Remove the pan from the heat.
6. Beat the egg yolks and whisk in a small amount of the hot chocolate sauce. Slowly pour the egg mixture into the saucepan, stirring rapidly. Cook over low heat stirring, for 10–15 minutes, until the mixture is very thick and creamy. Do not allow to boil.
7. Remove from the heat. Stir in the butter and vanilla, then pour into the cold pastry case. Cover to prevent a skin forming and chill for about 4 hours until set.
8. Just before serving, whip the cream lightly and spread evenly over the chocolate filling. Decorate the top with chocolate curls or grated chocolate. Serve chilled.

To freeze: open freeze the set pie at the end of step 7 until firm, then wrap and freeze. Defrost overnight in the refrigerator.

MISSISSIPPI MUD PIE

SERVES 16

This rich and sticky pie originated here in the United States, where it is served warm with hot fudge sauce or cold topped with whipped cream and grated chocolate. Either way, a small portion is all that is needed.

FOR THE BASE
generous 1 cup ginger cookies, crushed
generous 1 cup Graham cracker crumbs
¾ cup butter, melted
scant ¼ cup light brown soft sugar

FOR THE FILLING
2 sticks butter or margarine
6 squares semi sweet chocolate
8 tablespoons corn syrup
4 eggs, beaten
½ cup pecans, chopped

1. Grease a 9 inch loose-based cake pan.
2. To make the base, mix the cookies with the butter and sugar. Press into the bottom and 1½ inches up the sides of the prepared pan. Chill while making the filling.
3. To make the filling, put the butter, chocolate and syrup in a saucepan and heat very gently until melted, stirring all the time. (Alternatively, put the ingredients in a bowl and microwave on LOW for 4–6 minutes or until melted, stirring frequently.) Cool, then beat in the eggs and pecans. Pour the mixture into the cookie crust.
4. Bake in the oven at 350° for 1¼ hours or until just firm to the touch but still soft in the center. Serve warm or cold.

To freeze: wrap and freeze the cold pie. Defrost overnight in the refrigerator. Serve cold.

Illustrated on page 89

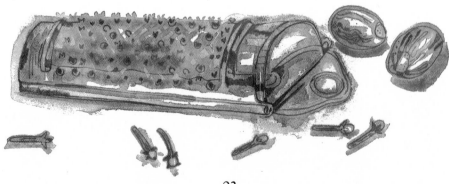

MAGIC CHOCOLATE PUDDING

SERVES 4–6

This delicious chocolate pudding, which is a great hit with children, is called 'magic' because it separates magically during baking into a rich chocolate sauce at the bottom and a sponge cake on top.

½ stick butter or margarine
scant ½ cup superfine sugar
2 eggs, separated
1½ cups milk
3 tablespoons self raising flour
5 teaspoons cocoa

1. Grease a 3½ cup heatproof dish.
2. Cream the butter and sugar together in a bowl until light and fluffy. Beat in the egg yolks and stir in the milk.
3. Sift the flour and cocoa together over the creamed mixture, then beat in until evenly mixed. Whisk the egg whites until stiff and fold into the mixture. Pour into the prepared dish.
4. Bake in the oven at 350° for 35–45 minutes until the top is set and spongy to the touch. This pudding will separate into a custard layer with a sponge topping. Serve hot.

Not suitable for freezing.

Below: MAGIC CHOCOLATE PUDDING.

Chocolate Filo Pie

SERVES 9–12

An unusual way to use up stale cake crumbs.

4 sheets of filo pastry (see page 46)
½ stick melted butter

FOR THE FILLING
¾ stick butter, softened
¾ cup icing sugar
4 eggs, separated
1 cup ground almonds
2 cups chocolate cake crumbs
¾ cup chopped candied fruit
4 squares semi sweet chocolate, grated
1 tablespoon cocoa, sifted
½ cup heavy cream

FOR THE DECORATION
½ cup slivered almonds
1 tablespoon icing sugar, sifted

1. To make the filling, cream the butter and icing sugar together in a bowl until pale and fluffy. Gradually beat in the egg yolks, then the almonds, cake crumbs, candied fruit, chocolate, cocoa and cream. Whisk the egg whites until stiff, then fold into the chocolate mixture.

2. Fold one sheet of filo pastry in half and trim to fit an 8½ × 11½ inch baking pan. Repeat with the remaining sheets of pastry, reserving the trimmings.

3. Lay one of the folded sheets of pastry in the dish and spread with one third of the chocolate filling. Cover with a second folded sheet of pastry. Repeat the layers twice more ending with a pastry layer. Brush the top with the melted butter. Cut the pastry trimmings into neat strips and sprinkle on top. Brush with more melted butter. Sprinkle with the almonds and icing sugar.

4. Bake in the oven at 375° for 40 minutes or until golden brown. Serve hot or cold, cut into squares, with vanilla ice cream.

Not suitable for freezing.

Zuccotto

SERVES 6

A rich, Italian version of tipsy cake.

3 tablespoons brandy
2 tablespoons orange-flavored liqueur
2 tablespoons cherry or almond-flavored liqueur
12 ounces yellow sponge cake
5 squares semi sweet chocolate
1½ cups heavy cream
1 cup icing sugar
½ cup blanched almonds, roasted and chopped
½ cup hazelnuts, roasted and chopped

FOR THE DECORATION
icing sugar
cocoa

1. Line a 5 cup ceramic bowl or round-bottomed bowl with a damp cheesecloth.

2. In a separate bowl, mix together the brandy and liqueurs and set aside.

3. Cut the cake into ½ inch slices. Sprinkle with the brandy and liqueurs. Line the bowl with the moistened sponges, reserving enough to cover the top.

4. Using a sharp knife, chop 3 squares of the chocolate into small pieces and set aside.

5. In a separate bowl, whip the cream and icing sugar together until stiff, then fold in the chopped chocolate and nuts.

6. Divide this mixture in two and use one half to spread over the sponge lining in an even layer.

7. Break the remaining chocolate into small pieces. Place in a small heatproof bowl standing over a pan of simmering water and heat gently until the chocolate melts. (Alternatively, microwave on LOW for 2–3 minutes or until melted, stirring occasionally.) Cool slightly, then fold into the remaining cream mixture. Use this to fill the center of the pudding.

8. Level the top of the Zuccotto and cover with the remaining moistened cake. Trim the edges. Cover and chill for at least 12 hours.

9. To serve, uncover, invert a flat serving plate over the bowl and turn upside down. Lift off the bowl, and carefully remove the cheesecloth. Serve cold, dusted with icing sugar and cocoa.

To freeze: open freeze the unmolded Zuccotto until firm, then wrap and freeze. Defrost overnight in the refrigerator.

Opposite: Petits Pots au Chocolat.

PETITS POTS AU CHOCOLAT

SERVES 6

These little chocolate pots rely heavily on the flavor of the chocolate used. So it is essential to use a good quality chocolate.

1 tablespoon coffee beans
3 egg yolks
1 egg
scant ½ cup superfine sugar
2½ cups milk and light cream mixed
3 squares semi sweet chocolate

FOR THE DECORATION

½ cup whipping cream
Chocolate shapes (see page 78) or coffee dragées

1. Roast the coffee beans under a moderate broiler for a few minutes, then set aside.

2. Beat the egg yolks, egg and sugar together in a bowl until very pale.

3. Place the milk, cream and coffee beans in a saucepan and bring to the boil. Strain the hot milk on to the egg mixture, stirring all the time. Discard the coffee beans. Return the mixture to the saucepan.

4. Break up the chocolate and add to the pan. Stir over gentle heat (do not boil) for about 5 minutes until the chocolate has almost melted and the mixture is slightly thickened. Whisk lightly until the mixture is evenly blended.

5. Stand six individual ½ cup custard pots in a roasting pan, then pour in enough hot water to come halfway up the sides of the dishes. Pour the custard mixture slowly into the dishes, dividing it equally between them. Cover.

6. Bake in the oven at 300° for 1–1¼ hours or until the custard is lightly set. Leave to cool completely.

7. To serve, whip the cream and spoon into a pastry tube fitted with a large star tip. Pipe a whirl on top of each dessert. Decorate with chocolate shapes or coffee dragées.

Not suitable for freezing.

POIRES BELLE HÉLÈNE

SERVES 6

generous ½ cup sugar
thinly pared peel and juice of 2 oranges
6 firm pears
8 squares semi sweet chocolate
4 tablespoons orange-flavored liqueur
orange slices, to decorate

1. Put the sugar, 3 cups water and half the orange peel in a large heavy-based saucepan and heat gently, without stirring, until the sugar has dissolved.

2. Meanwhile, peel the pears quickly (to prevent discoloration), leaving the stalks on. Cut out the cores from the bottom and level them so that the pears will stand upright.

3. Stand the pears in the syrup, cover the pan and simmer gently for 20 minutes or until tender. Remove from the heat and leave to cool, covered tightly. Spoon the syrup over the pears occasionally during cooling.

4. Cut the remaining orange peel into thin matchstick (julienne) strips. Blanch in boiling water for 2 minutes, then drain and immediately refresh under cold running water. Leave to drain on kitchen paper.

5. To make the chocolate sauce, break the chocolate into small pieces. Place in a heatproof bowl with the liqueur. Stand the bowl over a pan of simmering water and heat gently until the chocolate melts. (Alternatively, microwave on LOW for 7–8 minutes or until melted, stirring occasionally.)

6. Remove the pears from the syrup and stand them on a large serving dish or six dishes and chill for 2 hours.

7. Discard the orange peel from the syrup. Stir the melted chocolate into ½ cup of the syrup with the orange juice, then slowly bring to the boil, stirring constantly. Simmer, stirring, until the sauce is thick and syrupy.

8. To serve, pour the hot chocolate sauce over the cold pears and sprinkle with the orange julienne. Decorate with orange slices and serve immediately.

Not suitable for freezing.

WHITE CHOCOLATE AND SHERRY MOUSSE

SERVES 8

The chocolate horns can be made in advance. The filled horns will keep in the refrigerator for up to two days. Pack them in a single layer in a rigid container. Serve with a refreshing red fruit salad.

4 squares white chocolate
3 tablespoons dry sherry or eau de vie
½ cup heavy cream
2 eggs, separated
1 teaspoon gelatin
1 tablespoon milk
16 Chocolate horns, to serve (see page 98)
Chocolate shapes, to decorate (see page 78)

1. Break the chocolate into small pieces. Place in a medium heatproof bowl with the sherry and 2 tablespoons water. Stand the bowl over a pan of simmering water and heat until the chocolate melts. (Alternatively, microwave on LOW for 2–3 minutes or until melted, stirring occasionally.) Stir well until the mixture is smooth.

2. Lightly whip the cream in a bowl until it just holds its shape. Fold in the egg yolks and chocolate mixture.

3. Sprinkle the gelatin over the milk in a small bowl and leave to soak for 2–3 minutes. Place the bowl over a pan of simmering water and stir until dissolved. (Alternatively, microwave on HIGH for 30 seconds or until dissolved.) Stir into the chocolate mixture. Chill until beginning to set.

4. Whisk the egg whites until stiff but not dry, then fold into the chocolate mixture. Leave to set until the consistency of whipped cream.

5. Stand the chocolate horns in tall glasses and spoon in the mousse. Chill the horns for at least 1 hour before serving decorated with chocolate shapes.

To freeze: pack and freeze the filled horns. Defrost in the refrigerator for 2 hours.

Opposite: WHITE CHOCOLATE AND SHERRY MOUSSE.

CHOCOLATE AND LIME MOUSSE

SERVES 2

Lime adds a refreshing tang to the chocolate flavor.

3 squares semi sweet chocolate
2 eggs, separated
1 tablespoon superfine sugar
finely grated peel and strained juice of 1 small lime
½ cup heavy cream
½ teaspoon gelatin
grated chocolate or twists of lime, to decorate

1. Break the chocolate into small pieces. Place in a small heatproof bowl standing over a pan of simmering water and heat gently until the chocolate melts. (Alternatively, microwave on LOW for 4–5 minutes or until melted, stirring occasionally.) Cool slightly.

2. Whisk the egg yolks, sugar and lime peel in a bowl, using an electric mixer, until thick and mousse-like. Whisk in the chocolate, then 2 tablespoons of the cream.

3. Sprinkle the gelatin over the lime juice in a small bowl and leave to soak for 2–3 minutes. Place the bowl over a saucepan of simmering water and stir until dissolved. (Alternatively, microwave on HIGH for 30 seconds or until melted.) Whisk into the chocolate mixture.

4. Whisk the egg whites until stiff but not dry, then fold into the chocolate mixture.

5. Divide the mousse between two glasses and chill until set. Whip the remaining cream and use to decorate the desserts with grated chocolate or twists of lime. Leave at cool room temperature for about 30 minutes before serving.

Not suitable for freezing.

Illustrated on page 82

CHOCOLATE HORNS

MAKES 8

Start making chocolate horns the day before you intend to use them. Once made, they will keep in the refrigerator for two weeks or they can be frozen. Serve filled with mousses, fools, sherbets or ice creams. See the recipe for White chocolate and sherry mousse on page 96.

6 squares semi sweet chocolate

1. Line eight cream horn pans with non-stick wax paper.

2. Break the chocolate into small pieces. Place in a small heatproof bowl standing over a pan of simmering water and heat gently until the chocolate melts. (Alternatively, microwave on LOW for 3–4 minutes or until melted, stirring occasionally.)

3. Using a pastry brush, brush the inside of the paper with a thick layer of the chocolate, making sure it goes right down to the tip. Chill until set.

4. If necessary re-melt the remaining chocolate as above. (If using the microwave, cook on LOW for 1–2 minutes.) Repeat step 3.

5. Carefully remove the chocolate lined paper from the pans, then peel away the wax paper. Store the chocolate horns in the refrigerator until required.

To freeze: pack in a rigid container and freeze. Defrost overnight in the refrigerator.

CHOCOLATE MOUSSE GÂTEAU

SERVES 10–12

The richest of chocolate desserts, this gâteau will keep in the refrigerator for 3–4 days, where it will gradually become more fudge-like. It can be filled with chocolate ganache or served on its own with lightly whipped cream or a light vanilla custard.

9 squares semi sweet chocolate
1 tablespoon instant coffee powder
2 tablespoons brandy
4 eggs
1 teaspoon vanilla
4 tablespoons superfine sugar
2 teaspoons cornstarch
2 tablespoons cocoa, sifted
¼ quantity Ganache (see page 90)
cocoa, for dusting

1. Lightly oil a 10 × 4¾ inch ribbed Balmoral pan or 4 cup pan. Line the base and sides of the pan with non-stick wax paper.

2. Break the chocolate into small pieces. Place in a medium heatproof bowl with the coffee powder, brandy and 2 tablespoons water. Stand the bowl over a pan of simmering water and heat gently until the chocolate melts. Stir until smooth and set aside to cool.

3. Using an electric mixer, whisk the eggs, vanilla, sugar and cornstarch together in a bowl until very thick and pale. Fold in the cool, but not cold, chocolate mixture with the cocoa. Pour the mixture into the prepared pan.

4. Bake in the oven at 350° for about 1 hour or until a tester inserted into the center comes out clean. (The cake may be cracked slightly.) Remove from the pan. Leave to cool.

5. Slice the cake at 1 inch intervals and sandwich together with two-thirds of the ganache. Spread the remaining mixture over the top and sides of the cake. Chill for 10 minutes. Dust with cocoa.

To freeze: pack and open freeze without the cocoa at the end of step 5. Cover tightly when solid. Defrost overnight in the refrigerator.

BLACK BREAD PUDDING

SERVES 6

This unlikely combination of flavors makes an unusual bread pudding. It works well with other tart fruits such as redcurrants and cranberries.

3 eggs, separated
generous $\frac{1}{2}$ cup superfine sugar
$\frac{1}{2}$ teaspoon cinnamon
pinch of salt
6 cups dark rye breadcrumbs
4 squares semi sweet chocolate, grated
4 cups blackcurrants, stalks removed
2 tablespoons light brown soft sugar
icing sugar, for dusting

1. Grease an 8 inch soufflé dish.
2. Whisk the egg yolks, sugar and cinnamon together in a bowl until pale and fluffy.
3. Whisk the egg whites and salt until stiff. Fold into the egg yolk mixture with the breadcrumbs and chocolate. Arrange the blackcurrants in the base of the prepared dish and sprinkle with the brown sugar. Pour the bread mixture over the fruit.
4. Bake in the oven at 350° for 40 minutes or until firm to the touch. Dust with icing sugar and serve hot or cold with sour cream.

Not suitable for freezing.

CHOCOLATE SNOWBALL

SERVES 4–6

This luscious dessert should be left for at least 24 hours before eating. The outer layer forms a crust while the center remains a soft fudge.

6 squares semi sweet chocolate
1$\frac{1}{2}$ teaspoons instant coffee granules
scant 1 cup superfine sugar
1$\frac{1}{2}$ sticks sweet butter, diced
4 eggs
1 tablespoon dark rum
FOR THE DECORATION
1 cup heavy cream
Frosted petals (see page 10)

1. Line a 2$\frac{1}{2}$ cup ceramic bowl with foil.
2. Break the chocolate into pieces and place in a saucepan. Dissolve the coffee in 3 tablespoons water and add it to the pan with the sugar. Heat gently until the chocolate melts. (Alternatively, put the ingredients in a bowl and microwave on HIGH for 1–2 minutes or until the chocolate has melted.)

3. Transfer the chocolate mixture to a bowl, if necessary, and beat well with an electric hand-held mixer or a balloon whisk. Slowly whisk in the butter until evenly combined. Whisk in the eggs, one at a time. Stir in the rum. Pour the mixture into the prepared bowl.
4. Bake in the oven at 350° for about 1$\frac{1}{4}$ hours or until risen and firm, but still slightly wobbly like a soufflé, with a thick, cracked crust.
5. Leave to cool at room temperature, then press down with your fingertips to level the surface. Cover and chill for at least 24 hours. Unmold on to a serving plate.
6. Whip the cream until it holds its shape. Fill a pastry tube fitted with a star tip and pipe rosettes on the pudding until completely covered. Decorate with a sprinkling of frosted petals, if wished.

Not suitable for freezing.

CHOCOLATE COOKIE CAKE

SERVES 8

Serve this easy dessert with cups of strong coffee to round off an informal dinner.

4 squares semi sweet chocolate
1 tablespoon corn syrup
1 stick butter
2 tablespoons heavy cream
1$\frac{1}{4}$ cups Graham Crackers, broken up
2 tablespoons raisins
$\frac{1}{4}$ cup candied cherries, halved
$\frac{1}{4}$ cup slivered almonds, roasted

1. Butter a loose-bottomed 6–7 inch pan or ring.
2. Break the chocolate into pieces and place in a bowl over a pan of hot water. Add the syrup, butter and cream.
3. When the chocolate and butter have melted, remove the pan from the heat and cool slightly. (Alternatively, microwave on HIGH for 2–3 minutes or until melted, stirring occasionally.)
4. Mix the Graham Crackers, fruit and nuts into the chocolate mixture.
5. Turn the mixture into the prepared pan, lightly level the top, then chill for at least 1 hour before serving.

To freeze: pack and freeze once the mixture is set. Defrost at cool room temperature.

CHOCOLATE AND PRALINE RING

SERVES 4–6

Before adding the cream and egg whites, the custard must be the right consistency. It should be cold and just beginning to thicken. Too runny, and the pudding separates into layers; too set, and the finished result will be lumpy.

2 squares semi sweet or milk chocolate
scant 1 cup milk
1 tablespoon gelatin
5 tablespoons cold black coffee
3 eggs, separated
scant $\frac{1}{3}$ cup superfine sugar
$\frac{1}{2}$ teaspoon cornstarch
2 ounces praline powder (see page 104)
5 tablespoons heavy cream

FOR THE DECORATION
whipped cream
marrons glacés (optional)

1. Lightly oil a 4 cup ring mold.
2. Break the chocolate into small pieces. Place in a medium saucepan and add the milk. Heat gently until the chocolate melts. Bring to the boil, stirring all the time, until the chocolate mixture is smooth—about 2–3 minutes.
3. Sprinkle the gelatin over the cold black coffee in a small bowl and leave to soak for 2–3 minutes. Place the bowl over a saucepan of simmering water and stir until dissolved. (Alternatively, microwave on HIGH for 30 seconds or until dissolved.)
4. Whisk the egg yolks, 2 tablespoons of the sugar and the cornstarch together in a bowl until very thick and pale. Slowly add the hot chocolate mixture, whisking all the time.
5. Return the mixture to the rinsed-out pan and stir over a very gentle heat until it thickens enough to coat the back of a wooden spoon. Do not allow to boil. Pour the mixture into a bowl.
6. Stir the dissolved gelatin into the chocolate mixture with 2 tablespoons of the praline powder. Leave to cool completely.
7. When the custard is cool and just beginning to set, whip the cream until it just begins to hold its shape. Fold into the mixture. Whisk the egg whites until stiff but not dry. Whisk in the remaining sugar, then fold into the custard.
8. Pour into the prepared ring mold and chill for about 3 hours to set.
9. To serve, dip the mold briefly into hot water and invert the ring on to a serving plate. Decorate with the remaining praline, whipped cream and marrons glacés, if using.

Not suitable for freezing.

CHOCOLATE MOUSSE CUPS

SERVES 6

This must be the most delicious chocolate mousse you can imagine, encased in crisp, sugar-dusted filo pastry.

3 large sheets filo pastry, about 10 × 20 inches
$\frac{1}{4}$ stick butter
4 squares semi sweet chocolate
2 tablespoons brandy
1 tablespoon instant coffee powder
2 eggs, separated
$\frac{1}{2}$ cup heavy cream, lightly whipped
roasted slivered almonds, to decorate
icing sugar, for dusting

1. Cut each filo pastry sheet into 12 squares. Line 12 deep muffin pans with three overlapping squares, brushing with melted butter between each layer.
2. Bake blind in the oven at 400° for 10–12 minutes or until the pastry is crisp, golden brown and cooked through. Turn out on to a wire rack and leave to cool.
3. Break the chocolate into small pieces. Place in a heatproof bowl with the brandy, coffee powder and 1 tablespoon water. Stand the bowl over a pan of simmering water and heat gently until the chocolate melts. Stir the mixture until smooth. (Alternatively, microwave on LOW for 4–6 minutes or until melted, stirring occasionally.)
4. Stir in the egg yolks, cool slightly, then mix in the cream. Whisk the egg whites until stiff but not dry, then fold into the chocolate mixture. Leave to set until the consistency of thick cream. Spoon the mousse into the pastry cups and chill for 1 hour.
5. Sprinkle the mousse cups with the roasted slivered almonds and dust heavily with icing sugar before serving with light cream.

Not suitable for freezing.

Above: CHOCOLATE AND PRALINE RING.
Below: CHOCOLATE MOUSSE CUPS.

BANANA AND CHOCOLATE CHIP SPONGE

SERVES 4

A favorite with children. If you own a microwave, this dessert can be reheated successfully, a portion at a time, covered, on HIGH for 2 minutes.

1 stick butter or margarine
generous ½ cup superfine sugar
2 eggs, beaten
1½ cups self raising flour
about 3 tablespoons milk
1 small banana, peeled and chopped
⅓ cup chocolate chips

1. Grease a 3 cup ceramic bowl.
2. Cream the butter and sugar together in a bowl until pale and fluffy. Gradually beat in the eggs.
3. Using a metal spoon, fold in the flour. Add enough milk to give a soft dropping consistency. Stir in the banana and chocolate.
4. Spoon the mixture into the prepared bowl. Cover with greased wax paper and foil, then secure with string. Steam for about 1½ hours or until firm to the touch. (Alternatively, cover with wax paper only and microwave on HIGH for 5–6 minutes.) Turn out on to a warmed plate and serve with hot Chocolate sauce (see page 244).

Not suitable for freezing.

BAKED CHOCOLATE MARBLE SPONGE

SERVES 8

A delicious family dessert to serve on cold winter days.

3 squares semi sweet chocolate
1½ sticks butter or margarine
scant 1 cup light brown soft sugar
3 eggs, beaten
1¾ cups self raising flour
3 tablespoons milk
1 cup macaroons

1. Grease a 4¼ cup loaf pan.
2. Break the chocolate into small pieces. Place in a small heatproof bowl standing over a pan of simmering water and heat until the chocolate melts. (Alternatively, microwave on LOW for 3–4 minutes or until melted, stirring occasionally.) Leave to cool.
3. Cream the butter and sugar together in a bowl until pale and fluffy. Gradually beat in the eggs. Using a metal spoon, fold in the flour and milk.

4. Divide the mixture in two and flavor half with the cooled chocolate, folding it evenly through the mixture.
5. Place alternate spoonfuls of the mixtures in two layers in the prepared pan and zig-zag a knife through the mixture to make a marbled pattern. Roughly crush the macaroons and scatter over the top. Cover with foil.
6. Bake in the oven at 350° for about 1¼ hours or until firm to the touch. Turn out and serve thickly sliced with hot Chocolate sauce (see page 244) or Chocolate fudge sauce (see page 253).

Not suitable for freezing.

Illustrated on page 252.

CHOCOLATE AND CHESTNUT GINGER PIE

SERVES 12

1½ quantity Pâte sucrée (see page 43)
FOR THE FILLING
2 squares semi sweet or bitter chocolate
5 tablespoons stem ginger syrup
2 eggs
scant ⅓ cup superfine sugar
½ cup heavy or whipping cream
15 ounce can unsweetened chestnut paste
white and semi sweet Chocolate curls (see page 78), to decorate

1. Roll out the pastry on a lightly floured work surface and use to line the base and sides of a 14 × 4 inch shallow rectangular pie ring or a round 9 inch pie ring.
2. Bake blind in the oven at 375° for 15 minutes, then remove the beans and continue to bake for 5–10 minutes or until golden brown and cooked through. Cool completely in the dish.
3. Meanwhile to make the filling, break the chocolate into small pieces. Place in a heatproof bowl with the ginger syrup. Stand the bowl over a pan of simmering water and heat gently until the chocolate melts. Stir only once or twice after the chocolate has started to melt. (Alternatively, microwave on LOW for 4 minutes, stirring occasionally.) Remove from the heat.
4. Whisk the eggs and sugar together in a bowl with an electric whisk, until very pale and thick. Whip the cream until it holds its shape and fold in the cool but not cold chocolate. Fold into the egg mixture.
5. Using an electric whisk, whip the chestnut paste with a quarter of the chocolate mixture until smooth. Gradually whisk in the remaining mixture. Cover and chill for at least 1 hour.
6. About 30 minutes before serving, spoon the mixture into the cold pastry case. Decorate.

To freeze: pack and freeze the filled pastry case. Unwrap and defrost at cool room temperature. Decorate as above.

DOUBLE CHOCOLATE MUFFINS

SERVES 12

A very popular recipe and no wonder too, as they are quick to make and taste delicious, especially if served fresh from the oven.

4 squares semi sweet chocolate
$\frac{2}{3}$ cup cocoa
2 cups self raising flour
1 teaspoon baking powder
$\frac{1}{4}$ cup dark brown soft sugar
pinch of salt
$\frac{2}{3}$ cup chocolate chips
1 cup milk
4 tablespoons vegetable oil
1 teaspoon vanilla
1 egg

1. Thoroughly grease 12 deep muffin pans. Place a large paper cake case in each.
2. Break the chocolate into small pieces. Place in a large heatproof bowl standing over a pan of simmering water and heat gently until the chocolate melts. (Alternatively, microwave on LOW for 3–4 minutes or until melted, stirring occasionally.)
3. Remove from the heat and stir in the remaining ingredients. Beat thoroughly together. Spoon the mixture into the paper cases.
4. Bake in the oven at 425° for 15 minutes until well risen and firm to the touch. Serve warm.

To freeze: wrap and freeze the cooled muffins. Defrost at cool room temperature. Reheat at 350° for 5–10 minutes.

STEAMED CHOCOLATE PUDDING

SERVES 4

Vary this favorite English nursery pudding by adding $\frac{1}{2}$ cup chopped nuts, chocolate chips, raisins or dry apricots to the basic mixture, or $\frac{1}{4}$ cup chopped stem ginger.

1 stick butter or margarine
generous $\frac{1}{2}$ cup superfine sugar
4 tablespoons cocoa
2 eggs, beaten
$1\frac{1}{2}$ cups self raising flour
about 3 tablespoons milk

1. Grease a 3 cup ceramic bowl.
2. Cream the butter and sugar together in a bowl until pale and fluffy. Blend the cocoa and 2 tablespoons hot water to a smooth cream, then gradually add to the creamed mixture.
3. Add the beaten eggs, a little at a time, beating well after each addition. Using a metal spoon, fold in the flour. Add enough milk to give a soft dropping consistency.
4. Spoon the mixture into the prepared bowl. Cover with greased wax paper and secure with string. Steam for $1\frac{1}{2}$ hours. (Alternatively, microwave on HIGH for 5–6 minutes.) Turn out on to a warmed plate and serve with Chocolate sauce (see page 244).

Not suitable for freezing.

CHOCOLATE AND ORANGE TRIFLE

SERVES 8

$\frac{3}{4}$ pound chocolate cake
4 oranges
8 tablespoons orange-flavored liqueur
4 egg yolks
scant $\frac{1}{3}$ cup superfine sugar
3 tablespoons cornstarch
vanilla
2 cups milk
3 tablespoons stem ginger syrup
1 cup heavy cream
roasted almonds and stem ginger, to decorate

1. Thinly slice the cake and use to line the base of a shallow serving dish.
2. Peel and segment the oranges. Place the segments on top of the cake. Spoon the liqueur evenly over the cake and orange.
3. In a saucepan, combine the egg yolks, sugar, cornstarch and vanilla. Gradually stir in the milk and ginger syrup; bring the mixture almost to the boil and simmer for 4–5 minutes until thickened, stirring all the time.
4. Pour the custard evenly into the dish. Leave to cool.
5. Whip the cream until it just holds its shape then spoon on top of the custard. Decorate with almonds and stem ginger.

Not suitable for freezing.

DARK AND LIGHT CHOCOLATE TERRINE

SERVES 6–8

A wickedly delicious chocaholic's dream! Be careful when slicing, as the terrine softens very quickly.

FOR THE PRALINE

1½ cups blanched almonds or peeled hazelnuts

generous ½ cup sugar

FOR THE DARK CHOCOLATE MOUSSE

6 squares semi sweet chocolate

¾ stick sweet butter

scant ½ cup superfine sugar

2 tablespoons cocoa, sifted

3 egg yolks

2 tablespoons rum or brandy

1 cup heavy or whipping cream

FOR THE WHITE CHOCOLATE MOUSSE

6 squares white chocolate

½ stick sweet butter, softened

2 egg yolks

generous ½ cup heavy or whipping cream

1. Grease and line a 2½ cup loaf pan with plastic wrap. Lightly oil a cookie sheet.
2. To make the praline, toast the nuts in the oven at 350° or until golden brown, stirring occasionally. Put the sugar with 1 tablespoon water into a heavy-based saucepan. Melt over a gentle heat until the sugar has dissolved. Stir in the warm nuts and boil until the syrup starts to brown. Immediately pour on to the prepared cookie sheet. Leave to cool completely, then roughly crush with a rolling pin or in a blender or food processor. Store in an airtight container until needed.
3. To make the mousses, break both chocolates into small pieces. Place in two small heatproof bowls standing over pans of simmering water and heat gently until the chocolates melt. Stir until smooth. (Alternatively, microwave on LOW for 2–3 minutes or until melted, stirring occasionally.) Cool slightly.
4. To make the dark chocolate mousse, cream the butter and half the sugar together until pale and creamy. Beat in the cocoa powder. In another bowl, beat the egg yolks and the remaining sugar until pale. Stir in the rum. Whip the cream until it just holds its shape. Working quickly, beat the melted semi sweet chocolate into the creamed butter. Stir this into the yolk mixture, then carefully fold in the cream. Set aside.
5. To make the white chocolate mousse, beat the butter into the melted white chocolate. Stir in the yolks and 2 tablespoons crushed praline. Whip the cream until it just holds its shape and fold into the chocolate mixture.
6. Drop large spoonfuls of each mousse alternately into the prepared pan until full. Tap the pan on the work surface to level. Cover and chill for at least 4 hours (or overnight preferably) until very firm.

7. To serve, turn out the mousse on to a flat serving dish and peel off the plastic wrap. With a spatula, press the remaining praline over the top and sides. Chill for 30 minutes to firm, then serve cut into slices. This dessert is so rich it needs nothing extra to accompany it.

Not suitable for freezing.

CHOCOLATE LACE BASKETS

SERVES 6

These dainty lace baskets are made with chocolate-flavored cake covering. When set, it is less brittle than semi sweet chocolate and is therefore less likely to crack. Don't attempt these unless you have time to spare, as they require patience.

5 squares chocolate-flavored cake coating

1 small mango

¼ fresh pineapple

12 strawberries

1 passion fruit

1. Break the cake coating into small pieces. Place in a heatproof bowl standing over a pan of simmering water and heat gently until it melts. (Alternatively, microwave on LOW for 4–6 minutes or until melted, stirring occasionally.)
2. Invert six 3½ inch ring molds and stretch plastic wrap over the rounded bases to cover completely.
3. Spoon half the melted chocolate cake coating into a wax paper pastry tube and snip off the point. Pipe three of the ring molds with a lacy pattern of cake covering.
4. Fill a second bag with melted cake coating and pipe the remaining three molds. Chill until set.
5. Meanwhile, peel the mango and chop the flesh. Cut the pineapple flesh into pieces. Hull the strawberries. Halve the passion fruit and scoop out the pulp.
6. Carefully lift the chocolate baskets with the plastic wrap, then remove the plastic wrap from the shells. Fill the baskets with the fruit. Serve with whipped cream.

To freeze: pack the unfilled chocolate baskets in a rigid container. Defrost in the refrigerator overnight, then finish as above.

Opposite: CHOCOLATE LACE BASKETS.

LIGHT BATTERS AND OMELETS

Luscious fillings and light, golden pancakes combine to
make truly sublime ensembles from classic Crêpes Suzette
to sensational Crêpes soufflés au framboise. For other
wonderful ways with batters such as beignets, fritters and
Clafoutis plus sweet soufflé omelets, read on!

Batter is a liquid and flour mixture, with a consistency similar to light cream. Pouring batter is used to make pancakes or crêpes, waffles and biscuits, and a thicker, coating batter is used to give a crisp, protective coating to food to make fritters or beignets.

A blender or food processor takes the work out of batter making. Put the eggs and other liquid ingredients into the machine, spoon the flour on top of them and process for a second or two, just enough to blend the ingredients together. Not long enough to create lots of bubbles.

Alternatively, make the batter by hand. Put the dry ingredients in a large bowl, make a deep well in the center, using a wooden spoon, then add the eggs and a little of the liquid. Blend the liquid ingredients together in the well, then gradually incorporate the surrounding flour. Do this slowly, keeping the central mixture smooth and free of lumps. As the mixture becomes thicker, add the remaining liquid, a little at a time and keep beating until all of the flour is incorporated. Once all the flour is added and the mixture is absolutely smooth, add the remaining liquid.

If you have time, 'rest' the batter for about 30 minutes to give the starch grains a chance to swell. This will give a lighter, less doughy batter. Re-mix the batter before cooling.

An essential for pancake and omelet making is a good heavy-based skillet. Ideally it should be kept solely for pancake or omelet making and should never be scrubbed, just wiped out with kitchen paper after use. Store the pan wrapped, to prevent the surface being scratched. Choose a pan with a base area of about 8–9 inches, with or without a non-stick coating. If available, follow the manufacturer's instructions for use, otherwise, first heat a new pan with plenty of oil to 'season' or seal it. Repeat the process once or twice until it has a perfect surface. Then pour out the oil and start pancake making. Once you get in the swing and your confidence grows, make several batches of pancakes at once, freezing the extras for another day.

BASIC PANCAKE BATTER
MAKES 8 THIN PANCAKES OR CRÊPES

1 cup All Purpose flour
pinch of salt
1 egg
1 cup milk
oil, for frying

1. Sift the flour and salt into a bowl and make a well in the center. Break in the egg and beat well with a wooden spoon. Gradually beat in the milk, drawing in the flour from the sides to make a smooth batter.

2. Heat a little oil in a 7 inch heavy-based skillet, running it around the base and sides of the pan, until hot. Pour off any surplus.

3. Pour in just enough batter to thinly coat the base of the pan. Cook for 1–2 minutes until golden brown. Turn or toss and cook the second side until golden.

4. Transfer the pancake to a plate and keep hot. Repeat with the remaining batter to make eight pancakes. Pile the cooked pancakes on top of each other with wax paper in between each one and keep warm in the oven while cooking the remainder.

5. Serve as soon as they are all cooked, sprinkled with sugar and lemon juice.

VARIATIONS

Buckwheat Pancakes Replace half the flour with buckwheat flour and add an extra egg white.

Orange, Lemon or Lime Pancakes Add the finely grated peel of 1 lemon, ½ an orange or 1 lime with the milk.

Chocolate Pancakes Replace 1 tablespoon of the flour with sifted cocoa.

To freeze: interleave with wax paper and wrap in foil. Defrost at room temperature for 2–3 hours or overnight in the refrigerator. To defrost quickly, spread out separately and leave at room temperature for about 20 minutes. Reheat the foil-wrapped pancakes in the oven at 375° for 20–30 minutes. Alternatively, separate the pancakes and heat in an oiled skillet for 30 seconds on each side.

Previous Page: PANCAKES WITH FRUIT AND CREAM.

FRITTER OR COATING BATTER

MAKES ABOUT 1 CUP

Fritter or coating batter is thicker than pancake batter, so it will cling to foods dipped into it, which can then be deep-fried.

1 cup All Purpose flour
pinch of salt
1 egg
½ cup milk or milk and water mixed

1. Sift the flour and salt into a bowl and make a well in the center. Break in the egg and beat well with a wooden spoon.
2. Gradually beat in the liquid, drawing in the flour from the sides to make a smooth batter.

VARIATION

To make a lighter batter, use 1 tablespoon oil instead of the egg. Just before cooking, whisk two egg whites stiffly and fold them into the batter. Use the batter immediately.

APPLE FRITTERS

SERVES 4

These mouth watering apple fritters can be made successfully using pineapple or bananas. Serve them with cream.

3 medium tart apples
oil, for deep-frying
1 quantity Fritter batter (see above)
FOR THE COATING
sugar
cinnamon

1. Peel and core the apples and cut into ¼ inch thick rings.
2. Heat the oil in a deep fat fryer to 350°. Dip the apple rings in the fritter batter and deep fry for 2–3 minutes until golden.
3. Drain on kitchen paper. Toss in sugar and cinnamon, then serve.

VARIATIONS

Pineapple Fritters Use a well drained 8 ounce can pineapple rings instead of the apples.

Banana Fritters Use 4 small bananas, peeled and cut in half lengthways, instead of the apples.

Pear Fritters Use 3–4 medium pears, peeled, cored and cut into thick rings, instead of the apples.

Not suitable for freezing.

RICH PANCAKES

MAKES 12–14

These work equally well if you replace the brandy or rum with your favorite liqueur.

½ cup icing sugar
1 cup All Purpose flour
pinch of salt
½ stick butter, melted
1 tablespoon brandy, rum or liqueur
1 egg, beaten

1. To make the batter, sift the icing sugar, flour and salt into a bowl. Make a well in the center, then pour in the butter, brandy and egg.
2. Beat the mixture well, then gradually add about ½ cup warm water. Continue beating and adding water until a thin batter is obtained.
3. Make 12–14 pancakes (see page 108). Serve with orange juice and sugar to taste.

To freeze: interleave with wax paper and wrap in foil. To defrost and reheat, see page 108.

CRÊPES SUZETTE

SERVES 4–6

A classic French dessert; with its spectacular flambéed finish, Crêpes Suzette is just perfect for a special dinner party. Traditionally flambéed at the table in a copper chafing dish in restaurants specializing in haute cuisine, the crêpes can look just as good at home carried flaming to the table on a silver of china plate.

7 tablespoons orange-flavored liqueur
1 quantity Pancake batter (see page 108)
1 stick sweet butter
generous ½ cup superfine sugar
finely grated peel and juice of 1 large orange

1. Stir 1 tablespoon of the liqueur into the batter. Make 8–12 crêpes (see page 108). Stack with wax paper in between and keep warm in the oven.
2. To serve, heat the butter and sugar together in a large, heavy-based skillet until thick and syrupy. Add 2 tablespoons of the liqueur and the orange peel and juice and heat through.
3. Fold the crêpes into triangle shapes by folding each one in half, then in half again. Place them in the skillet and spoon over the sauce to coat evenly.
4. Heat the remaining liqueur gently in a ladle or separate small pan. Transfer the crêpes and sauce to a warmed serving dish, pour over the warmed liqueur and set alight. Carefully carry the crêpes to the table while still flaming.

To freeze: freeze and defrost the crêpes (see page 108). Finish as above.

BANANA PANCAKES

SERVES 4

These lightly spiced pancakes will be popular with all the family.

1 tablespoon superfine sugar
large pinch of mixed spice
½ quantity Pancake batter (see page 108)
4 large ripe bananas
oil and butter, for frying
lemon juice, for sprinkling

1. Stir the sugar and mixed spice into the batter.
2. Peel and slice the bananas into ¼ inch pieces.
3. Heat a little oil and butter in a medium non-stick skillet. Add the slices from one banana and brown on one side. Turn the slices over.
4. Pour in a thin layer of batter and fry over a moderate heat until browned. Slide out the pancake and keep warm, lightly covered, in a low oven.
5. Fry remaining three pancakes in the same way. Sprinkle the pancakes with lemon juice.

Not suitable for freezing.

CRÊPES ANNETTE

SERVES 6

Kirsch-flavored pancakes filled with a rich mixture of cream cheese and cherries.

FOR THE CRÊPES

1¾ cups All Purpose flour
1 teaspoon baking powder
½ teaspoon soda
pinch of salt
9 tablespoons kirsch
2 cups milk
¼ stick butter, melted
2 eggs, beaten
oil, for frying

FOR THE FILLING

15 ounce can black cherries
¾ cup full fat soft cream cheese
scant ⅓ cup superfine sugar

1. To make the crêpes, sift the flour, baking powder, soda and salt into a bowl. Add 6 tablespoons of the kirsch, the milk, butter and eggs, then beat until smooth.
2. Heat a little oil in a heavy-based skillet. Pour in 2 tablespoons batter. Swirl around the pan and cook until golden underneath. Turn over and cook on the other side. Makes 12 crêpes.

3. Stack the crêpes with wax paper in between and keep warm in the oven.
4. To make the filling, drain the cherries; reserve the juice and a few cherries. Pit the cherries, if necessary. Beat the cream cheese and sugar together until soft and fluffy. Chop the remaining cherries roughly and fold them into the cheese mixture.
5. Spread a little filling on each crêpe and fold into triangles; or put the filling in the center and roll up the crêpes. Arrange in a serving dish and keep warm.
6. Heat the reserved cherries and syrup in a pan. Gently warm the remaining kirsch. Drizzle the cherries and syrup over the crêpes, then add the kirsch and set alight.

To freeze: freeze the crêpes (see page 108).

ORANGE AND NECTARINE CRÊPES

SERVES 4–6

Peaches can be used in place of the nectarines.

1 quantity Pancake batter (see page 108)
finely grated peel and juice of 2 oranges
scant ⅓ cup superfine sugar
4 large ripe nectarines
2 tablespoons orange-flavored liqueur
3 tablespoons brandy

1. Grease a heatproof dish.
2. Make 8–12 crêpes (see page 108). Stack the crêpes with wax paper in between and keep warm in the oven.
3. Make the orange juice up to ½ cup with water. Place the peel and juice in a saucepan with the sugar. Warm gently until the sugar dissolves, then boil for 1 minute.
4. Meanwhile, quarter each nectarine, skin and roughly chop the flesh. Place the flesh in the syrup and simmer gently for 3–4 minutes.
5. Remove from the heat and stir in the liqueur. Strain off the syrup and reserve.
6. Fill the pancakes with the nectarines, then fold each pancake into a fan shape. Place, slightly overlapping, in the prepared heatproof dish. Pour over the syrup and cover tightly with greased foil.
7. Bake in the oven at 375° for about 25 minutes or until thoroughly hot.
8. Place the brandy in a small saucepan. Warm slightly, then set alight with a match and immediately pour over the crêpes. Serve straight away, with cream or yogurt.

To freeze: freeze the pancakes (see page 108).

Opposite: ORANGE AND NECTARINE CRÊPES.

PANCAKES CREOLE

SERVES 4–6

All the best flavors of Creole cooking combine to make these mouthwatering pancakes.

1 quantity Pancake batter (see page 108)
finely grated peel and juice of 1 lime
½ stick butter or margarine
¼ cup brownulated sugar
4 tablespoons dark rum
½ teaspoon cinnamon
3–4 bananas

FOR THE DECORATION

twists of orange
twists of lime

1. Make 8–12 pancakes (see page 108). Stack the pancakes with wax paper in between and keep warm in the oven.
2. Put the lime peel and juice in a saucepan with the butter, sugar, rum and cinnamon. Heat gently until the butter has melted and the sugar dissolved, stirring occasionally.
3. Peel the bananas and slice thinly into the sauce. Cook gently for 5 minutes until tender.
4. Remove the banana slices from the sauce with a slotted spoon. Place a few slices in the center of each pancake, then fold the pancakes into 'envelopes' around the cooked bananas.
5. Place in a warmed serving dish and pour over the hot sauce. Decorate with orange and lime twists. Serve with cream.

To freeze: freeze the pancakes (see page 108).

GINGER AND APPLE PANCAKE LAYER

SERVES 8

Using sweet apples means that they retain their shape and you will not need to add much sugar.

1 teaspoon ginger
1 quantity Pancake batter (see page 108)
2 pounds sweet apples
sugar, to taste
⅓ cup white raisins
8 tablespoons ginger preserve

1. Grease a shallow heatproof dish.
2. Stir the ginger into the pancake batter. Make 8 pancakes (see page 108). Stack the pancakes with wax paper in between and keep warm in the oven.

3. Peel, quarter and core the apples, then roughly chop. Place the apples in a medium saucepan with 2 tablespoons water and sugar to taste. Cover and cook gently for about 5 minutes or until the apples soften. (Alternatively, put the ingredients in a bowl. Cover and microwave on HIGH for 6–8 minutes or until soft.) Add the white raisins.
4. Place one pancake in the prepared dish and spread with a little of the apple mixture. Repeat the layers until all of the pancakes and apple mixture are used, finishing with a pancake. Cover with buttered foil.
5. Bake in the oven at 400° for about 30 minutes or until really hot.
6. Meanwhile, place the ginger preserve and 4 tablespoons water in a pan and heat gently until melted. (Alternatively, put the ingredients in a bowl and microwave on HIGH for 2 minutes.) Strain the mixture and pour over the pancake layer just before serving. Serve cut into wedges.

To freeze: pack and freeze at the end of step 4. To use, defrost overnight at cool room temperature, then finish as above.

APRICOT AND ALMOND CRÊPE GÂTEAU

SERVES 6–8

An unusual cold gâteau where the custard changes into a sauce when cooked. This would be very good served with extra stewed fruits and cream.

16 Orange crêpes (see page 108)

FOR THE FILLING

¾ pound dry apricots
1 cup orange juice
2½ cups ground almonds
2 tablespoons superfine sugar
2–4 tablespoons heavy cream
¾ cup white raisins

FOR THE CUSTARD

5 egg yolks
scant ½ cup superfine sugar
1½ cups milk or light cream, scalded

1. Grease a 3½ cup charlotte mold or soufflé dish. The diameter of the dish should be a little wider than the diameter of the crêpes.
2. Make the crêpes (see page 108). Stack the crêpes with wax paper in between and keep warm in the oven.
3. To make the filling, place the apricots and orange juice in a saucepan. Cover and simmer for about 10 minutes or until just tender. (Alternatively, microwave, covered, on HIGH for 5–7 minutes.) Strain off any liquid and reserve. Blend or strain the apricots to make a thick purée.

4. Mix the ground almonds with the sugar and enough cream to bind to a spreadable paste.

5. Spread each crêpe with almond paste, then apricot purée. Layer the crêpes in the prepared dish, sprinkling with raisins between each layer.

6. To make the custard, beat the egg yolks and sugar together in a bowl until pale and fluffy. Add the scalded milk or cream and stir well. Carefully ladle over the crêpes. Cover with buttered wax paper.

7. Bake in the oven at 300° for 30–40 minutes or until the custard is set. Leave to cool completely.

8. When cold, run a thin-bladed knife around the edge to loosen and turn out on to a serving plate. Serve the gâteau, cut into wedges with the reserved orange cooking liquid poured over.

Not suitable for freezing.

CHOCOLATE CINNAMON CRÊPES

SERVES 4–5

This makes ten generously filled crêpes, enough for five, allowing two each, or enough for four hungry people, allowing for second helpings.

3 teaspoons cinnamon
1 quantity Pancake batter (see page 108)
1 cup All Purpose flour
scant ⅓ cup superfine sugar
1 cup milk
2 squares semi sweet chocolate, cut into pieces
grated peel of 1 lemon
4 eggs
grated white and semi sweet chocolate, to decorate

1. Lightly grease a large shallow heatproof dish.

2. Stir 2 teaspoons of the cinnamon into the batter. Make ten crêpes (see page 108). Stack the crêpes with wax paper in between and keep warm in the oven.

3. Mix the flour, sugar and remaining cinnamon together in a bowl. Blend to a smooth paste with a little of the milk. Heat the remaining milk to boiling point and whisk in the flour mixture. Bring to the boil, whisking all the time; it should be very thick. Remove from the heat.

4. Stir the chocolate and lemon peel into the mixture until completely blended and smooth. Gradually beat the egg yolks into the chocolate mixture. Whisk the egg whites until stiff, then fold in the mixture.

5. Spoon about 4 tablespoons mixture on to the center of each crêpe. Fold in the sides to completely enclose. Place in one layer in the prepared dish, seam side downwards.

6. Bake in the oven at 425° for 15–20 minutes until just set. Decorate with grated chocolate. Serve hot or cold.

To freeze: freeze the unfilled crêpes (see page 108).

CRÊPES SOUFFLÉES AU FRAMBOISE

SERVES 4

The delicious soufflé filling puffs up as the crêpes bake in the oven. Serve immediately before they collapse.

8 Orange crêpes (see page 108)
2 tablespoons superfine sugar
1 tablespoon All Purpose flour
½ cup milk
2 eggs, separated
3 tablespoons raspberry-flavored liqueur
2 cups raspberries, hulled
1 tablespoon icing sugar, sifted

1. Grease a heatproof dish.

2. Make the crêpes (see page 108). Stack the crêpes with wax paper in between and keep warm in the oven.

3. Put the sugar, flour and milk in a heavy-based saucepan and bring to the boil, whisking all the time. Cool slightly, then stir in the egg yolks and liqueur. Whisk the egg whites until stiff, then fold lightly into the mixture.

4. Place a few raspberries on one half of each crêpe, reserving a few for decoration. Top the raspberries with the soufflé mixture, then fold the crêpes in half to enclose the raspberries and filling. As each one is filled, transfer it to the prepared dish, arranging them side by side.

5. Bake in the oven at 425° for 5 minutes. Sprinkle with the icing sugar and bake for a further 5 minutes. Serve immediately, with Raspberry Fruit Purée Sauce (see page 244), decorated with the reserved raspberries.

Not suitable for freezing.

STRAWBERRY SAVARIN

SERVES 6

A savarin is an open-textured, spongy yeast cake. Once cooked, it is soaked in a sugar or liqueur syrup.

1 packet fresh yeast or 1½ teaspoons dry
3 tablespoons warm milk
2 eggs, lightly beaten
½ stick butter, melted and cooled
1 cup All Purpose flour
1 tablespoon superfine sugar
¼ cup sweet shredded coconut
6 tablespoons redcurrant jelly or strained strawberry jelly
5 tablespoons lemon juice
1 pound strawberries, hulled

1. Lightly oil a 4½ cup savarin pan or ring mold and turn it upside down on kitchen paper to drain off the excess oil.
2. Blend the fresh yeast with the milk. If using dry yeast, sprinkle it on to the milk and leave in a warm place for 15 minutes or until frothy. Gradually beat the eggs and butter into the yeast liquid.
3. Mix the flour, sugar and coconut together in a bowl. With a wooden spoon, gradually stir in the yeast mixture to form a thick smooth batter. Beat together.
4. Turn the batter into the prepared pan, cover with oiled plastic wrap and leave in a warm place for about 30 minutes or until the savarin is nearly doubled in size.
5. Bake in the oven at 375° for 35–40 minutes until golden. Turn out on to a wire rack placed over a large plate.
6. Put the jelly and lemon juice into a small pan over a low heat. (Alternatively, microwave on HIGH for 1–2 minutes.) When the jelly has melted, spoon over the warm savarin until well glazed, allowing any excess to collect on the plate under the wire rack. Transfer the savarin to a serving plate.
7. Return the excess jelly mixture to the pan and add the strawberries; stir to coat. Remove from heat and cool for 15–20 minutes or until almost set. Spoon into the center of the savarin. Serve warm or cold.

VARIATIONS

Strawberry Babas   Divide the yeast batter between six 3½ inch ring pans. Leave to rise until the molds are nearly two-thirds full, then bake for 15–20 minutes. Replace the lemon juice with brandy or kirsch, soak each baba well and place on individual serving plates. Finish with strawberries and sour cream as above.

Rum Babas   Make as strawberry babas but soak the warm babas in a rum syrup made with 8 tablespoons clear honey, 8 tablespoons water and rum or rum flavoring to taste. Serve filled with whipped cream.

To freeze: wrap and freeze the cooled savarin. Defrost overnight at cool room temperature, then warm gently, covered, in a low oven. Spoon over the warm jelly and finish as above.

FRUIT AND RUM SAVARIN

SERVES 6

Served filled with fresh fruits, this savarin is soaked in a rum syrup.

1 packet fresh yeast
3 tablespoons warm milk
1 cup strong All Purpose flour, sifted with a pinch of salt
2 tablespoons superfine sugar
2 eggs, beaten
½ stick sweet butter, softened
generous 1 cup sugar
8 tablespoons dark rum
2 bananas, peeled and sliced
1 pound black seedless grapes, halved
2 kiwi fruit, peeled and sliced
2 small oranges, peeled and segmented

1. Grease and flour a 4 cup savarin or ring mold.
2. Put the yeast in a warmed small bowl and add the milk; cream together. Add ¼ cup of the flour and beat well with a fork. Leave in a warm place for 10–15 minutes until frothy.
3. Put the remaining flour in a warmed large bowl with 1 teaspoon of the sugar and the eggs. Add the frothy yeast mixture, then beat until an elastic dough is formed. Cover with a floured cloth and leave in a warm place until doubled in size.
4. Beat the softened butter into the dough a little at a time until evenly incorporated.
5. Put the dough in the prepared mold. Cover with a floured cloth and leave to prove in a warm place until it has risen to the top of the mold. Uncover the mold.
6. Bake in the oven at 400° for 25–30 minutes until risen and golden brown.
7. Meanwhile, make the rum sugar syrup. Put the sugar and scant 1 cup water in a heavy-based saucepan and heat gently until the sugar has dissolved. Bring to the boil and boil steadily, without stirring, for 5 minutes until syrupy. Remove from the heat and stir in 6 tablespoons of the rum.
8. Turn the savarin out on to a wire rack placed over a large plate or tray. Prick all over the savarin with a fine tester, then slowly spoon over the warm syrup. Collect any syrup that drips on to the plate or tray and spoon it back over the savarin. Leave until completely cold.
9. Toss the prepared fruits together with the remaining sugar and rum. Place the savarin on a serving plate and pile the fruits in the center. Serve immediately with light cream.

To freeze: wrap and freeze the cooled savarin. Defrost overnight at cool room temperature, then warm gently, covered, in a low oven. Spoon over the warm syrup and finish as above.

Opposite: STRAWBERRY BABAS.

WAFFLES

SERVES 4

These crisp, light wafers, made from batter, are cooked in a special waffle iron. The cooking time varies with different kinds of waffle irons, but as a rule 2–3 minutes is sufficient. Follow the manufacturer's instructions.

1 cup self raising flour
pinch of salt
1 tablespoon superfine sugar
1 egg, separated
2 tablespoons butter or margarine, melted
½ cup milk
½ teaspoon vanilla (optional)

1. Heat the waffle iron according to the manufacturer's instructions.
2. Mix the flour, salt and sugar together in a bowl. Add the egg yolk, melted butter, milk and vanilla. Beat to give a smooth coating batter. Whisk the egg white until stiff and fold into the batter.
3. Pour just enough batter into the iron to run over the surface. Close the iron and cook for 2–3 minutes, turning the iron if using a non-electric type.
4. When the waffle is cooked, it should be golden brown and crisp and easily removed from the iron—if it sticks, cook for 1 minute longer.
5. Serve immediately with butter and maple syrup, or a fruit conserve of your choice.

To freeze: interleave with wax paper and wrap in foil. Defrost at room temperature for 2–3 hours or overnight in the refrigerator. Reheat the foil-wrapped waffles in the oven at 375° for 30 minutes.

ENGLISH DROP SCONES

MAKES 16–18

Drop scones take their name from the fact that the mixture is 'dropped' from the mixing spoon on to a hot griddle. Made with kitchen ingredients, they are ideal for an impromptu dessert. Serve with maple syrup and lashings of whipped cream.

1¼ cups self raising flour
pinch of salt
1 tablespoon superfine sugar
1 tablespoon oil
1 egg, beaten
½ cup milk
lard or oil, for greasing

1. Sift the flour, salt and sugar into a bowl. Add the oil, egg and milk. Stir with a wooden spoon to combine to a thick batter the consistency of heavy cream.
2. Grease a griddle or heavy skillet with a little lard or oil and place over moderate heat until hot.

3. Drop spoonfuls of the mixture from the point of a spoon on to the griddle, keeping them well apart to allow for spreading.
4. Cook over moderate heat for 2–3 minutes until bubbles rise and burst all over the surface of the scones and the undersides are golden brown. Turn them over with a spatula and cook for 2–3 minutes.
5. Transfer the cooked scones to a clean cloth and fold the cloth over to enclose them while making the remaining scones. Serve hot.

To freeze: pack and freeze the cold scones. Defrost at cool room temperature. Reheat in the oven, wrapped in foil, at 375° for 15–20 minutes.

GULAB JAMUN

SERVES 4–6

Gulab Jamun are popular in India; they are very sweet and syrupy, with a wonderfully exotic aroma of rose water, which is worth adding at the end for an authentic Gulab Jamun. Rose water is available in bottles at drug stores, delicatessens and herbalists.

generous 1 cup sugar
6 green cardamon pods, lightly crushed
1½ cups powdered low fat milk with vegetable fat
2 teaspoons baking powder
½ cup self raising flour
1 tablespoon Farina
about ½ cup milk
oil, for deep-frying
rose water, for sprinkling

1. Put the sugar and 1½ cups water in a saucepan. Bring slowly to the boil, stirring until the sugar has dissolved. Add the crushed cardamoms and boil rapidly for 4 minutes. Remove from the heat and cover.
2. Mix the powdered milk, baking powder, flour, Farina and enough milk together in a bowl to mix to a stiff dough rather like shortcrust pastry.
3. Knead the dough on a work surface until smooth. Divide into 24 pieces. Keep covered with plastic wrap to prevent the dough drying out. Roll each piece of dough into a completely smooth ball.
4. Heat the oil in a deep fat fryer to 325°. Deep fry the dough pieces in batches for 2–3 minutes until golden brown on all sides, turning them with a slotted spoon to ensure even browning. They must not fry too quickly as they have to cook all the way through before becoming too brown on the outside. Remove with a slotted spoon, drain on kitchen paper and keep warm while frying the remainder.
5. While the Gulab Jamuns are still hot, transfer them to a warmed serving dish. Pour over the warm syrup and sprinkle with rose water. Serve warm or cold.

Not suitable for freezing.

Opposite: GULAB JAMUN.

LE CLAFOUTIS

SERVES 6

A Clafoutis is a baked batter dessert popular throughout France. It is usually made with black cherries. Traditionalists insist that the cherries must not be pitted; we found that with pitted cherries it was much easier and daintier to eat! The choice is yours.

3 tablespoons kirsch
1 pound black cherries, pitted
FOR THE BATTER
$\frac{3}{4}$ cup All Purpose flour
$\frac{1}{2}$ cup icing sugar
pinch of salt
$\frac{1}{4}$ stick butter, melted
1 cup creamy milk
3 eggs, beaten
icing sugar, for dusting

1. Generously grease a shallow heatproof dish or pan.
2. Pour the kirsch over the cherries and leave to macerate for at least 30 minutes.
3. To make the batter, mix the flour, icing sugar and salt together in a bowl, then make a well in the center. Pour in the butter, milk and eggs. Beat together to make a smooth batter. Pour a very thin layer of batter into the prepared dish.
4. Bake in the oven at 425° for 5–10 minutes or until just set.
5. Drain the cherries, reserving the liquid, and arrange in a layer over the batter. Stir the reserved liquid into the remaining batter, pour evenly over the cherries. Return to the oven and bake for a further 40–45 minutes or until risen and golden brown.
6. Leave to cool for 5 minutes, then dust generously with icing sugar and serve while still warm with light cream.

Not suitable for freezing.

BEIGNETS DE FRUITS

SERVES 8

Most fruits make delicious beignets. Remember that soft fruits like apricots or peaches will require a much shorter cooking time than fruits such as apples and pears.

2 cups All Purpose flour
large pinch of salt
1 tablespoon icing sugar
1 cup beer
2 eggs, separated
1 tablespoon oil
oil, for deep-frying
2 large sweet apples, peeled, cored and cut into rings
2 firm nectarines, pitted and cut into quarters
2 bananas, peeled and cut into chunks
sugar, for sprinkling

1. To make the batter, mix the flour, salt and sugar together in a bowl, then make a well in the center. Add the beer and egg yolks. Beat together to make a smooth batter. Add the oil. Whisk the egg whites until stiff, then fold into the batter.
2. Heat the oil in a deep fat fryer to 375°. Dip the prepared fruits in the batter and deep fry in batches. The apples will take about 4 minutes and the nectarines and banana about 3 minutes.
3. Drain on kitchen paper and keep warm while frying the remainder. Serve hot, sprinkled with sugar.

Not suitable for freezing.

Opposite: BEIGNETS DE FRUITS.

FRESH STRAWBERRY FRITTERS

SERVES 4

Serve with a mixture of Greek yogurt and cream flavored with a little orange liqueur and orange peel.

$\frac{3}{4}$ *pound large firm, ripe strawberries*
4 tablespoons icing sugar
1$\frac{1}{2}$ cups All Purpose flour
pinch of salt
oil, for deep-frying

1. Hull the strawberries and toss in 2 tablespoons of the icing sugar.
2. To make the batter, mix the flour, salt and remaining icing sugar together in a bowl, then make a well in the center. Add $\frac{3}{4}$ cup water and beat vigorously with a wooden spoon to make a smooth batter. Chill.
3. Heat the oil in a deep fat fryer or a wok to 375°. Dip the strawberries in the batter, then remove with a slotted spoon taking up plenty of the batter with the fruit.
4. Deep fry for 3–4 minutes until crisp. Remove with a slotted spoon and drain on kitchen paper. Keep warm in the oven while cooking the remainder.

Not suitable for freezing.

DAMSON AND APPLE TANSY

SERVES 4

Tansies originally included the bitter-sweet herb, tansy.

2 large apples, peeled, cored and thinly sliced
$\frac{1}{2}$ *pound damsons, halved, pitted and quartered*
1 tablespoon butter
3 tablespoons sugar
pinch of cloves
pinch of cinnamon
4 eggs, separated
3 tablespoons sour cream

1. Put the apples, damsons, butter and half of the sugar in a large skillet. Cook over a gentle heat until the fruit is softened, stirring continuously. Stir in the cloves and cinnamon, then remove from the heat.
2. Beat the egg yolks and cream together and stir into the fruit. Whisk the egg whites until stiff, then fold in.
3. Cook over a low heat until the mixture has set. Sprinkle the top with the remaining sugar, then brown under a hot broiler. Serve immediately, straight from the pan, with sour cream.

Not suitable for freezing.

RUM SOUFFLÉ OMELET

SERVES 1

2 eggs, separated
1 teaspoon superfine sugar
1 tablespoon dark rum
1 tablespoon butter
1 tablespoon apricot jelly, warmed
2 tablespoons icing sugar

1. Mix the egg yolks, sugar and rum together in a bowl.

2. Whisk the egg whites until stiff and standing in peaks.

3. Melt the butter in a heavy-based omelet pan until foaming. Fold the egg whites quickly into the egg yolk mixture, then pour into the foaming butter.

4. Cook over moderate heat for 2–3 minutes until the underside of the omelet is golden brown. Place the pan under a preheated hot broiler and cook for a few minutes more until the top is golden brown.

5. Slide the omelet on to a sheet of foil placed on a warmed serving plate. Spread with the warmed jelly, then tip the foil to fold over the omelet.

6. Sift the icing sugar thickly over the top of the omelet, then mark in a criss-cross pattern with hot metal skewers, if liked. Carefully remove the foil and serve immediately.

VARIATIONS

Fruit Soufflé Omelet Replace the jelly with sliced fresh fruit or berries, such as raspberries or strawberries.
Chocolate Soufflé Omelet Omit the jelly and drizzle the omelet with 1½ squares melted chocolate (in step 5). Add a few chopped nuts. Sprinkle the omelet with a mixture of icing sugar and cinnamon.

Not suitable for freezing.

Opposite: DAMSON AND APPLE TANSY.
Above: RUM SOUFFLÉ OMELET.

SPECTACULAR GÂTEAUX

Blissfully self-indulgent and as far from the maddening diet as you could possibly wish, these are special treats for all those occasions when you want to spoil yourself, friends and family with some really mouthwatering confection.

You can't beat a light-as-a-feather sponge cake to create a mouthwatering dessert. Lots of gâteaux are based on a basic Genoese or whisked sponge. These are delicious enough simply to split and fill with fruit and cream, or can be transformed into totally irresistible, decadent desserts with nuts, liqueurs and praline.

Lightness, the essence of a good sponge, comes from using the freshest eggs possible and whisking them with sugar until thick and creamy. There is no fat in the classic sponge and the cake rises simply because of the air incorporated during whisking.

A moister version of the whisked sponge is a Genoese cake. This is also made by the whisking method, but melted butter is added with the flour. This gives a delicate sponge with a moister texture than the plain whisked sponge and a more delicious rich and buttery taste.

When adding melted butter, make sure it is just liquid and pour into the mixture around the sides of the bowl and fold in very light. Do not try to substitute margarine for butter in this recipe or the flavor and texture will be lost. A Genoese cake keeps better than a plain whisked sponge.

To make a really good sponge
- The eggs and sugar must be whisked until thick enough to leave a trail when the whisk is lifted from the surface. If you use a balloon whisk or a hand-held electric mixer, place the bowl over a saucepan of hot water to speed the thickening process. When whisking in an electric table top mixer, additional heat is not required.
- Do not let the bottom of the bowl touch the water or the mixture will become too hot. When the mixture is really thick and double in volume, take the bowl off the heat and continue to whisk until it is cool.
- Add the flour carefully. Sift it first, then add a little at a time to the whisked mixture and fold it in with a metal spoon until evenly blended. Do not stir or the air bubbles will be broken and the cake will not rise.
- Once the pan is filled, give it a sharp bang on a work surface to release any large air bubbles that may be trapped. If left, they will give the sponge an uneven texture.
- Make a Genoese cake the day before filling, it will be easier to cut. Wrap and chill to firm it up.
- Preheat the oven before starting to make cakes so that it will be at the correct temperature by the time the cake is ready to go in. Check that the shelves are in the correct position—place in the center of the oven where possible. To test whether a cake is cooked, press the center top of the cake very lightly with your fingertip. The cake should be spongy and should give only very slightly to the pressure, then rise again immediately, retaining no impression.
- It should have shrunk slightly away from the sides of the pan. Allow the cake a few minutes to cool, then loosen the sides with a blunt edged knife and turn out on to a wire rack. Invert once turned out so that the delicate crust is not cut by the wire rack.

BASIC GENOESE CAKE

MAKES ONE 9 inch CAKE

A Genoese cake is the basis for many gâteaux. It is important to add the butter slowly, carefully and lightly, in step 5, or the cake will have a heavy texture.

$\frac{3}{4}$ stick butter
6 eggs
scant 1 cup superfine sugar
$1\frac{1}{4}$ cups All Purpose flour
2 tablespoons cornstarch

1. Grease a 9 inch spring-release cake pan and line with wax paper.
2. Put the butter into a saucepan and heat gently until melted, then remove from the heat and leave for a few minutes to cool slightly.
3. Put the eggs and sugar in a heatproof bowl standing over a pan of hot water. Whisk until pale and creamy and thick enough to leave a trail on the surface when the whisk is lifted. Remove from the heat and whisk until cool.
4. Sift the flours together into a bowl. Fold half the flour into the egg mixture with a metal spoon.
5. Pour half the cooled butter around the edge of the mixture. Gradually fold in the remaining butter and flour alternately. Fold in very lightly or the butter will sink and result in a heavy cake. Pour the mixture into the prepared pan.
6. Bake in the oven at 350° for 35—40 minutes until well risen, firm to the touch and beginning to shrink away from the sides of the pan. Turn out on to a wire rack and leave to cool.

VARIATION

Chocolate Genoese Substitute $\frac{1}{4}$ cup of the All Purpose flour with cocoa. Sift the cocoa with the flours and proceed as above.

To freeze: wrap and freeze after cooling. Defrost at cool room temperature.

Previous page: RED FRUIT GÂTEAU (PAGE 138).

Basic Whisked Sponge

MAKES TWO 7 inch SPONGES

This classic fatless sponge also forms the basis of gâteaux, however it does not keep as well as a Genoese cake and should be eaten on the day of making.

3 eggs
scant ½ cup superfine sugar
¾ cup All Purpose flour

1. Grease two 7 inch layer cake pans, line with wax paper, then dust with a mixture of flour and sugar.
2. Put the eggs and sugar in a large heatproof bowl standing over a pan of hot water. Whisk until doubled in volume and thick enough to leave a thin trail on the surface when the whisk is lifted.
3. Remove from the heat and continue whisking for a further 5 minutes until the mixture is cool.
4. Sift half the flour over the mixture and fold in very lightly, using a large metal spoon. Sift and fold in the remaining flour in the same way.
5. Pour the mixture into the prepared pans, tilting the pans to spread the mixture evenly. Do not use a spatula to smooth the mixture as this will crush out the air bubbles.
6. Bake in the oven at 375° for 20–25 minutes until well risen, firm to the touch and beginning to shrink away from the sides of the pans. Turn out on to a wire rack and leave to cool.

To freeze: wrap and freeze after cooling. Defrost at cool room temperature.

VARIATIONS

To make two 8 inch sponges, use 4 eggs, generous ½ cup sugar and 1 cup flour.

Jelly Roll   **1.** Line a 13 × 9 inch jelly roll pan with wax paper.
2. Make the sponge as above but use 1 cup flour and fold in with 1 tablespoon hot water. Pour into the prepared pan. Tilt the pan backwards and forwards to spread the mixture in an even layer.
3. Bake in the oven at 400° for 10–12 minutes until golden brown, well risen and firm.
4. Meanwhile, place a sheet of wax paper over a damp cloth. Dredge the paper with sugar.
5. Quickly turn out the cake on to the paper, trim off the crusty edges and spread with jelly. Roll up the cake with the aid of the paper. Make the first turn firmly so that the whole cake will roll evenly and have a good shape when finished, but roll the cake more lightly after this turn.
6. Place seam-side down on a wire rack and dredge with sugar.

Chocolate Jelly Roll   Make the sponge as for jelly roll, above, but replace 1 tablespoon All Purpose flour with 1 tablespoon sifted cocoa. Turn out the cooked sponge and trim as above, then cover with a sheet of wax paper and roll with the paper inside. When cold, unroll and remove the paper. Spread with whipped cream and re-roll. Dust with icing sugar.

To freeze: roll up the cake with the wax paper inside. Overwrap and freeze. Defrost at cool room temperature, unroll and finish as above.

Apple Hazelnut Genoese

SERVES 6

Home-made apple jelly or purée gives the best flavor, but do not add too much sugar; the seven-minute frosting is very sweet.

3 eggs
generous ½ cup superfine sugar
½ cup All Purpose flour
1 tablespoon cornstarch
⅓ cup ground hazelnuts
¾ stick butter, melted and cooled
6 tablespoons apple jelly or purée
FOR THE FROSTING
1 egg white
scant 1 cup superfine sugar
pinch of salt
pinch of cream of tartar
2 tablespoons thick apple purée

1. Grease two 7 inch layer cake pans, line the bases with wax paper and grease the paper.
2. Whisk the eggs and sugar together in a bowl until very thick. Sift in the flour and cornstarch. Add the hazelnuts, then fold in the butter. Turn the mixture into the prepared pans.
3. Bake in the oven at 350° for about 25 minutes or until the sponge springs back when pressed lightly with a finger and has shrunk away a little from the pans. Turn out on to a wire rack and leave to cool for 1–2 hours. Sandwich the layers with apple jelly. To prepare the seven-minute frosting put all the ingredients into a bowl and whisk lightly. Place the bowl over a pan of hot water and heat, whisking continuously, until the mixture thickens sufficiently to stand in peaks. This will take about 7 minutes.
5. Cover the cake with the frosting, peaking up the surface. Leave for 2–3 hours before serving to allow the frosting to firm up.

To freeze: wrap and freeze the cakes at the end of step 3. Defrost at cool room temperature, then finish as above.

DOBOS TORTE

SERVES 8

The old Austro-Hungarian empire is the home of this elaborate 'drum cake'. Versions of the traditional sponge rounds, layered with chocolate cream and glazed with caramel, are still to be found in the best cafés and pastry shops from Vienna to Budapest. Be sure to mark the caramel into portions before it hardens or it will be extremely difficult to cut.

4 eggs
1½ cups superfine sugar
1¼ cups All Purpose flour
4 squares semi sweet chocolate
1 cup crushed cookies or chopped nuts, for coating

FOR THE FILLING
3 egg whites
1½ cups icing sugar, sifted
2 sticks butter

1. Line two cookie sheets with non-sticking wax paper.
2. Whisk the eggs and scant 1 cup of the sugar in a bowl standing over a pan of hot water. Whisk until the mixture is thick enough to leave a trail on the surface when the whisk is lifted. Remove from the heat.
3. Sift half the flour over the mixture and fold in lightly with a metal spoon. Add the remaining flour in the same way. Carefully spread some of the mixture out on the prepared cookie sheets in large rounds measuring about 8 inches in diameter.
4. Bake in the oven at 375° for 7–10 minutes until golden brown. Loosen from the cookie sheets and trim each round to a neat shape with a sharp knife, using a saucepan top as a guide. Transfer them to wire racks and leave to cool for about 15 minutes.
5. Re-line the cookie sheets, spread on more mixture. Bake, trim and cool as before. There will be enough mixture to make six or seven rounds.
6. Select the round with the best surface and lay it on an oiled cookie sheet.
7. Put the remaining sugar in a small, heavy-based saucepan. Dissolve the sugar, without stirring, over a gentle heat and boil it steadily to a rich brown.
8. Pour it over the round on the cookie sheet, spreading it with a knife brushed with oil. Mark into eight sections and trim round the edge.
9. Break the chocolate into small pieces. Place in a heatproof bowl standing over a pan of simmering water and heat gently until the chocolate melts. (Alternatively, microwave on LOW for 5–6 minutes, stirring occasionally until the chocolate melts.) Remove from the heat.
10. To make the filling, put the egg whites and icing sugar into a heatproof bowl standing over a pan of simmering water. Whisk until very thick, then remove from the heat.
11. Put the butter into a bowl and beat until pale and soft. Gradually beat in the egg and sugar mixture, then stir in the melted chocolate.
12. Sandwich the remaining rounds together with some of the filling and put the caramel-covered one on top.
13. Spread the sides of the torte with the remaining filling and press the crushed cookie crumbs or chopped nuts round the sides.

To freeze: wrap and freeze the cooled cakes at the end of step 5. Defrost at cool room temperature, then finish as above.

RASPBERRY CINNAMON TORTE

SERVES 6

A crumbly almond cake with a soft center surrounding moist raspberries. Serve just warm to enjoy the torte at its best.

1¼ sticks butter or margarine
scant ¾ cup superfine sugar
1½ cups ground almonds
1¼ cups self raising flour
1 egg
1 teaspoon cinnamon
1 cup raspberries, hulled
mixed icing sugar and cinnamon, for dusting

1. Grease an 8½ inch spring-release cake pan and line the base with wax paper.
2. Place the butter, sugar, almonds, flour, egg and ground cinnamon in a bowl. Beat well.
3. Spread half the almond mixture into the prepared pan, using a fork to flatten lightly. Sprinkle over the raspberries, then dot over the remaining almond mixture so it almost covers the fruit. Stand the pan on a cookie sheet.
4. Bake in the oven at 350° for about 1 hour, covering lightly when well browned. The torte should feel just firm to the touch with a springy texture. Cool in the pan for about 1 hour.
5. Dust with mixed cinnamon and icing sugar and serve warm.

Not suitable for freezing.

Opposite: DOBOS TORTE.

ANGEL CAKE

SERVES 8–10

This angel cake is served with cream and figs. Truly a
cake from heaven.

FOR THE CAKE

¾ *cup superfine sugar*
¾ *cup All Purpose flour*
½ *teaspoon salt*
6 *egg whites*
1 *teaspoon cream of tartar*
¼ *teaspoon almond flavoring*
¼ *teaspoon vanilla*
2 *teaspoons lemon juice*

FOR THE FILLING AND DECORATION

½ *cup heavy cream*
2 *fresh figs, sliced*

1. Grease and flour an 8 cup angel food cake pan or
savarin mold.
2. To make the cake, sift half of the sugar, the flour and
salt together three times.
3. Using an electric mixer, whisk the egg whites until
foamy. Add the cream of tartar and continue whisking
until the egg whites are stiff but not dry. Gradually add
the remaining sugar, about 1 tablespoon at a time,
whisking well between each addition. Whisk in the
almond flavoring, vanilla and the lemon juice.
4. Sift about a quarter of the flour and sugar mixture
over the egg mixture and fold in very lightly using a
metal spoon. Repeat until all of the mixture is added.
Spoon into the prepared pan.
5. Bake in the oven at 350° for about 35–40 minutes or
until the cake is risen and springs back when pressed
gently.
6. Invert the pan on to a wire rack and leave to cool
with the pan covering the cake. When cold, carefully
run a spatula around the sides and center of the pan,
then remove the cake.
7. Transfer the cake to a serving plate. Whip the cream
until it just holds its shape and use to fill a pastry tube
fitted with a star tip. Pipe around the bottom edge of the
cake. Decorate with the figs.

*To freeze: wrap and freeze the cake at the end of step 6.
Defrost overnight, wrapped, at cool room temperature, then
finish as above.*

STRAWBERRY ALMOND LAYER GÂTEAU

SERVES 8

To make this gâteau, a basic jelly roll mixture is cooked
and, instead of being rolled up, it is cut into three and
layered with strawberries and cream. Make a jelly roll
up to the end of step 3 (see page 125), then turn out on
to a sheet of wax paper dredged with sugar. Leave to
cool on the paper.

1 *jelly roll (see page 125)*

FOR THE FILLING AND DECORATION

1½ *pounds small strawberries*
1 *tablespoon icing sugar*
2 *tablespoons strawberry liqueur*
3 *squares semi sweet chocolate*
2 *tablespoons strawberry jelly*
1¼ *cups whipping cream*
few drops of almond flavoring
¾ *cup slivered almonds, roasted*

1. Hull and slice 1 pound of the strawberries and put in
a bowl with the icing sugar and liqueur. Leave to stand
for 20 minutes, stirring occasionally.
2. Trim the edges of the jelly roll, then cut widthways
into three even pieces.
3. Meanwhile, break the chocolate into small pieces.
Place in a small heatproof bowl standing over a pan of
simmering water and heat gently until the chocolate
melts. (Alternatively, microwave on LOW for 2 minutes
or until melted, stirring occasionally.)
4. Halve the remaining strawberries (leaving the stalks
attached). Dip the base of each piece of strawberry in
the melted chocolate. Place on a sheet of wax paper and
leave to set.
5. Drain the strawberry slices, reserving the juice. Stir
the jelly into the juice and mix together. Brush a little of
the jelly and juice mixture over two pieces of the cake.
Top with the strawberry slices.
6. Whip the cream until it stands in soft peaks, then
flavor to taste with a little almond flavoring. Spread a
little cream on top of the strawberries.
7. Place the strawberry covered pieces of cake on top
of one another, then cover with the remaining piece of
cake. Spread the top and sides with the remaining jelly
mixture, then cover completely with the cream. Press
the roasted nuts on the sides. Decorate the top with the
chocolate dipped strawberries.

*To freeze: cut the jelly roll to size then wrap and freeze.
Defrost at cool room temperature, then finish as above.*

Above: ANGEL CAKE.
Below: STRAWBERRY ALMOND LAYER GÂTEAU.

SACHERTORTE

SERVES 8–10

Famous the world over, Sachertorte was the invention of Franz Sacher, a master sugar baker, in Vienna in 1832. It is a very rich, moist, chocolate cake. The traditional cake is covered with a chocolate fondant, but as this is rather sweet, a ganache frosting is used here.

FOR THE CAKE

5 squares semi sweet chocolate
1 stick sweet butter or margarine, softened
generous ½ cup superfine sugar
generous 1 cup ground almonds
4 eggs, separated
1 cup fresh brown breadcrumbs
2 tablespoons apricot jelly, melted

FOR THE FROSTING

7 squares semi sweet chocolate
scant 1 cup heavy cream

1. Grease a 9 inch spring-release cake pan, line with wax paper and grease the paper.

2. To make the cake, break the chocolate into small pieces. Place in a heatproof bowl standing over a pan of simmering water and heat gently until the chocolate melts. (Alternatively, microwave on LOW for 4–5 minutes or until melted, stirring occasionally.) Remove from the heat.

3. Cream the butter and sugar together in a bowl until pale and fluffy. Stir in the almonds, egg yolks, breadcrumbs and melted chocolate, then beat until well combined.

4. Whisk the egg whites until stiff and fold half into the chocolate mixture, then fold in the other half. Pour the mixture into the prepared pan and level the surface.

5. Bake in the oven at 350° for 40–45 minutes until firm to the touch.

6. Cover with a damp cloth, leave for 5 minutes to cool slightly, then unclip the sides of the pan and invert on to a wire rack. Remove the base. Turn the cake the right way up, cover again and leave to cool. When cold, brush the top with the melted apricot jelly.

7. To make the frosting, break the chocolate into small pieces. Place in a heatproof bowl with the cream. Stand the bowl over a pan of simmering water and heat until the chocolate melts and blends with the cream. (Alternatively, microwave on LOW for 6–7 minutes, stirring

Above: SACHERTORTE.

occasionally until the chocolate melts.) Cool for a few minutes until the frosting just coats the back of a spoon.

8. Stand the cake and the wire rack on a cookie sheet and pour over the frosting. Gently shake the cake to spread the frosting evenly and use a spatula, if necessary, to ensure that the sides are completely covered. Leave in a cool place to set, but do not put in the refrigerator or the frosting will lose its shine.

To freeze: wrap and freeze the cake before icing. Defrost at cool room temperature, then finish as above.

CARAMEL BANANA TORTE

SERVES 8

In step 6, work quickly, so that the caramel does not set before you have a chance to spread it over the top of the gâteau.

FOR THE CAKE
1½ cups self raising flour
¼ teaspoon baking powder
¼ teaspoon soda
½ stick butter or margarine, cut into pieces
¾ cup superfine sugar
6 ounces ripe bananas
½ teaspoon nutmeg
3 tablespoons milk
1 egg, beaten

FOR THE CARAMEL
scant ½ cup sugar

FOR THE FILLING AND DECORATION
¾ cup full fat soft cream cheese
2 tablespoons lemon juice
2 tablespoons icing sugar
6 ounces ripe bananas
½ cup slivered almonds, roasted

1. Grease an 8 inch round cake pan, line the base with wax paper and grease the paper.

2. Sift the flour, baking powder and soda into a bowl. Rub in the butter until the mixture resembles fine breadcrumbs, then stir in the sugar.

3. Peel the bananas and mash them in a bowl, then beat in the nutmeg, milk and egg. Stir the banana mixture into the dry ingredients. Turn the mixture into the prepared pan and level the surface.

4. Bake in the oven at 350° for about 40 minutes. Cool in the pan for 5 minutes, then turn out on to a wire rack and leave to cool. Cut the cake into two layers.

5. To make the caramel, put the sugar into a small saucepan. Dissolve, without stirring, over gentle heat, then boil until a rich brown color.

6. When the caramel is ready, immediately pour it on to the top of the cake. Use an oiled knife to spread the

caramel so that it completely covers the top. Mark into eight portions with the point of a knife.

7. To make the filling, put the cream cheese, lemon juice and icing sugar into a bowl and beat together. Peel and chop the bananas and add to half of the cheese mixture. Use this mixture to sandwich the cakes together.

8. Spread a little of the remaining cheese mixture around the sides of the cake and cover with most of the almonds. Decorate the caramel top with the remaining cheese mixture and almonds.

To freeze: wrap and freeze at the end of step 4. Defrost at cool room temperature, then finish as above.

NUSSKUCHEN

SERVES 12

Nusskuchen comes in many forms, but is always made with nuts of some kind. This is a light cake filled with a hazelnut butter cream.

9 inch Genoese cake (see page 124)

FOR THE FILLING AND DECORATION
2¼ cups hazelnuts
4 egg whites
2 cups icing sugar, sifted
2 sticks sweet butter
1 teaspoon vanilla

1. Put the hazelnuts on to a cookie sheet. Bake in the oven at 350° for 10–15 minutes until their skins become loose. Put the nuts in a clean cloth and rub until the skins are removed. Put the skinned nuts on a cookie sheet and return to the oven for 5–10 minutes until lightly browned. Remove from the oven and leave to cool. Put about 24 nuts aside for decoration, then chop the remainder finely.

2. To make the filling, put the egg whites and icing sugar in a large bowl standing over a pan of hot water. Whisk until they form a stiff shiny meringue—do not allow the meringue to become too hot. Remove from the heat and continue whisking until the meringue is cooled, and forms stiff peaks.

3. Beat the butter until very pale and fluffy, then beat in the vanilla. Gradually beat the meringue into the butter. Divide the butter cream in two and mix half the chopped nuts into one half.

4. Cut the cake into three even layers. Sandwich the sponge layers together with the hazelnut butter cream. Spread plain butter cream over the top and around the sides of the cake. Coat the sides with the remaining chopped hazelnuts. Place the gâteau on a plate.

5. Put the remaining butter cream into a pastry tube fitted with a small star tip. Pipe a decorative edge around the top of the gâteau, then decorate with the reserved whole hazelnuts. Keep in a cool place until ready to serve.

To freeze: open freeze until firm, then pack and freeze. Defrost at cool room temperature.

TORTA DI MELE

SERVES 6

This recipe for a Genoese sponge, which is heavy with sweet apples, is made in the classic way. If you are in a hurry, you can cut corners with this particular recipe, because the weight of the apples tends to disguise the texture of the cake! Simply beat the eggs and sugar together with a wooden spoon, then fold in the flour mixture, followed by the melted butter, milk, lemon peel and apples.

1–2 teaspoons oil
1–2 tablespoons dry breadcrumbs

FOR THE CAKE
1 stick butter, melted and cooled
4 eggs
$\frac{3}{4}$ cup superfine sugar
1$\frac{1}{4}$ cups All Purpose flour, sifted with 1 teaspoon baking powder and pinch of salt
finely grated peel of 1 lemon
1$\frac{1}{2}$ pounds green apples, peeled, cored and thinly sliced
icing sugar, for dusting

1. Brush the inside of a 9 inch loose-based cake pan with oil. Sprinkle with breadcrumbs, then shake off the excess.
2. To make the cake (see page 124), adding the lemon peel and apples last. Pour the mixture into the pan.
3. Bake in the oven at 350° for about 40 minutes until a tester inserted into the center comes out clean.
4. Leave the cake to rest in the pan for about 5 minutes, then turn out on to a wire rack and leave to cool completely for 2–3 hours. Dust icing sugar over the top of the cake just before serving.

To freeze: wrap and freeze the cake. Defrost overnight at cool room temperature.

BRANDY PRALINE RING

SERVES 8

Adding the brandy and coffee mixture to the warm cake ensures that it is absorbed.

$\frac{1}{3}$ cup whole unblanched almonds
generous 1 cup superfine sugar
4 eggs
1 cup All Purpose flour
4 tablespoons strong black coffee
5 tablespoons brandy
1 cup whipping cream

1. Grease a 5$\frac{1}{2}$–6 cup ring mold. Oil a cookie sheet.
2. Make the praline using the almonds and a quarter of

the sugar (see page 133). Roughly crush half the praline and reserve. Finely crush the remainder.
3. Place the eggs and $\frac{1}{2}$ cup of the sugar in a bowl. Using an electric whisk, whisk until very thick and pale in color—the mixture should leave a trail when the beaters are lifted from the bowl.
4. Using a metal spoon, carefully fold in the flour, finely crushed praline and 1 tablespoon of the coffee. Gently pour the mixture into the prepared mold.
5. Bake in the oven at 375° for about 30–40 minutes until well risen and just firm to the touch.
6. Meanwhile prepare the brandy syrup. Pour 3 cups water into a saucepan, add the remaining sugar and heat gently until the sugar dissolves. Bring to the boil then boil for 1 minute. Cool slightly and add 4 tablespoons of the brandy with the remaining coffee.
7. Remove the cake from the oven and prick the surface with a fine tester. Spoon over half the syrup and leave to soak for about 20 minutes. Invert the ring on to a plate and spoon over the remaining syrup. Cool.
8. Lightly whip the cream, stir in the remaining brandy and spoon into the center of the ring. Decorate the cake as liked with the roughly crushed praline.

To freeze: wrap and freeze at the end of step 7. Defrost overnight, wrapped, at cool room temperature, then finish as above.

COFFEE PRALINE GÂTEAU

SERVES 6

Praline can be made in large quantities and stored in an airtight container for decorating cakes or flavoring mousses and ice creams.

FOR THE SPONGE
2 eggs
scant $\frac{1}{2}$ cup superfine sugar
$\frac{1}{2}$ cup All Purpose flour
1 tablespoon coffee flavoring

FOR THE PRALINE
2 tablespoons superfine sugar
$\frac{1}{4}$ cup blanched almonds

FOR THE FILLING
$\frac{1}{2}$ cup heavy cream
2 tablespoons coffee-flavored liqueur
icing sugar, for dusting

1. Grease an 8 inch round cake pan, line the base with wax paper and grease the paper. Dust with sugar and flour.
2. To make the sponge, put the eggs and sugar in a large heatproof bowl standing over a pan of hot water. Whisk until pale and creamy and thick enough to leave a trail on the surface when the whisk is lifted. Remove from the heat and whisk until cool.

3. Sift the flour evenly over the surface of the mixture and fold in lightly, using a large metal spoon. Lightly fold in the coffee flavoring. Turn the mixture into the prepared pan.

4. Bake in the oven at 350° for about 30 minutes or until the sponge springs back when pressed lightly with a finger and has shrunk away a little from the sides of the pan. Turn out on to a wire rack and leave to cool.

5. Meanwhile to make the praline, grease a cookie sheet. Put the sugar and almonds into a small skillet and heat gently, shaking the pan occasionally, until the sugar dissolves and caramelizes to a rich brown color.

6. Pour the mixture on to the cookie sheet and leave for 10–15 minutes to cool and harden. When cold, grind or crush with the end of a rolling pin in a strong bowl.

7. To make the filling, whip the cream until it holds its shape, then whisk in the liqueur and fold in three-quarters of the praline.

8. Cut the sponge into two layers and sandwich with the cream. Dust the top with icing sugar and decorate with the remaining praline. Chill for 1–2 hours.

To freeze: wrap and freeze the sponge at the end of step 4. Defrost overnight at cool room temperature, then finish as above.

Passion Fruit Gâteau

SERVES 8–10

This layered cake, with its exotic passion fruit filling, is ideal for a summer wedding buffet. (Make two cakes for about 20 guests.) If liked, make the cakes well in advance and freeze them. On the day, fill, frost and decorate.

FOR THE CAKE
4 eggs, separated
generous $\frac{1}{2}$ cup superfine sugar
1 cup self raising flour
pinch of salt
$\frac{1}{4}$ stick sweet butter, melted

FOR THE PASSION FRUIT CREAM
$1\frac{1}{2}$ cups fromage blanc
5 tablespoons thick plain yogurt
few drops of orange flower water
$1\frac{1}{2}$ tablespoons icing sugar
5 ripe passion fruit, halved

FOR THE DECORATION
$\frac{1}{2}$ cup heavy cream, lightly whipped
3–4 tablespoons pistachios, chopped
shelled pistachios

1. Grease a 9 inch loose-based cake pan and line the base with wax paper.

2. To make the cake, whisk the egg yolks and sugar together in a bowl until thick and pale. Sift the flour and salt over and fold in lightly.

3. Whisk the egg whites until stiff but not dry, then lightly fold into the yolk mixture. Trickle the butter over and carefully fold in. Turn the mixture into the prepared pan.

4. Bake in the oven at 350° for 25–35 minutes until risen and springy to the touch when lightly pressed in the center. Leave to cool slightly in the pan, then turn out on to a wire rack covered with a cloth. Remove the lining paper and leave to cool completely.

5. To make the passion fruit cream, mix the fromage blanc, yogurt, orange flower water and icing sugar together in a bowl. Stir in the passion fruit flesh.

6. Cut the cake into three equal layers. Spread about one-third of the passion fruit cream over the bottom layer. Place the second layer gently on top and cover with another third of the passion fruit cream, not taking it right to the edge. Spread the remaining passion fruit cream over the top cake layer, not taking it right to the edge, and gently place this on top of the cake.

7. For the decoration, reserving a little of the whipped cream for piping around the top of the cake, spread the remainder over the sides of the cake. Coat the sides with the chopped pistachios.

8. Spoon the reserved cream into a pastry tube fitted with a small star tip and pipe a border around the top edge of the cake. Decorate with the pistachios.

To freeze: open freeze the completed gâteau until firm then overwrap. Defrost overnight in the refrigerator.

STRAWBERRY ROSE RING

SERVES 6–8

---

1 quantity Genoese cake, made in a 10 inch ring mold (see page 124)

FOR THE SYRUP

generous ½ cup sugar

3 tablespoons rose water

4 tablespoons kirsch or orange-flavored liqueur

FOR THE FILLING

1 pound strawberries

2 tablespoons rose water

2 tablespoons icing sugar

⅓ cup pistachios, chopped

FOR THE DECORATION

1 cup heavy cream

orange shreds

---

1. To make the syrup, put the sugar in a pan with ½ cup water and heat gently, stirring occasionally until the sugar has dissolved. Bring to the boil and boil rapidly for 1 minute until slightly thickened. Cool completely, then stir in the rose water and liqueur.

2. Put the cake back into the washed mold and spoon over the syrup until it is all absorbed. Leave for 1–2 hours for the syrup to sink through.

3. To make the filling, hull the strawberries, keeping some unhulled ones for the decoration. Halve or quarter the remaining strawberries and toss them with the rose water and icing sugar.

4. Turn the cake out on to a serving plate and fill the center with the strawberries. Whip the cream until just holding its shape and fill a pastry tube fitted with a star tip. Pipe a decorative border around the ring. Scatter the pistachios over the strawberries. Scatter the orange shreds over the cake and decorate with the remaining whole strawberries and strawberry leaves, if liked.

To freeze: wrap and freeze the cake at the end of step 2. Defrost at cool room temperature, then finish as above.

MARZIPAN SURPRISE GÂTEAU

SERVES 6

Make the decoration for this gâteau as simple or elaborate as you like.

---

13 × 9 inch jelly roll, filled with raspberry jelly (see page 125)

FOR THE FILLING

1½ cups fresh or frozen raspberries, defrosted

little icing sugar

2 tablespoons kirsch (optional)

FOR THE DECORATION

1½ cups white marzipan

pink food coloring

4 tablespoons warmed raspberry jelly, strained

1 cup whipping cream

fresh flowers

---

1. Line a 4 cup ceramic bowl with plastic wrap. Slice the jelly roll and use to line the bottom and sides of the bowl, reserving a few slices to cover the top.

2. To make the filling, mix the raspberries with icing sugar to taste and the kirsch, if using. Spoon into the center of the sponge. Press down well and cover with the remaining slices of jelly roll. Place the saucer on top and lightly weigh down. Chill in the refrigerator overnight.

3. Turn out the cake on to a board and remove the plastic wrap. Color the marzipan with a few drops of pink food coloring and roll out to a round just large enough to cover the cake. Paint the cake with the warmed jelly and carefully drape over the marzipan, molding it to fit the shape. Trim away any excess marzipan.

4. Stand the cake on a cake stand. Whip the cream until it just holds its shape and spoon into a pastry tube fitted with a large star tip. Pipe around the base of the cake. Decorate with flowers.

Not suitable for freezing.

Opposite: MARZIPAN SURPRISE GÂTEAU.

PRUNE AND WALNUT GÂTEAU WITH BRANDY BUTTER

SERVES 8

Prunes and nuts keep this gâteau moist.

FOR THE CAKES
1½ *sticks butter or margarine, softened*
¾ *cup self raising Graham flour*
¾ *cup self raising flour*
scant 1 cup superfine sugar
2 eggs
1 teaspoon mixed spice
2 tablespoons milk
¾ *cup pitted no-soak dry prunes, roughly chopped*
1 cup walnut halves, chopped

FOR THE FILLING AND DECORATION
1 stick butter, softened
1 cup icing sugar, sifted
2 tablespoons brandy
icing sugar, for dusting

1. Grease three 7 inch layer cake pans and line the bases with wax paper.
2. To make the cakes, put the butter, flours, sugar, eggs, mixed spice and milk in a blender or food processor and process until smooth. Stir in the prunes and nuts. Pour the mixture into the prepared pans.
3. Bake in the oven at 350° for 30–35 minutes or until risen and firm to the touch. Turn out on to a wire rack and leave to cool.
4. To make the filling, cream the butter until very pale and soft, then beat in the icing sugar. Add the brandy, a little at a time, taking care not to allow it to curdle.
5. When the cakes are cool, sandwich them together with the brandy filling. Dust the cake with icing sugar to decorate.

To freeze: wrap and freeze before decorating with icing sugar. Defrost overnight, wrapped, at cool room temperature.

PARSNIP, APRICOT AND NUT GÂTEAU

SERVES 8

No one will guess that this gâteau contains parsnips. It is delicious and moist, and has the added bonus of being packed with fiber.

FOR THE CAKE
1 cup light brown soft sugar
2½ *cups self raising flour*
1 teaspoon mixed spice
large pinch of salt
½ *cup walnut oil*
½ *stick butter, melted and cooled*
2 eggs
2 cups parsnips, peeled and finely grated
1 cup walnuts, finely chopped

FOR THE FILLING AND DECORATION
1 cup no-soak dry apricots
½ *cup orange juice*
scant 1 cup low fat soft cream cheese
1 tablespoon clear honey
icing sugar, to decorate

1. Grease and line three 8 inch layer cake pans.
2. To make the cake, put all the ingredients except the parsnips and walnuts in a blender or food processor and process until smooth. Add the parsnips and walnuts. Divide the mixture evenly between the prepared pans.
3. Bake in the oven at 350° for 30–40 minutes or until risen and firm to the touch. Change over the positions of the pans halfway through cooking so that they cook evenly. Turn out on to a wire rack and leave to cool.
4. Meanwhile to make the filling, put the apricots and orange juice in a saucepan. Cover and simmer until the apricots are tender. (Alternatively, put the apricots and orange juice in a bowl, cover and microwave on HIGH for 6–8 minutes or until tender.) Cool, then purée until smooth.
5. When the cakes are cold, spread two of them with the apricot purée. Beat the cheese with the honey and spread carefully on top of the apricot purée. Sandwich the cakes together, putting the unfilled one on top.
6. To decorate the cake, cut some 1 inch wide strips of wax paper and lay across the top of the cake. Sift icing sugar over the top of the cake to cover completely. Carefully remove the paper to reveal a striped pattern.

Not suitable for freezing.

Opposite: ORANGE CHARLOTTE GÂTEAU.

Orange Charlotte Gâteau

SERVES 6

A really special gâteau, a little bit like an English trifle!

20–24 lady fingers
FOR THE FILLING
7 inch Whisked sponge (see page 125)
8 tablespoons orange-flavored liqueur
1 orange
$\frac{1}{2}$ cup heavy or whipping cream
1 tablespoon icing sugar
FOR THE DECORATION
$\frac{1}{2}$ cup heavy or whipping cream
kumquats or orange shreds
orange segments

1. Line an 8 inch charlotte mold with non-stick wax paper. Line the base and sides of the mold with the lady fingers.

2. Cut the whisked sponge into $\frac{1}{2}$ inch cubes. Press one third of the sponge cubes into the base of the mold and sprinkle with one third of the liqueur.

3. Finely grate the peel of the orange and place in a bowl with the cream and icing sugar. Whip until very stiff.

4. Remove the pith from the orange like peeling an apple. Cut the orange into segments. Chop the segments roughly and fold into the cream. Spread half the cream over the soaked sponge.

5. Cover the cream with the second third of the sponge and sprinkle with half the remaining liqueur. Press down gently. Cover with the remaining cream and top with the remaining sponge. Sprinkle with the remaining liqueur and press down gently. Cover and chill for 2–3 hours.

6. To serve, turn out on to a serving plate, remove the paper and decorate with whipped cream, kumquats or orange shreds and segments.

Not suitable for freezing.

PEAR AND HAZELNUT GÂTEAU WITH CARAMEL LATTICE

SERVES 6

Do not add the caramel lattice more than 1 hour in advance of serving or it will start to dissolve.

9 inch Genoese cake (see page 124), made with 1¼ cups roasted ground hazelnuts folded in with the flour

FOR THE FILLING

2 ripe pears, peeled, cored and chopped

little lemon juice

½ cup heavy cream

½ cup sour cream

pinch of nutmeg

FOR THE TOPPING

3 ripe pears, peeled, quartered and thinly sliced

little lemon juice

½ cup peeled hazelnuts, roasted and roughly chopped

½ cup granulated sugar

1. Cut the cake into two layers with a serrated knife. To make the filling, toss the pears in a little lemon juice to prevent discoloration. Pour the heavy cream, sour cream and nutmeg into a bowl. Whip until just holding its shape, then fold in the pears. Use to fill the cake.

2. To make the topping, toss the sliced pears in a little lemon juice and arrange in a wheel-like pattern on top of the cake. Scatter the hazelnuts over the pears.

3. Put the sugar in a small, heavy-based saucepan with 2 tablespoons water. Dissolve the sugar over a gentle heat without boiling. When dissolved, bring to the boil and boil rapidly until the sugar turns amber. Working quickly, remove from the heat and dip the base of the pan in a bowl of cool water to prevent further cooking.

4. Once the bubbles have subsided, quickly pour the caramel in a thin steady stream over the top of the cake to form a zig-zag lattice pattern. Leave to set for 5 minutes, then serve.

To freeze: freeze the unfilled cake. Defrost at cool room temperature, then finish as above.

RED FRUIT GÂTEAU

SERVES 8–10

This is the cake to capture the spirit of summer. A melt-in-the-mouth sponge covered with a sauce made from fruits of the forest.

FOR THE CAKE

1 cup All Purpose flour

½ stick sweet butter

4 medium eggs

generous ½ cup superfine sugar

few drops of vanilla (optional)

FOR THE SAUCE

1½ pounds mixed red summer fruit, such as raspberries, strawberries, redcurrants, loganberries

sugar, to taste

3 tablespoons lemon juice

1 tablespoon rose water (optional)

FOR THE DECORATION AND FILLING

1 egg white

1 pound mixed red summer fruit

a few pink or red rose petals

sugar

1–1½ cups heavy cream

1. Line the base of a 10 inch spring-release cake pan with non-stick wax paper. Grease the pan and the paper. When set, dust out the pan with flour.

2. To make the cake (see page 124), adding the vanilla. Pour the mixture into the prepared pan.

3. Bake in the oven at 350° for 35–40 minutes. When cooked, the cake will look evenly brown, will spring back when lightly pressed, and will have shrunk slightly from the sides of the pan. Cool for 5 minutes, then turn out on to a wire rack and cool.

4. To make the sauce, put all the ingredients into a pan and heat gently until the juice starts to run from the fruit and the sugar melts. Add a little water and press through a nylon strainer, or purée then strain. Chill.

5. Prepare the frosted fruit for the decoration. Lightly beat the egg white. Brush a few berries or fruit and rose petals with a thin coating of egg white. Sprinkle with sugar and lay on non-stick wax paper to dry. Pick over the remaining fruit.

6. Whip the cream until it just holds its shape. Chill until ready to use.

7. To assemble the cake, using a long serrated knife, carefully cut the cake into two layers. Sandwich together with some of the fruit sauce and the prepared fruit. Spread the cream evenly over the top and sides of the cake. Decorate with the frosted fruit and petals. Serve the remaining fruit sauce separately.

To freeze: wrap and freeze the sponge at the end of step 3. Defrost at cool room temperature, then finish as above.

Illustrated on pages 122–123

Coconut Rum Gâteau

SERVES 20

A rich, coconut-flavored gâteau, layered with pineapple and generously flavored with a coconut and rum liqueur.

FOR THE CAKES

2 sticks butter or margarine
generous 1 cup superfine sugar
3 eggs, separated
4 cups self raising flour
pinch of salt
1 teaspoon baking powder
scant 1 cup coconut milk
1 cup sweet shredded coconut

FOR THE FILLING AND DECORATION

6–8 tablespoons coconut rum liqueur
12 ounces fresh or canned pineapple
2 cups whipping cream
$\frac{1}{2}$ cup shredded or flaked coconut, toasted

1. Grease and line two 9 inch round cake pans.
2. To make the cakes, cream the butter and sugar together in a bowl until pale and fluffy. Gradually beat in the egg yolks. Sift the flour, salt and baking powder together.

3. Add half of the coconut milk with half of the dry ingredients to the creamed mixture. Fold in the coconut, then add the remaining coconut milk and dry ingredients. Whisk the egg whites until stiff, then fold lightly into the mixture. Pour the mixture into the prepared pans.
4. Bake in the oven at 350° for 40–45 minutes or until risen and firm to the touch. Turn out on to a wire rack and leave to cool.
5. When cold, prick the cakes with a fine cake tester and sprinkle with 4 tablespoons liqueur. Leave for at least 30 minutes.
6. To make the filling, cut the pineapple into small pieces. Whip the cream with the remaining liqueur to taste until it forms soft peaks. Spread a little cream over each cake. Sprinkle one cake with two thirds of the pineapple, place the other cake, cream side down, on top of the first cake. Press together with the flat of your hand.
7. Sprinkle the remaining pineapple pieces over the top of the cake. Spread the remaining cream all over the top and sides of the cake and sprinkle with the coconut. Chill until ready to serve.

To freeze: wrap and freeze the cake at the end of step 4. Defrost, wrapped, at cool room temperature, then finish as above.

Above: COCONUT RUM GÂTEAU.

CHOCOLATE-WRAPPED ORANGE LIQUEUR GÂTEAU

SERVES 12

The sponge is soaked in a liqueur syrup, and coated in an intriguing chocolate frill that is easy to make but never fails to impress.

FOR THE SPONGE
1¾ cups self raising flour
½ cup cornstarch
1½ teaspoons baking powder
scant 1 cup superfine sugar
3 eggs, separated
finely grated peel and juice of 1 small orange
7 tablespoons oil
3 tablespoons milk

FOR THE LIQUEUR SYRUP
generous ½ cup sugar
finely grated peel and juice of 1 orange
3 tablespoons orange-flavored liqueur

FOR THE DECORATION
2 large oranges
1 cup heavy cream
8 squares semi sweet chocolate
cocoa, for dusting

1. Grease a deep 8½ inch spring-release cake pan and line the base with wax paper.
2. To make the sponge, mix the flours, baking powder and sugar together in a bowl. Blend the egg yolks with the orange peel and juice, oil and milk, then mix into the dry ingredients. Beat thoroughly with a wooden spoon to make a smooth batter. Whisk the egg whites until stiff, then fold into the mixture. Pour into the pan.
3. Bake in the oven at 350° for about 55 minutes or until well risen and firm to the touch.
4. Meanwhile to make the syrup, put the sugar, orange peel and juice and 4 tablespoons water in a heavy-based saucepan and heat gently until the sugar has dissolved. Bring to the boil and boil rapidly for 2 minutes. Stir in the liqueur.
5. Prick the hot cake all over with a fork, then spoon over the hot syrup. Leave to cool.
6. To make the decoration, peel the oranges, discarding all of the white pith. Roughly chop the flesh. Whip the cream until it forms soft peaks.
7. Remove the cooled cake from the pan and place on a serving plate. Arrange the chopped orange on top. Spread the cream all over the top and sides.
8. Break the chocolate into small pieces. Place in a bowl standing over a saucepan of simmering water and heat until the chocolate melts. (Alternatively, microwave on LOW for 4–5 minutes, stirring occasionally.)

9. Meanwhile, cut a strip of wax paper long enough to go round the sides of the cake and wide enough to come 1½ inches above the cake. When the chocolate is melted, spread it evenly all over the paper with spatula. Leave to cool until no longer runny but still sticky when pressed with a finger.
10. Wrap the chocolate around the gâteau, pressing it gently on to the cream so that it sticks. Carefully pinch the chocolate and paper into pleats where it extends above the cake. Leave until set then carefully peel away the paper. Dust the top with a little cocoa.

To freeze: wrap and freeze at the end of step 5. Defrost overnight at cool room temperature, then finish as above.

FARINA CAKE

SERVES 12

This cake is popular throughout Greece and Turkey.

FOR THE CAKE
generous 1 cup superfine sugar
6 eggs
3 cups Farina
finely grated peel of 1 lemon
½ cup ground rice
1½ teaspoons baking powder
large pinch of salt
4 tablespoons lemon juice
⅓ cup blanched almonds

FOR THE SYRUP
10 green cardamom pods, crushed
2 bay leaves
1 cinnamon stick
1 strip of lemon peel
2¼ cups superfine sugar

1. Grease a 9 inch square cake pan.
2. To make the cake, put all the ingredients, except the almonds, in a bowl and whisk together with a hand held whisk until well mixed. Pour into the pan.
3. Bake in the oven at 350° for 1–1¼ hours or until firm to the touch and golden brown. Arrange the almonds in a pattern on top of the cake halfway through the cooking time.
4. Meanwhile to make the syrup, put all the ingredients in a saucepan with 1 cup water. Heat gently until the sugar has dissolved, stirring all the time. Bring to the boil, then simmer for 10 minutes. Strain and cool.
5. When the cake is cooked, spoon over the syrup. Leave to cool in the pan. Turn out on to a work surface, then invert on to a serving plate. Serve, cut into squares or diamonds, with Greek yogurt.

To freeze: wrap and freeze the cooled, syrup soaked cake. Defrost overnight at cool room temperature.

Opposite: CHOCOLATE-WRAPPED ORANGE LIQUEUR GÂTEAU.

FRUIT SALAD GÂTEAU

SERVES 14

A hollowed-out cake filled with fruit and passion fruit cream.

---

9 inch Genoese cake (see page 124)

FOR THE FILLING

1 small ripe mango

6 fresh lychees

1¾ cups strawberries

few blueberries

finely grated peel of 1 lime

½ cup heavy cream

5 tablespoons Greek yogurt

2 passion fruit

FOR THE DECORATION

½ cup heavy cream

1 cup chopped mixed nuts

2 small ripe star fruit, sliced

few gooseberries

juice of 1 lime

1 tablespoon superfine sugar

2 teaspoons arrowroot

---

1. Using a serrated knife, make a cut around the cake that is about 1 inch in from the edge and about 1½ inches deep.

2. Holding the knife almost horizontally and following the first cut, cut through to the center to remove a thin layer of sponge. This will be the top.

3. Scoop out the sponge in the center of the cake, being careful not to cut through to the bottom. Save the scooped out sponge crumbs for making Truffles or Chocolate filo pie (see page 94).

4. To make the filling, slice the mango each side of the pit. Peel, then cut the flesh into small chunks. Peel the lychees and pit. Hull the strawberries and halve. Mix all the fruits with the blueberries and the lime peel.

5. Whip the cream until it holds its shape and mix with the yogurt. Halve the passion fruit, scoop out the pulp and mix with the cream and yogurt.

6. Spoon the passion fruit cream into the sponge case. Top with the fruit salad. Replace the top of the sponge and push down firmly.

7. Whip the cream for the decoration until it just holds its shape. Spread thinly over the top and around the sides of the cake. Using a spatula, press the nuts on to the sides of the cake. Arrange the fruit on the top of the cake.

8. Put the lime juice and sugar in a small saucepan and heat gently until the sugar dissolves. Blend the arrowroot to a smooth paste with 6 tablespoons cold water.

9. When the sugar has dissolved, add the arrowroot mixture to the saucepan. Bring to the boil, stirring all the time. The mixture should be thick enough to coat the back of a spoon. Cool slightly, stirring all the time, then spoon the glaze over the fruit. Leave until set.

To freeze: wrap and freeze at the end of step 3. Defrost overnight at cool room temperature, then finish as above.

CHERRY AND KIRSCH GÂTEAU

SERVES 10

A dessert to make the most of ripe summer cherries.

---

two 8 inch Whisked sponges (see page 125)

FOR THE FILLING

2½ pounds cherries

2 tablespoons sugar

2 tablespoons kirsch

1 cup heavy cream

½ cup Greek yogurt

---

1. Reserve about 1 pound of the best cherries for the decoration. To make the filling, pit the remaining cherries and put them in a saucepan with the sugar and 6 tablespoons water. Cover and simmer gently until tender, stirring occasionally. Drain, reserving the juice. Cool, then purée the cherries in a blender or food processor with the kirsch. Stir half the purée into the reserved juice to make a sauce.

2. Whip the cream until stiff, then fold in the yogurt. Spread one of the sponges with the cherry purée, allowing it to run down the sides a little. Spread with half of the cream. Place the second sponge on top.

3. For the decoration, spread the remaining cream on top of the cake. Pit most of the reserved cherries, leaving some whole with the stalks attached. Decorate the top with the cherries. Serve with the cherry sauce handed separately.

To freeze: wrap and freeze the cooked sponges. Freeze the cherry purée and sauce in rigid containers. Defrost overnight at cool room temperature, then finish as above.

Opposite: FRUIT SALAD GÂTEAU.

THE CHEESECAKE COLLECTION

Creamily rich, velvety smooth, these cheesecake recipes
will set your tastebuds tingling. From the traditional
European baked cheesecake to the sumptuous and
squidgy Marbled chocolate fudge cheesecake. Bake one
soon and treat yourself to a new taste experience.

Cheesecakes are always made from unripened cheeses. These may be full fat soft cream cheese, curd cheese or cottage cheese. Full fat soft cream cheese is creamy rich made from full milk, enriched with heavy cream to give a high fat content. This gives cheesecakes a superbly smooth texture. Low fat soft cream cheese is a low fat alternative, useful if you are counting calories, but will not give such a rich texture and flavor. Curd cheese is made from full milk and has the most pronounced (cheesy) flavor. Its texture is slightly grainy. Cottage cheese is lighter than either, made from skim milk. The texture of cottage cheese is lumpy and the flavor mild. There is often a good deal of whey left in the cheese, making it rather moist. Push it through a fine strainer and drain off any excess whey before adding to the mixture.

Bake cheesecakes in spring-release cake pans to make turning out easy. If you do not own a spring-release pan, a cake pan with a loose base works almost as well. Baked cheesecakes should be cooked on a low temperature to make sure that the eggs do not curdle.

When making chilled cheesecakes, set with gelatin. All the rules for using gelatin apply (see page 188). Once the cheesecake has set, remove it from the pan to prevent any reaction between the metal pan and the acid in the cheesecake causing discoloration.

Store leftover cheesecake, closely wrapped, in the refrigerator and serve within a day or two. Some cheesecakes freeze well (see the recipes). Freeze in the pan until solid, then turn out and wrap in freezer film or foil. Defrost slowly, overnight in the refrigerator.

TRADITIONAL EUROPEAN BAKED CHEESECAKE

SERVES 8

Lemon and white raisins are the traditional flavorings for a European baked cheesecake.

FOR THE BASE

½ cup self raising flour
½ teaspoon baking powder
½ stick butter, softened
scant ⅓ cup superfine sugar
1 egg

FOR THE FILLING

4 eggs, separated
generous 1 cup superfine sugar
2 cups full fat soft cream cheese
3 tablespoons All Purpose flour
grated peel and juice of 1 lemon
1 cup sour cream
½ cup white raisins
pinch of nutmeg, for sprinkling

1. Grease an 8 inch round spring-release cake pan and line the base with wax paper, then grease the paper.
2. To make the base, sift the self raising flour and baking powder into a bowl. Add the butter, sugar and egg. Mix well and beat for 2–3 minutes. Spread the mixture evenly over the bottom of the prepared pan.
3. To make the filling, whisk the egg yolks with the sugar until the mixture is thick and creamy.
4. Beat the soft cheese lightly in a bowl. Add the whisked egg mixture and mix until smooth. Sift in the All Purpose flour and stir in. Add the lemon peel and juice, half of the sour cream and the raisins.
5. Whisk the egg whites until stiff, then fold into the mixture. Pour on to the mixture in the pan.
6. Bake in the oven at 325° for 1 hour or until firm but still spongy to the touch. Turn off the heat and leave in the oven for 1 hour with the door just open.
7. Remove from the oven and cool completely for 2–3 hours. Carefully remove the cheesecake from the tin. To serve, spread the remaining sour cream over the top and sprinkle with nutmeg.

To freeze: pack and freeze the cold cheesecake before covering with cream. Defrost in the refrigerator overnight, then finish as above.

Previous page: BAKED BLENDER CHEESECAKE WITH RED FRUIT SAUCE (PAGE 158). Above: TRADITIONAL EUROPEAN BAKED CHEESECAKE. Below: CALCIONI ALL'ASCOLANA (PAGE 148).

RICOTTA CHEESECAKE

SERVES 8

This classic Italian cheesecake does not have a base and is flavored with chopped candied fruit, rum and almonds.

2 cups ricotta cheese
3 eggs, separated
generous ½ cup superfine sugar
¼ cup rum or brandy
scant 1 cup ground almonds
½ cup chopped candied fruit
finely grated peel of 1 lemon
sugar, for dredging

1. Grease and flour an 8 inch spring-release cake pan and line the base with wax paper.
2. Beat the ricotta cheese with the egg yolks and half of the sugar in a bowl. Fold in the rum, almonds, candied fruit and lemon peel.
3. Whisk the egg whites with the remaining sugar until stiff. Fold into the cheese mixture. Spoon into the prepared pan.
4. Bake in the oven at 350° for 45 minutes or until firm to the touch and slightly shrunk away from the sides of the pan.
5. Turn the oven off. Leave the cheesecake to cool in the oven, with the door just open.
6. To serve, carefully remove the cheesecake from the pan and dredge with sugar.

Not suitable for freezing.

CALCIONI ALL'ASCOLANA

SERVES 16

Individual cheesecake turnovers filled with a delicious ricotta and candied fruit mixture.

FOR THE PASTRY
2 cups All Purpose flour
pinch of salt
2 eggs, beaten
2 tablespoons olive oil

FOR THE FILLING
1 cup ricotta cheese
scant 1 cup ground almonds
25 g (1 oz) caster sugar
1 egg yolk
finely grated peel of 1 lemon
½ cup candied fruit, finely chopped
beaten egg, to glaze
icing sugar, for dusting

Above: RICOTTA CHEESECAKE. *Below:* CENCI (PAGE 68).

1. To make the pastry, put the flour and salt in a bowl. Make a well in the center and stir in the eggs and olive oil. Using your fingertips, knead the mixture together to make a smooth dough.
2. Turn out on to a floured work surface and knead for about 5 minutes. Wrap and chill for 30 minutes.
3. To make the filling, mix the ingredients together.
4. Roll out the pastry on a lightly floured work surface until it is very thin. Cut out 4 inch rounds, using a plain cookie cutter. Re-roll the pastry trimmings and use to make more rounds, making 16 rounds in total.
5. Divide the filling between the pastry rounds. Brush the edges with the beaten egg, then fold each round in half to enclose the filling. Brush with beaten egg to glaze. Transfer to cookie sheets.
6. Bake in the oven at 375° for 25–30 minutes or until golden brown. Serve cold, dusted with icing sugar.

To freeze: wrap and freeze the cold cheesecakes. Defrost overnight at cool room temperature.

Illustrated on page 147

BAKED BANANA CHEESECAKE

SERVES 8–10

FOR THE BASE
2 cups chocolate Graham Cracker crumbs
¾ stick butter, melted

FOR THE FILLING
½ stick butter or margarine
¼ stick self raising flour
1 cup low fat soft cream cheese
4 firm, ripe bananas, peeled and chopped
generous ½ cup superfine sugar
4 eggs
¾ cup chocolate chips

FOR THE TOPPING
1 cup sour cream
2 squares chocolate, grated

1. Grease an 8 inch spring-release cake pan.
2. To make the base, mix the crumbs and butter together. Press into the base of the prepared pan and level the surface. Chill while making the filling.
3. To make the filling, put all the ingredients, except the chocolate chips, in a blender or food processor and purée until smooth and well mixed. Stir in the chocolate chips. Pour the filling over the base and level the surface.
4. Bake in the oven at 350° for 1¼ hours or until just set. Leave to cool in the pan.
5. To serve, remove from the pan and spread the cream on top of the cheesecake. Sprinkle with the grated chocolate.

Not suitable for freezing.

BAKED LEMON AND BLACKCURRANT CHEESECAKE

SERVES 8

Use frozen blackcurrants straight from the freezer. Stir them quickly and lightly into the cheesecake mixture.

FOR THE BASE

¾ stick butter or margarine, melted

scant ⅓ cup superfine sugar

1½ cups Graham Cracker crumbs

FOR THE FILLING

1 cup low fat soft cream cheese

grated peel and juice of 1 lemon

3 eggs, separated

generous ½ cup superfine sugar

2 tablespoons All Purpose flour

1¼ cups frozen or fresh blackcurrants

icing sugar, for dusting

1. Grease a loose-based 7–8 inch round cake pan.
2. To make the base, mix the butter, sugar and crumbs together. Press the mixture evenly over the base of the prepared pan. Chill to firm while preparing the filling.
3. To make the filling, beat the cheese with the grated lemon peel and juice, the egg yolks, half of the sugar and the flour. Whisk the egg whites until stiff but not dry, then whisk in the remaining sugar. Carefully fold into the cheese mixture with the blackcurrants. Spoon on to the base and level the top.
4. Bake in the oven at 350° for about 1¼ hours or until well risen and fairly firm to the touch. Reduce the oven temperature to 325° and cook for about another 30 minutes or until quite firm to the touch. Cover loosely with foil during baking to prevent overbrowning. The cheesecake will sink slightly in the center.
5. Leave the cheesecake to stand for a few minutes then, using a spatula, ease the sides away from the pan. Carefully push the cake out of its pan base, then slide off the base. Cool, then dust with icing sugar.

To freeze: cool, pack and freeze. Defrost overnight in the refrigerator.

LEMON MUESLI CHEESECAKE

SERVES 6

If you are buying muesli specially to make the base for this cheesecake, select a sugar-free variety or at least one that is low in sugar.

FOR THE BASE

1½ cups muesli

¾ stick butter or margarine, melted

FOR THE FILLING

3 lemons

1 tablespoon gelatin

1 cup low fat soft cream cheese

½ cup plain yogurt

4 tablespoons clear honey

2 egg whites

1. Grease an 8 inch spring-release cake pan.
2. To make the base, mix the muesli and melted butter together. Press the mixture over the base of the prepared pan, using the back of a metal spoon. Chill to set while making the filling.
3. To make the filling, finely grate the peel of 2 of the lemons. Set aside. Squeeze the juice from the 2 lemons and make up to ½ cup with water.
4. Sprinkle the gelatin over the lemon juice and water in a bowl and leave to soak for 2–3 minutes. Place the bowl over a pan of simmering water and stir until dissolved. (Alternatively, microwave on HIGH for 30 seconds or until dissolved.) Leave to cool slightly.
5. Whisk the cheese, yogurt and honey together in a separate bowl. Stir in the grated lemon peel and dissolved gelatin until evenly incorporated. Whisk the egg whites until standing in stiff peaks. Fold into the cheesecake mixture until evenly incorporated. Spoon the mixture into the prepared pan and level the surface. Chill for at least 4 hours until set.
6. Coarsely grate the peel from the remaining lemon over the center of the cheesecake, to decorate. Alternatively, slice the lemon thinly and arrange on top of the cheesecake. Remove the cheesecake from the pan and place on a serving plate. Serve chilled.

To freeze: wrap and freeze at the end of step 5. Defrost overnight in the refrigerator, then finish as above.

APPLE AND RAISIN CHEESECAKE

SERVES 8

This is rather like a cheesecake pie.

1 quantity Shortcrust pastry (see page 42)

FOR THE FILLING
1 cup dry apple rings
⅔ cup white raisins
grated peel and juice of 1 lemon
2 tablespoons rum
¼ stick butter, softened
½ cup low fat soft cream cheese
2 tablespoons self raising flour
sugar
½ cup cottage cheese, strained
2 tablespoons milk
3 eggs

1. To make the filling, soak the apple rings overnight in cold water. Soak the raisins overnight with the grated lemon peel, 3 tablespoons lemon juice and the rum.

2. Line the base of a 5–6 cup loaf pan with wax paper.

3. Roll out three quarters of the pastry and use to line the base and sides of the prepared pan.

4. Beat the butter, soft cheese, flour, 2 tablespoons sugar and the cottage cheese together in a bowl. Whisk the milk, 2 eggs and 1 egg yolk together, then whisk into the cheese mixture.

5. Well drain and chop the apple. Stir the apple and raisins into the cheese mixture. Spoon into the pastry base.

6. Roll out the remaining pastry and use to cover the filling, sealing the edges well. Beat the remaining egg white and brush over the pastry. Sprinkle with a little sugar.

7. Bake in the oven at 375° for about 1½ hours. Leave to cool in the pan for 20 minutes before turning out. Cool for a further 1 hour. Serve cut into thick slices.

Not suitable for freezing.

MARBLED CHOCOLATE FUDGE CHEESECAKE

SERVES 16

The cold cheesecake has a much heavier, fudgier texture than when served hot.

FOR THE BASE
8 ounces chocolate chip cookies
⅓ cup chocolate chips
¾ cup butter, melted

FOR THE FILLING
4 squares semi sweet chocolate
1¼ sticks butter or margarine
1 cup superfine sugar
3 eggs
1 cup All Purpose flour
vanilla
generous ½ cup low fat soft cream cheese

1. Grease an 8 inch loose-based cake pan.

2. To make the base, roughly crush the chocolate chip cookies and mix with the chocolate chips and butter. Spoon into the prepared pan and pack down with the back of a spoon. Chill while making the filling.

3. To make the filling, break the chocolate into small pieces. Place in a large bowl with the butter. Stand the bowl over a pan of simmering water and heat gently until the chocolate melts. (Alternatively, microwave on LOW for 4–5 minutes or until melted, stirring occasionally.)

4. Add half of the sugar, 2 of the eggs, the flour and a few drops of vanilla to the chocolate and beat together. Pour the mixture into the prepared pan.

5. Beat the cheese, remaining sugar and egg and a few drops of vanilla together. Spoon on top of the chocolate mixture. Pull a knife through the two mixtures to give a marbled effect.

6. Bake in the oven at 350° for 1 hour 10–20 minutes or until firm to the touch. Leave to cool in the pan for 5 minutes. Serve hot with Greek yogurt or cold with vanilla ice cream.

To freeze: wrap and freeze after baking. Defrost overnight in the refrigerator.

RUM AND RAISIN CHEESECAKE

SERVES 8

A light, fluffy baked cheesecake with a pastry base.

FOR THE PASTRY
2 cups self raising flour
1 teaspoon soda
1 teaspoon cream of tartar
$\frac{3}{4}$ stick butter
finely grated peel of 1 lemon
$\frac{1}{2}$ cup sour cream

FOR THE FILLING
$\frac{1}{2}$ cup raisins
5 tablespoons dark rum
$\frac{1}{2}$ cup cottage cheese
$\frac{1}{2}$ cup full fat soft cream cheese
2 eggs, separated
scant $\frac{1}{3}$ cup superfine sugar
$\frac{1}{2}$ cup heavy cream
1 tablespoon icing sugar, for dusting

1. Grease a 10 inch pie plate.
2. To make the filling, put the raisins and rum in a saucepan and bring to the boil. Remove from the heat and leave to cool for 15 minutes.
3. Meanwhile, to make the pastry, sift the flour, soda and cream of tartar into a bowl. Rub in the butter until the mixture resembles fine breadcrumbs. Add the lemon peel. Bind to a smooth dough with the sour cream. Roll out and use to line the prepared plate.
4. Beat the cottage and cream cheeses together in a bowl. Stir in the rum and raisins.
5. In a separate bowl, whisk the egg yolks and sugar together until pale and fluffy. Whisk in the heavy cream, and continue whisking until the mixture is the consistency of lightly whipped cream. Fold into the cheese, rum and raisin mixture. Whisk the egg whites until stiff, then fold into the mixture. Pour into the pastry case.
6. Bake in the oven at 350° for about 1 hour. Turn off the heat and leave to cool in the oven for 15 minutes. Remove from the oven and cool for a further 45 minutes. Dust with icing sugar.

Not suitable for freezing.

HOT CHOCOLATE CHEESECAKE

SERVES 10–12

This cheesecake has a rich, irresistible flavor. Unusually for a cheesecake, it is served straight from the oven; however, should there be any left it tastes good cold as well.

FOR THE CHOCOLATE PASTRY
$\frac{1}{3}$ cup All Purpose flour
$\frac{3}{4}$ stick butter or margarine
2 tablespoons cocoa, sifted
2 tablespoons superfine sugar
$\frac{1}{3}$ cup ground hazelnuts
1 egg yolk

FOR THE FILLING
2 eggs, separated
scant $\frac{1}{2}$ cup superfine sugar
$1\frac{1}{2}$ cups curd cheese
scant $\frac{1}{2}$ cup ground hazelnuts
$\frac{1}{2}$ cup heavy cream
2 tablespoons cocoa, sifted
2 teaspoons dark rum
icing sugar, for dusting

1. Grease an 8 inch round loose-based cake pan.
2. To make the chocolate pastry, put the flour in a bowl and rub in the butter until the mixture resembles fine breadcrumbs. Stir in the cocoa, sugar and hazelnuts. Add the egg yolk and sufficient water to give a soft dough.
3. Roll out the pastry on a lightly floured work surface and use to line the prepared pan. Chill while making the filling.
4. To make the filling, whisk the egg yolks and sugar together in a bowl until thick enough to leave a trail on the surface when the whisk is lifted. Whisk in the cheese, nuts, cream, cocoa and rum until blended.
5. Whisk the egg whites until stiff, then fold into the cheese mixture. Pour into the pastry case and fold the edges of the pastry over the filling.
6. Bake in the oven at 325° for $1\frac{1}{2}$ hours until risen and just firm to the touch. Remove carefully from the pan and dust icing sugar over the top. Serve while still hot.

Not suitable for freezing.

Opposite: HOT CHOCOLATE CHEESECAKE.

GINGER AND BANANA CHEESECAKE

SERVES 6–8

The flavor of banana and ginger go very well together, but you can make it a little different by using chocolate Graham Crackers for the base of this cheesecake instead of ginger cookies, and omitting the preserved ginger from the filling. Decorate the top with banana slices arranged alternately with chocolate chips.

FOR THE BASE

| 8 ounces ginger cookies, crushed |
| 1 stick sweet butter, melted and cooled |

FOR THE FILLING

| 1 cup full fat soft cream cheese |
| $\frac{1}{2}$ cup sour cream |
| 3 bananas |
| 2 tablespoons clear honey |
| 1 tablespoon chopped preserved ginger (with syrup) |
| 1 tablespoon gelatin |
| 4 tablespoons lemon juice |

FOR THE DECORATION

| banana slices |
| preserved ginger slices |

1. To make the base, mix the cookies and melted butter together. Press the mixture over the base of an 8 inch spring-release pan or deep cake pan with a removable base. Chill for about 30 minutes.
2. To make the filling, beat the cheese and cream together in a bowl until well mixed. Peel and mash the bananas, then beat into the cheese mixture with the honey and ginger.
3. Sprinkle the gelatin over the lemon juice in a small bowl and leave to soak for 2–3 minutes. Place the bowl over a pan of simmering water and stir until dissolved. (Alternatively, microwave on HIGH for 30 seconds or until dissolved.)
4. Stir the dissolved gelatin slowly into the cheesecake mixture. Spoon on to the cookie base. Chill for about 3–4 hours until the cheesecake is set.
5. To serve, remove the cheesecake carefully from the pan and place on a serving plate. Decorate around the edge with banana and ginger slices. Serve as soon as possible or the banana will discolor.

To freeze: wrap and freeze at the end of step 4. Defrost overnight in the refrigerator, then finish as above.

RASPBERRY RIPPLE CHEESECAKE

SERVES 12

This cheesecake looks best made in a heart-shaped pan. Or use any other pan with an 8 cup capacity.

FOR THE BASE

| $\frac{1}{4}$ cup blanched almonds |
| 8 ounces almond butter cookies, crushed |
| 1 stick butter or margarine, melted |
| few drops of almond flavoring |

FOR THE FILLING

| 1 pound raspberries |
| 1 cup Greek yogurt |
| generous $\frac{1}{2}$ cup low fat soft cream cheese |
| 1 tablespoon gelatin |
| 2 egg whites |
| $\frac{1}{2}$ cup icing sugar |
| mint leaves, to decorate |

1. Grease a 4 pint loose-based cake pan or spring-release cake pan.
2. To make the base, lightly roast the almonds, then finely chop. Mix with the cookies and butter. Add a few drops of almond flavoring. Spoon the mixture into the base of the prepared pan and pack down with the back of a metal spoon. Chill while making the filling.
3. To make the filling, purée half of the raspberries in a blender or food processor, then press through a strainer. Pour three-quarters of the purée into a bowl and reserve. Add the yogurt and cheese to the purée remaining in the blender and process until well blended.
4. Sprinkle the gelatin over 2 tablespoons water in a small bowl and leave to soak for 2–3 minutes. Place the bowl over a pan of simmering water and stir until dissolved. (Alternatively, microwave on HIGH for 30 seconds or until dissolved.) Leave to cool, then add to the cheese mixture.
5. Whisk the egg whites with the icing sugar until very thick and shiny. Fold into the cheese mixture.
6. Arrange half of the reserved raspberries over the cookie base. Pour the cheese mixture into the pan. Sprinkle with the remaining raspberries. Spoon in the reserved purée and mark in a swirl with a knife to make a marbled pattern. Chill for 3–4 hours or until set.
7. To serve, unmold and decorate with mint leaves.

Not suitable for freezing.

Opposite: RASPBERRY RIPPLE CHEESECAKE.

MINI GRAPE CHEESECAKES

SERVES 24

These creamy individual baked cheesecakes are
decorated with halved black grapes.

FOR THE PASTRY

$2\frac{1}{2}$ cups All Purpose flour
pinch of salt
$1\frac{1}{2}$ sticks butter or margarine, cut into pieces
scant $\frac{1}{3}$ cup superfine sugar

FOR THE FILLING

1 cup full fat soft cream cheese
2 eggs, beaten
2 tablespoons superfine sugar
2 teaspoons All Purpose flour
finely grated peel and juice of $\frac{1}{2}$ lemon

FOR THE DECORATION

6 ounces seedless black grapes, halved
$\frac{1}{2}$ cup whipping cream, whipped

1. To make the pastry, put the flour and salt into a
bowl. Rub in the butter until the mixture resembles
breadcrumbs. Stir in the sugar and add sufficient water,
about 4 tablespoons, to mix to a smooth dough.
2. Roll out the pastry on a lightly floured work surface
and cut out twelve 3 inch rounds, using a fluted pastry
cutter. Use to line 24 deep muffin pans.
3. Bake blind in the oven at 400° for 10 minutes.
Remove the foil and baking beans, then return to the
oven for a further 5 minutes.
4. Meanwhile to make the filling, beat the soft cheese,
eggs, sugar, flour and lemon peel and juice together in a
bowl until evenly mixed. Pour the filling into the pastry
cases.
5. Lower the oven temperature to 300° and bake the
cheesecakes for 15 minutes until the fillings are set.
Leave to cool on a wire rack for 30 minutes, then
refrigerate the cheesecakes for at least 1 hour before
serving.
6. Just before serving, decorate the top of each cheesecake with the grapes and piped whipped cream.

*To freeze: wrap and freeze at the end of step 5. Defrost
overnight in the refrigerator, then finish as above.*

TROPICAL CHEESECAKE

SERVES 8

Sweet, aromatic and juicy mangoes are used in the
cheesecake filling, with kiwi fruit slices to decorate.

FOR THE BASE

$\frac{3}{4}$ stick butter, melted
2 cups chocolate Graham Crackers, finely crushed
$\frac{1}{2}$ cup sweet shredded coconut

FOR THE FILLING

2 medium mangoes
2 tablespoons gelatin
$\frac{1}{2}$ cup orange juice
$1\frac{1}{2}$ cups full fat soft cream cheese
generous $\frac{1}{2}$ cup superfine sugar
2 eggs, separated
2 tablespoons lemon juice
1 cup heavy cream
3 kiwi fruit, peeled and sliced, to decorate

1. Lightly oil an $8\frac{1}{2}$ inch spring-release cake pan. Line
the base with wax paper and grease the paper.
2. To make the base, stir the melted butter into the
crumbs and coconut. Mix well together. Press into the
prepared pan. Chill for 30 minutes.
3. To make the filling, peel the mangoes and cut the
flesh from the pit. Discard the pit. Roughly chop or
mash the flesh.
4. Sprinkle the gelatin over the orange juice in a bowl
and leave to soak for 2–3 minutes. Place the bowl over a
pan of simmering water and stir until dissolved.
(Alternatively, microwave on HIGH for 30 seconds or
until dissolved.) Leave the gelatin to cool for 5 minutes.
5. Beat the soft cheese and sugar together in a bowl
until smooth, then beat in the egg yolks and lemon
juice. Stir in the mango flesh and dissolved gelatin.
Lightly whip the cream and fold into the mixture.
6. Whisk the egg whites until stiff, then carefully fold
into the cheese mixture. Pour on to the base. Chill for
3–4 hours until firm. Carefully remove the cheesecake
from the pan. Decorate with the kiwi fruit.

*To freeze: wrap and freeze at the end of step 6. Defrost
overnight in the refrigerator, then finish as above.*

REDCURRANT CHEESECAKE

SERVES 4–6

Fresh redcurrants are only to be had during the height of summer but their sharpness does go very well with the sweet cheesecake base. Substituting a fruit-flavored yogurt for plain gives more fruit flavor and a hint of extra color.

FOR THE BASE

generous ½ stick butter, melted
1¾ cups Graham Cracker crumbs

FOR THE FILLING

1½ cups redcurrants
1 tablespoon gelatin
½ cup cottage cheese
1 egg, separated
3 tablespoons superfine sugar
½ cup plain yogurt
½ cup heavy cream
1 tablespoon redcurrant jelly
redcurrants, to decorate

1. To make the base, mix the butter and crumbs together. Press the mixture into a loose-based 8 inch cake pan, lining the base and sides.

2. To make the filling, put the redcurrants in a medium saucepan with 3 tablespoons water and simmer gently for 5–6 minutes until just soft. (Alternatively, cover and microwave on HIGH for 3–4 minutes.) Leave to cool.

3. Sprinkle the gelatin over 3 tablespoons water in a small bowl and leave to soak for 2–3 minutes. Place the bowl over a pan of simmering water and stir until dissolved. (Alternatively, microwave on HIGH for 30 seconds or until dissolved.) Leave until lukewarm.

4. Put the cheese, egg yolk, sugar and yogurt in a food processor or blender and work until smooth. Whip the cream until it just holds its shape. Fold the cooked redcurrants, redcurrant jelly, dissolved gelatin and most of the cream into the cheese mixture. Whisk the egg white until stiff, then fold into the mixture.

5. Pour the mixture on to the base and chill until set. Remove from the pan and decorate with the remaining cream and redcurrants.

Not suitable for freezing.

Above: REDCURRANT CHEESECAKE.

BAKED BLENDER CHEESECAKE WITH RED FRUIT SAUCE

SERVES 8

The cheesecake will rise quite dramatically in the oven at first, then settle back down in the pan. If using a fan-assisted oven, reduce the temperature according to manufacturer's instructions.

FOR THE BASE
1 cup Graham Cracker crumbs
⅔ cup ground almonds
¾ stick butter, melted

FOR THE FILLING
1 cup full fat soft cream cheese
1 cup cottage cheese
4 tablespoons heavy cream
2 eggs, separated
1 egg yolk
1 tablespoon cornstarch
grated peel and juice of 3 lemons
generous ½ cup superfine sugar

FOR THE SAUCE
2½ cups strawberries, hulled
2¼ cups raspberries, hulled
scant ½ cup icing sugar
6 tablespoons orange-flavored liqueur or fresh orange juice

FOR THE DECORATION
whipped cream
halved strawberries
frosted rose petals (see page 10)
icing sugar, for dusting

1. Grease the base and sides of an 8 inch spring-release cake pan and line with wax paper.
2. To make the base, stir the crumbs and ground almonds into the melted butter and blend well. Press half the mixture into the base of the prepared pan.
3. To make the filling, blend the cheeses, cream, egg yolks, cornstarch, lemon peel and 4 tablespoons lemon juice together in a blender or food processor.
4. Whisk the egg whites until stiff but not dry. Whisk in 2 tablespoons of the sugar, then whisk again until stiff and shiny. Fold in the remaining sugar. Gently fold the egg whites into the cheese mixture. Spoon into the pan. Sprinkle the remaining crumb mixture on top.
5. Bake in the oven at 400° for 30 minutes. Reduce the oven temperature to 350° and bake for a further 45 minutes or until a tester inserted into the center comes out clean. Cover with foil if necessary during cooking. Leave to cool in the pan. Chill for at least 1 hour.
6. To make the sauce, blend the strawberries, rasp-berries, icing sugar and liqueur together in a blender or food processor. Strain to remove pits. Chill.
7. Carefully remove the pan from the sides of the cheesecake. Peel off the lining paper. Place a flat serving plate on top of the cheesecake and invert. Remove the base of the pan and lining paper. Decorate with whipped cream, halved strawberries and rose petals. Dust with icing sugar and serve with the chilled red fruit sauce.

To freeze: pack and freeze the undecorated cheesecake. Freeze the sauce separately. Defrost in the refrigerator overnight then decorate as above.

Illustrated on pages 144–145

COFFEE CHEESECAKE

SERVES 8

If you can find them, use sugar coffee beans, available from high class confectioners, to decorate.

FOR THE BASE
½ stick butter, melted
2 cups ginger cookies, finely crushed

FOR THE FILLING
1 tablespoon gelatin
1 tablespoon instant coffee powder
2 tablespoons coffee-flavored liqueur
1 cup light brown soft sugar
4 cups curd cheese
1 cup whipping cream
coffee beans, to decorate

1. Lightly oil an 8 inch loose-based deep cake pan or spring-release cake pan.
2. To make the base, stir the butter and crushed cookies together. Press firmly into the base of the prepared pan. Chill for 30 minutes until set.
3. To make the filling, sprinkle the gelatin over 3 tablespoons water in a small bowl and leave to soak for 10 minutes. Place the bowl over a pan of simmering water and stir until dissolved. (Alternatively, microwave on HIGH for 30 seconds or until dissolved.)
4. Stir the coffee and coffee liqueur into 1 cup boiling water. Stir in the gelatin, then the sugar.
5. Put the coffee mixture and curd cheese into a blender or food processor and work until just smooth. Leave until beginning to set. Lightly whip the cream and fold half into the cheese mixture.
6. Turn the mixture into the prepared pan and chill for 2–3 hours or until set.
7. When set, remove from the pan. Pipe whirls of the remaining cream around the cheesecake and decorate.

To freeze: wrap and freeze at the end of step 6. Defrost overnight in the refrigerator, then decorate as above.

Opposite: COFFEE CHEESECAKE.

PUMPKIN CHEESECAKE

SERVES 20

This makes a very large cheesecake, suitable for a buffet party.

FOR THE PUMPKIN LAYER

1½ pounds peeled and seeded pumpkin, chopped
scant ½ cup sugar
thinly pared peel and juice of 3 oranges
6 passion fruit
4½ teaspoons gelatin

FOR THE BASE

1 stick sweet butter
3 tablespoons corn syrup
2 cups Graham Cracker crumbs

FOR THE CHEESE LAYER

4 eggs, separated
scant 1 cup superfine sugar
finely grated peel of 3 lemons
4 tablespoons lemon juice
3 cups full fat soft cream cheese
3 tablespoons gelatin
1½ cups heavy cream

FOR THE DECORATION

1 cup heavy cream, whipped
few pistachios

1. To make the pumpkin layer, put the pumpkin, sugar and orange peel and juice into a large saucepan. Cover and cook gently for about 45 minutes until very soft. Cool slightly, then purée in a blender or food processor.

2. Cut each passion fruit in half and scoop out the pips into a nylon strainer placed over a small bowl. Work the seeds in the strainer with the back of a spoon until all of the juice is extracted into the bowl. Stir the juices into the pumpkin purée.

3. Sprinkle the gelatin over 3 tablespoons water in a small bowl and leave to soak for 2–3 minutes. Place the bowl over a pan of simmering water and stir until dissolved. (Alternatively, microwave on HIGH for 30 seconds or until dissolved.) Stir the dissolved gelatin into the pumpkin purée, then put the purée aside to cool.

4. To make the base, put the butter and syrup in a large pan and heat gently until the butter melts. (Alternatively, microwave on HIGH for 2 minutes or until melted, stirring once.) Stir in the crumbs and mix well. Spread the crumb mixture evenly over the base of a 12 inch spring-release cake pan, pressing gently to firm. Chill the base while making the cheese layer.

5. To make the cheese layer, whisk the egg yolks, sugar and lemon peel together in a bowl until the mixture is very thick and creamy, and leaves a trail when the whisk is lifted. Gradually, whisk in the lemon juice. Beat the soft cheese until very soft, then gradually beat in the lemon mixture.

6. Dissolve the gelatin in 6 tablespoons water, as above. Whip the cream until it holds soft peaks. Whisk the egg whites until stiff.

7. Mix the dissolved gelatin into the cheese and lemon mixture, then quickly fold in the cream, followed by the egg whites. Pour the mixture on to the biscuit base. Chill for at least 1 hour until set.

8. Very carefully pour the cold, but not yet set, pumpkin mixture on top of the set cheesecake. Smooth the surface. Chill for at least 3 hours, or preferably overnight, until well set.

9. To serve, carefully run a spatula around the side of the cheesecake then gently remove the side of the pan. Place the cheesecake on a serving dish. Decorate with whipped cream and pistachios. Chill until serving.

Not suitable for freezing.

CRANBERRY CHEESECAKE

SERVES 10

Cranberry cheesecake looks good as part of a buffet party spread. Serve with plenty of pouring cream or sour cream, for those who like it.

FOR THE FILLING

1 cup full fat soft cream cheese
2 eggs, separated
finely grated peel and juice of 2 lemons
generous 1 cup superfine sugar
1 cup plain yogurt
1 cup heavy cream
1 tablespoon gelatin
1 cup cranberries
2 teaspoons arrowroot

FOR THE BASE

1 cup Graham Cracker crumbs
¾ stick butter, melted

1. Lightly oil a 10 inch fluted savarin spring-release pan.

2. For the filling, beat the cheese, egg yolks, lemon peel, quarter of the sugar and the yogurt together in a bowl. Whip the cream lightly and fold into the cheese mixture.

3. In a small bowl, mix 5 tablespoons lemon juice with 2 tablespoons water. Sprinkle in the gelatin and leave to soak for 2–3 minutes. Place the bowl over a pan of simmering water and stir until dissolved. (Alternatively, microwave on HIGH for 30 seconds or until dissolved.) Stir into the cheese mixture and leave to cool.

4. Whisk the egg whites until standing in soft peaks, then fold into the cheese mixture until evenly incorporated. Pour the mixture into the prepared pan. Chill for 3–4 hours until completely set.

5. To make the base, mix the crumbs and melted butter together. Spoon the mixture over the set cheesecake and pat down firmly. Chill again for 1 hour until set.
6. Cook the cranberries, remaining sugar and ½ cup water in a pan for about 10 minutes until soft but still whole. Blend a little water with the arrowroot, stir into the cranberry mixture and slowly bring to boiling point. Cook for 2–3 minutes, then leave to cool for 30 minutes.
7. Invert the cheesecake on to a flat serving plate. Spoon the cranberry mixture into the center before serving.

To freeze: invert the cheesecake on to the top of a deep rigid container. Cover with the base. Defrost overnight in the refrigerator, then finish as above.

ORANGE LIQUEUR CHEESECAKE

SERVES 6

This is more like a cheesecake pie than a traditional cheesecake.

1 quantity Sweet pastry (see page 43)

FOR THE FILLING
1 cup full fat soft cream cheese
½ cup plain yogurt
2 tablespoons sugar
finely grated peel and juice of 1 medium orange
2 teaspoons gelatin
2 tablespoons lemon juice
3 tablespoons orange-flavored liqueur
1 egg white
grated chocolate, to decorate

1. Roll out the pastry very thinly and use to line an 8 inch fluted pie plate.
2. Bake blind in the oven at 400° for about 25 minutes.
3. To make the filling, beat the soft cheese, using a wooden spoon, in a bowl. Gradually beat in the yogurt, sugar, orange peel and 4 tablespoons orange juice.
4. Sprinkle the gelatin over the lemon juice in a small bowl and leave to soak for 2–3 minutes. Place the bowl over a pan of simmering water and stir until dissolved. (Alternatively, microwave on HIGH for 30 seconds or until dissolved.) Stir the dissolved gelatin into the cheese mixture with the liqueur. Whisk the egg white until stiff, then fold in.

5. Turn the mixture into the cold pastry case and leave to set. Decorate with grated chocolate.

To freeze: leave to set, open freeze without chocolate and wrap when frozen. Defrost overnight in the refrigerator, then finish as above.

CARROT CHEESECAKE

SERVES 8–10

Ginger cookies also make a good base for this unusual cheesecake.

FOR THE BASE
1½ cups Graham Cracker crumbs
1 stick butter or margarine, melted

FOR THE FILLING
1 stick butter or margarine
¼ cup light brown soft sugar
2 eggs, separated
1 cup low fat soft cream cheese
2 cups carrots, peeled and finely grated
1 teaspoon mixed spice
scant ½ cup self raising flour
½ cup ground almonds
⅓ cup raisins

FOR THE TOPPING
1 cup low fat soft cream cheese
1 tablespoon clear honey
2 teaspoons lemon juice
¼ cup blanched almonds, roasted and chopped

1. Grease a 7 inch square loose-based pan.
2. To make the base, mix the crumbs and butter together. Pack into the prepared pan. Chill.
3. To make the filling, cream the butter and sugar together in a bowl until pale and fluffy. Beat in the egg yolks, soft cheese, carrots, mixed spice, flour, almonds and raisins.
4. Whisk the egg whites until stiff, then fold into the mixture. Pour into the prepared pan and level the surface.
5. Bake in the oven at 350° for about 1¼ hours or until firm to the touch. Leave to cool, then remove from the pan.
6. To make the topping, beat the cheese, honey and lemon juice together. Spread over the top of the cheesecake and mark into a pattern with a fork. Sprinkle with the chopped almonds.

Not suitable for freezing.

SMOOTH CUSTARDS AND CREAMY PUDDINGS

From perennial dessert favorites such as light, silken baked Crème caramel through delicately flavored childhood treats like Rice pudding, Blancmange and Fruit fool to sophisticated, luxuriously creamy Bavarois and Syllabub, this chapter contains them all.

Egg Custard

Real egg custard forms the basis of a wide range of familiar and much loved desserts. Achieving a perfectly smooth, fine custard is not difficult, providing you take your time. Real custard cannot be hurried and will not tolerate rigorous boiling.

Always cook custard in a heavy-based saucepan or in the top of a double boiler over a very low heat. Stir frequently to prevent it overheating and curdling. It will only thicken slightly, just enough to coat the back of the spoon lightly.— Watch the froth on the top of the pan—this will be absorbed into the milk as the custard thickens slightly. As soon as the sauce thickens, pour it into a cold bowl to prevent further cooking.

Egg custard can be cooked in the microwave on LOW. Use a large bowl and whisk every 30 seconds.

Baked Custard

Custards are usually baked in a bain-marie. The surrounding water prevents the delicate mixture overcooking at the sides before the middle is set. In an overcooked custard, small holes will appear in the middle of the custard first, then it will curdle and eventually separate as the whey leaks out.

Cream

Custard mixed with cream and set with gelatin (see the notes on page 188) forms the basis of bavarois. Cream whipped and flavored makes light fools and syllabubs. Properly whipped cream is essential when a smooth, airy texture is required. Choose heavy or whipping cream for whipping. To achieve more volume, add 1 tablespoon milk to each ½ cup cream before starting. Chill the cream and all the utensils thoroughly beforehand. Whip quickly at first, using a balloon whisk or hand-held electric mixer, until the cream begins to look matt on the surface. Continue whipping, a little more slowly until it stands in soft peaks and does not fall off the upturned whisk. Extra care is needed if using an electric mixer. If overwhipped, the cream will look granular and the flavor will be affected. It is impossible to rescue if this happens. Overwhipped cream will not fold smoothly into mousses and bavarois.

Heavy and whipping cream freeze particularly well if they are first lightly whipped and then frozen in plastic containers. They will keep successfully for two months, It is best to add 1 tablespoon milk to each ½ cup cream before partially whipping. When defrosted, finish whipping to the consistency required. Take care when whipping cream which has been frozen, because it is easily overwhipped. Rosettes of cream for decorating can be open frozen on non-stick cookie sheets. Use while frozen to decorate cakes and trifles, then allow 45 minutes to defrost.

Serving

Smooth puddings such as fools, bavarois, syllabubs and creams are best served with crisp cookies to give a contrast in texture, see the recipes following.

Langues de Chats

MAKES ABOUT 12

½ stick butter or margarine
scant ⅓ cup superfine sugar
1 egg
½ cup self raising flour

1. Grease two cookie sheets.
2. Cream the butter and sugar together in a bowl until pale and fluffy, then beat in the egg. Work in the flour until mixture is of a piping consistency.
3. Put the mixture into a pastry tube fitted with a ½ inch plain tip. Pipe on to the prepared cookie sheets in fingers about 2½–3 inches long, spaced widely apart.
4. Bake in the oven at 425° for about 5 minutes until the edges of the cookies are lightly colored. Leave to cool on a wire rack.

To freeze: pack in a rigid container and freeze. Defrost at cool room temperature.

Florentines

MAKES 12

¼ cup hazelnuts, finely chopped
¼ cup blanched almonds, finely chopped
candied cherries, chopped
2 tablespoons white raisins, chopped
2 tablespoons mixed chopped fruit
½ stick butter or margarine
scant ⅓ cup superfine sugar
2 teaspoons creamy milk
4 squares semi sweet chocolate, melted

1. Line three cookie sheets with non-stick wax paper.
2. Mix together the nuts and fruits.
3. Melt the butter in a saucepan, stir in the sugar and bring slowly to the boil, stirring. Remove the pan from the heat immediately, then stir in the fruit and nut mixture with the milk. Leave the mixture to cool slightly, stirring occasionally, until evenly blended and no longer oily in appearance.
4. Spoon the mixture on to the prepared cookie sheets, allowing plenty of space to spread.
5. Bake in rotation in the oven at 350° for about 12 minutes until golden brown.
6. Using a small greased spatula, immediately push in the edges to give a neat round shape. Cool for 1–2 minutes, then slide them on to a wire rack to cool.
7. Spoon a little chocolate on to the smooth side of each florentine and carefully spread to coat. Leave the chocolate until creamy but not set.
8. Draw the prongs of a fork across the chocolate in a wavy line. Wipe the non-stick paper clean and replace the florentines on to the lined cookie sheet. Chill.

To freeze: see above.

ENGLISH BAKED CUSTARD

SERVES 4

A simply delicious family pudding. Be careful not to overcook or the custard will curdle.

2 cups milk
3 eggs
2 tablespoons superfine sugar
nutmeg

1. Grease a heatproof dish.
2. Warm the milk in a saucepan but do not boil. Whisk the eggs and sugar lightly in a bowl, then pour on the hot milk, stirring.
3. Strain the mixture into the prepared dish. Sprinkle the nutmeg on top. Stand the dish in a roasting pan and fill with hot water to come halfway up the sides.
4. Bake in the oven at 325° for about 1¼ hours or until set and firm to the touch. Serve hot or cold.

Not suitable for freezing.

Previous page: CRÈME CARAMEL (PAGE 166). Above: CRÈME BRÛLÉE.

CRÈME BRÛLÉE

SERVES 6

Delicious pots of rich baked custard, topped with a crisp caramelized sugar top. Serve with poached or fresh fruit.

2 cups whipping cream
4 egg yolks
generous ½ cup superfine sugar
1 teaspoon vanilla

1. Put the cream in the top of a double boiler or in a heatproof bowl over a pan of hot water. Heat gently; do not boil.
2. Meanwhile, beat the egg yolks, half of the sugar and the vanilla together in a bowl. Add the cream and mix well together.
3. Stand six individual custard pots in a roasting pan, then pour in enough hot water to come halfway up the sides of the pots. Pour the custard mixture slowly into the pots, dividing it equally between them.
4. Bake in the oven at 300° for about 1 hour or until set. Remove from pan and cool for 1 hour.
5. Chill for 2–3 hours, preferably overnight. Sprinkle the top of each crème brûlée with the remaining sugar and put under a hot broiler for 2–3 minutes until the sugar turns to caramel. Chill again for 2–3 hours before serving.

Not suitable for freezing.

CRÈME CARAMEL

SERVES 4–6

A perennial dessert favorite, this light silken, baked custard with a rich amber, caramel sauce, can be made with most types of milk. For richer results, however, use light cream. Different flavorings such as vanilla or cardamom pods, orange peel, or even scented geranium leaves may be infused in the milk. Confident cooks may crown the custard with a froth of spun sugar. See the photograph on pages 162–163. The recipe for spun sugar is on page 56.

FOR THE CARAMEL

scant 1 cup sugar

FOR THE CUSTARD

1 vanilla pod or a few drops of vanilla

2 cups milk

4 eggs

4 egg yolks

2 tablespoons superfine sugar or more to taste

1. To make the caramel, slightly warm six ½ cup custard pots. Put the sugar in a heavy saucepan with enough water to just moisten. Place over a low heat and heat without boiling until the sugar is dissolved. (If boiled before dissolved, the sugar will crystalize and never form a caramel.) Prod the sugar occasionally to help it dissolve.

2. Bring to the boil and boil rapidly for a few minutes until the sugar begins to turn pale brown. DO NOT LEAVE THE SUGAR. At this stage it will turn brown very quickly and could easily catch and burn. Gently swirl the caramel to ensure even browning.

3. Once the caramel has reached the desired color, dip the base of the pan in cool water to prevent further cooking. Pour a little caramel into each of the warm pots and rotate each one to coat the bottom and part way up the sides with caramel. Leave to cool.

4. To make the custard, split the vanilla pod to expose the seeds. Place in a pan with the milk and heat until almost boiling (if using vanilla flavoring, add after heating the milk first). Meanwhile, beat the eggs, yolks and sugar until well mixed. Strain on to the milk. Stir well and strain again into the pots.

5. Place the pots in a roasting pan and fill the pan with hot water to come two thirds up the sides of the pots.

6. Bake in the oven at 325° for 20–30 minutes or until just set. To test, insert the tip of a small sharp knife into the center of a custard—if cooked it should come out clean. Also, if sufficiently set, when gently tapped the custard will wobble slightly like jello. Remove from the water bath. Leave to cool, then chill overnight.

7. To turn out, allow the custards to come to room temperature for 15 minutes. Free the edges by pressing with fingertips, then loosen the sides with a thin-bladed, blunt-edged knife. Place a serving dish over the top and invert. Lift off the pot. Serve with a fruit compote.

Not suitable for freezing.

STRAWBERRY CUSTARD PIE

SERVES 6–8

1½ quantity Sweet pastry (see page 43)

FOR THE FILLING

3 tablespoons cornstarch

2 eggs, separated

1½ cups milk

scant ½ cup superfine sugar

few drops of vanilla

1½ cups strawberries, hulled

1. Roll out the pastry on a floured work surface and use to line a 9 inch pie plate. Chill for 30 minutes. Prick the base of the pastry.

2. Bake blind in the oven at 400° for 20 minutes or until pale golden and cooked through. Cool in the dish for 30–40 minutes.

3. To make the filling, mix the cornstarch to a smooth paste with a little of the milk. Mix the egg yolks with the cornstarch paste.

4. Put the rest of the milk in a saucepan with the sugar and vanilla. Bring to the boil. Remove from the heat and pour on to the cornstarch mixture. Return to the pan, then bring to the boil, stirring, and boil for 2 minutes until thickened. Cover with damp wax paper and leave to cool for 30 minutes.

5. Thinly slice the strawberries into the base of the pastry case, reserving a few for decoration. Whisk the egg whites until stiff, then fold into the cold custard mixture. Smooth the custard mixture evenly over the strawberries. Chill for 1 hour until set.

6. Serve the pie decorated with the reserved strawberry slices, preferably within 2 hours of completion.

Not suitable for freezing.

MINTED STRAWBERRY CUSTARDS

SERVES 6

Replace the mint with a few lemon geranium leaves, if preferred.

1½ cups milk
4 large sprigs mint
1 egg
2 egg yolks
3 tablespoons superfine sugar
4 teaspoons gelatin
1½ pounds strawberries, hulled
1 tablespoon icing sugar
strawberries, to decorate

1. Grease six ½ cup custard pots.

2. Place the milk and mint sprigs in a saucepan. Bring slowly to the boil, cover and leave to infuse for about 30 minutes.

3. Whisk the egg and yolks with the superfine sugar in a bowl. Strain over the milk. Return to the pan and cook gently, stirring, until the custard just coats the back of the spoon. Do not boil. Leave to cool.

4. Sprinkle the gelatin over 3 tablespoons water in a small bowl and leave to soak for 2–3 minutes. Place the bowl over a pan of simmering water and stir until dissolved. (Alternatively, microwave on HIGH for 30 seconds or until dissolved.) Stir the gelatin into the custard.

5. Purée and strain the strawberries. Whisk about two thirds into the cold, but not set, custard. Pour the custard into the dishes and chill to set—about 3 hours.

6. Meanwhile, whisk the icing sugar into the remaining strawberry purée. Chill.

7. To serve, turn out the custards. Surround with strawberry sauce, then decorate with strawberries.

Not suitable for freezing.

Above: MINTED STRAWBERRY CUSTARDS.

BAKED TANGERINE CUSTARDS

SERVES 6

Lightly set custards flavored with tangerines and served with a tangerine compote.

1 pound tangerines
scant ½ cup superfine sugar
2 cups milk
4 eggs
2 tablespoons orange-flavored liqueur

1. Using a potato peeler, pare the peel from one of the tangerines. Place in a saucepan with one-third of the sugar and 1 cup water. Bring slowly to the boil. Boil for 10 minutes. Strain, reserving the syrup.

2. Peel the remaining fruit, reserve the peel and flesh. Blend this peel, the milk, remaining sugar and eggs in a blender or food processor for 2 minutes or until the peel is very small.

3. Strain the mixture into six deep ½ cup heatproof dishes. Place in a roasting pan filled with enough hot water to come halfway up the dishes.

4. Bake in the oven at 325° for about 1 hour. They should be very lightly set. Cool, then chill.

5. Meanwhile, separate the segments of fruit. Carefully remove any pith. Place the segments in a small bowl with the reserved syrup and liqueur. Cover and marinate until required.

6. To serve, decorate each custard with a few marinated segments. Serve the remainder separately.

Not suitable for freezing.

CREMA FRITTA

SERVES 4–6

Literally translated, this simple dessert means 'fried cream', which is in fact exactly what it is. In Italy, it is traditional to celebrate *Carnevale*—the day before Lent—by eating *crema fritta*. Children and young people invite friends home and everyone eats *crema fritta* in the way that people in other countries eat pancakes.

3 eggs
scant ⅓ cup superfine sugar
½ cup All Purpose flour
1 cup milk
1 cup light cream
finely grated peel of ½ lemon
1 cup dry white breadcrumbs
oil, for shallow frying
sugar, for sprinkling

1. Grease a shallow 7 inch square cake pan.
2. Beat 2 of the eggs and the sugar together in a large bowl until the mixture is pale.
3. Add the flour, beating all the time. Very slowly, beat in the milk and cream. Add the lemon peel. Pour the mixture into the prepared pan.
4. Bake in the oven at 350° for about 1 hour until a tester inserted in the center comes out clean. Leave to cool for 2–3 hours, preferably overnight.
5. When completely cold, cut into 16 cubes and remove from the cake pan.
6. Beat the remaining egg in a bowl. Dip the cubes in the egg, then in the breadcrumbs until well coated.
7. Heat the oil in a skillet and, when hot, slide in the cubes. Fry for 2–3 minutes until golden brown and a crust is formed. Turn and fry the second side. Drain well on kitchen paper. Serve immediately, sprinkled with sugar.

Not suitable for freezing.

BAKED CUSTARD SPONGE

SERVES 6

You can use up slices of leftover sponge cake in this family favorite.

1½ cups milk
4 eggs, beaten
½ cup heavy cream
scant ⅓ cup superfine sugar
½ teaspoon vanilla
4 ounces sponge cake cut into squares
⅓ cup raisins
½ teaspoon nutmeg

1. Heat the milk in a saucepan until almost boiling. Place the eggs, cream, sugar and vanilla in a bowl and pour over the milk.
2. Dip the cake into the custard and use to line the sides of a 4 cup heatproof dish.
3. Place the raisins in the base of the dish and pour the rest of the custard over. Sprinkle with nutmeg.
4. Bake in the oven at 300° for about 1 hour until lightly set. Serve warm with light cream.

Not suitable for freezing.

ALMOND CUSTARD TARTS

SERVES 10

Here, pastry cases made in brioche pans make good deep containers for a delicious almond custard.

1 quantity Shortcrust pastry (see page 42)
FOR THE FILLING
scant 1 cup milk
2 eggs
scant ⅓ cup superfine sugar
¼ teaspoon almond flavoring
slivered almonds, roasted
icing sugar, for dusting

1. Grease ten 3 inch fluted brioche pans and place on a cookie sheet.
2. Roll out the pastry thinly on a floured work surface and use to line the pans. Chill for 20 minutes.
3. Bake blind in the oven at 400° for 15 minutes.
4. To make the filling, whisk the milk, eggs, sugar and almond flavoring together. Pour into the pastry cases. Scatter roasted almonds on top.
5. Reduce the oven temperature to 350° and bake for a further 15–20 minutes until just set. Leave the tarts to cool before serving. Dust lightly with icing sugar.

Not suitable for freezing.

Above: VANILLA BAVARIAN RING (PAGE 180). Below: ALMOND CUSTARD TARTS.

CHARLOTTE RUSSE

SERVES 6

A classic French dessert, this charlotte Russe (Russian charlotte) is made with a filling of *crème bavarois*—a rich vanilla-flavored egg custard. Sometimes the custard is flavored with chocolate, almond-flavored liqueur or kirsch. Fresh raspberries can also be added when they are in season.

lemon jello, to make up to 2 cups
3 tablespoons lemon juice
2 candied cherries, quartered
piece of angelica, cut into triangles
1 cup milk
1 vanilla pod
3 teaspoons gelatin
3 egg yolks
3 tablespoons superfine sugar
about 18 lady fingers
1 cup whipping cream

1. Dissolve the jello in a measuring container, according to the packet instructions, using the lemon juice and enough boiling water to make 2 cups. Leave to cool for 20 minutes.
2. Spoon a thin covering of cool jello into the base of a 4 cup charlotte pan. Chill for about 20 minutes or until set.
3. When set, arrange the cherry quarters and angelica triangles on top. Carefully spoon over cool liquid jello to a depth of about 1 inch. Chill for about 30 minutes to set, together with the remaining jello.
4. Bring the milk slowly to the boil with the vanilla pod in a pan. Remove from the heat, cover and leave to infuse for at least 10 minutes.
5. Sprinkle the gelatin over 3 tablespoons water in a small bowl and leave to soak for 2–3 minutes. Place the bowl over a pan of simmering water and stir until dissolved. (Alternatively, microwave on HIGH for 30 seconds or until dissolved.) Leave to cool slightly.
6. Using a wooden spoon, beat the egg yolks and sugar together until well mixed, then stir in the strained milk. Return to the pan and cook gently, stirring all the time until the custard is thick enough to just coat the back of the spoon—do not boil. Pour into a large bowl, stir in the dissolved gelatin and leave to cool for 30 minutes.
7. Trim the lady fingers so that they just fit the pan; reserve the trimmings. Stand the fingers closely together, sugar side out, around the edge of the pan.
8. Lightly whip the cream and stir into the cool custard. Place the bowl in a roasting pan. Pour in enough iced water to come halfway up the sides. Stir occasionally for about 10 minutes until the custard is on the point of setting and has a thick pouring consistency. Pour gently into the lined mold without disturbing the lady fingers.
9. Trim the lady fingers level with the custard. Lay the trimmings together with the reserved trimmings on top

of the custard. Cover with plastic wrap and chill for at least 3 hours to set.
10. To turn out, using fingertips, ease the lady fingers away from the pan, then tilt it slightly to allow an airlock to form between the two. Dip the base of the pan in hot water for about 5 seconds only—to loosen the jello. Invert the pudding on to a damp plate, shake the pan gently, then ease it carefully off the finished charlotte.
11. Loosen the remaining set jello by dipping the container in hot water for a few seconds only. Turn out on to a board lined with damp wax paper. Moisten a large knife and chop the jello into small pieces. Spoon the jello around the charlotte Russe.

Not suitable for freezing.

BLANCMANGE

SERVES 4

A real old-fashioned pudding. Set in one large mold or in individual molds.

4 tablespoons cornstarch
2 cups milk
strip of lemon peel
3 tablespoons sugar or to taste

1. Blend the cornstarch to a smooth paste with 2 tablespoons of the milk.
2. Put the remaining milk in a saucepan with the lemon peel. Bring to the boil, then strain the milk on to the blended mixture, stirring well.
3. Return the mixture to the pan and bring to the boil, stirring all the time, until the mixture thickens. Cook for 3 minutes. Add sugar to taste.
4. Pour into a dampened 2 cup mold or individual molds and leave until cool. Chill for several hours until set. Turn out to serve.

VARIATIONS

Chocolate Omit the lemon peel and add 2 squares melted chocolate to the cooked mixture.

Coffee Omit the lemon peel and add 2 tablespoons coffee flavoring.

Orange Substitute the lemon peel with 1 teaspoon grated orange peel.

Not suitable for freezing.

MILK PUDDING

SERVES 4

There's nothing nicer than a lovingly made milk pudding—use full cream milk though, and do not omit the butter or spice. Opt for rice, tapioca or Farina, whichever you have. The method is easy for them all.

½ cup short-grain white or brown rice, flaked rice or tapioca, or scant ½ cup Farina
2–3 cups milk
2 tablespoons sugar
1 tablespoon butter
¼ teaspoon cinnamon, mixed spice or nutmeg

1. Grease a 4 cup heatproof dish.
2. If using white rice, flaked rice or tapioca, place in the prepare dish and pour in 2 cups of the milk. If using brown rice, add an extra 1 cup milk. Add the sugar and butter. Sprinkle the top with the spice.
3. If using Farina, heat the milk in a saucepan until lukewarm, then gradually sprinkle in the Farina, stirring continuously. Add the sugar and butter and continue to cook for 10 minutes until thickened, stirring frequently. Pour into the prepared dish. Sprinkle the top with the spice.
4. Bake the rice, flaked rice or tapioca pudding in the oven at 325° for 2–2½ hours (brown rice for an extra 30 minutes). Stir the pudding two or three times during the first hour, but leave for the remaining time to form a crust.
5. Bake the Farina pudding in the oven at 350° for 30 minutes, without stirring.
6. Serve milk puddings hot or cold, plain or topped with fresh fruit, chopped nuts or thick plain yogurt.

Not suitable for freezing.

RUM AND COFFEE JUNKET

SERVES 4

A sophisticated version of the nursery pudding. Do not use preserved, powdered or sterilized milk—it will not set.

2 cups plus 4 tablespoons milk
2 tablespoons superfine sugar
2 teaspoons rennet
2 teaspoons rum
½ cup sour cream
2 teaspoons coffee and chicory flavoring
semi sweet and white chocolate, to decorate

1. Put the 2 cups milk in a saucepan and heat until just warm to the finger.
2. Add the sugar, rennet and rum, then stir until the sugar has dissolved.

3. Immediately, pour the mixture into four individual dishes or a 3 cup shallow, edged serving dish. Put in a warm place, undisturbed, for 4 hours to set.
4. Lightly whisk the sour cream. Gradually add the 4 tablespoons milk and the coffee flavoring, whisking until smooth.
5. Carefully flood the top of the junket with the coffee cream, taking care not to disturb the junket. Decorate with coarsely grated chocolate. Chill for 1 hour.

Not suitable for freezing.

RISENGRØD

SERVES 4–6

This elegant Danish Christmas rice pudding contains sherry, cream and chopped almonds. A single whole almond is always put in the pudding for luck. The finder receives a present and, if single, will be the next to marry. It is traditionally served with Kirsebaersauce, a Danish hot cherry sauce.

FOR THE PUDDING
2 cups milk
⅓ cup white rice
scant ⅓ cup superfine sugar
4–5 drops of vanilla
½ cup chopped almonds
1 glass of sherry
1 cup heavy cream
1 whole almond
FOR THE KIRSEBAERSAUCE
generous ½ cup sugar
1½ cups cherries, pitted
1 tablespoon arrowroot
chopped almonds, roasted, to decorate

1. To make the pudding, put the milk and rice in a saucepan and simmer for about 20 minutes until the rice is soft and most of the milk is absorbed.
2. Add the sugar, vanilla, almonds and sherry, then stir well. Leave to cool completely.
3. Stir in the cream. Transfer to a serving dish and push the whole almond into the pudding so that it is hidden. Cover and chill for several hours.
4. Meanwhile to make the kirsebaersauce, put the sugar in a heavy-based saucepan. Add 1 cup water and heat very gently until the sugar has dissolved.
5. Increase the heat and boil rapidly for 1 minute. Add the cherries and cook for 10 minutes until tender. Mix the arrowroot with 2 tablespoons water and stir into the cherries. Simmer for 2 minutes until the sauce is clear.
6. To serve, decorate the Risengrød with almonds and accompany with the sauce.

Not suitable for freezing.

GAJAR HALVA

SERVES 4–6

This unusual Indian carrot pudding is very sweet and rich. Serve in very small portions after an Indian-style meal.

1 pound carrots, peeled
2½ cups milk
½ cup light cream
scant ½ cup sugar
1 tablespoon molasses
3 tablespoons melted butter
1¼ cups ground almonds
seeds of 6 green cardamom pods, crushed
¼ cup white raisins
chopped pistachios, to decorate

1. Roughly grate the carrots and put into a large, heavy-based saucepan. Pour in the milk and cream and bring to the boil, stirring constantly.
2. Simmer gently, stirring occasionally to prevent any sticking, for at least 2 hours until the milk has evaporated and the mixture is greatly reduced.
3. Stir in the sugar and molasses, then simmer for a further 30 minutes, stirring occasionally to prevent sticking.
4. Add the melted butter, ground almonds, crushed cardamom seeds and raisins. Cook, stirring, for another 5–10 minutes until the mixture begins to look oily on the surface.
5. Transfer to a serving dish and decorate with the pistachios. Serve hot or cold.

Not suitable for freezing.

BANANA CHARTREUSE

SERVES 4–6

The word *chartreuse* in French culinary terms can mean several different things. It is the name of a yellow or green liqueur made by the monks at the abbey of Chartreuse. *En chartreuse* is a term used to describe a game bird which is stewed with cabbage. Or, as here, it can be used to describe a dessert made with jello.

4¾ ounce packet lemon jello
3 bananas
juice of ½ lemon
about 6 shelled pistachios
1 tablespoon gelatin
4 tablespoons dark rum
½ cup heavy cream
½ cup icing sugar, sifted

1. Chill a 6 inch Charlotte mold.
2. Make up the jello according to the packet instructions, using only 1 cup boiling water. Leave to cool for 30 minutes.
3. Pour about one third of the jello into the prepared mold. Chill for 30 minutes until set.
4. Peel 1 banana, slice thinly, then sprinkle with a little lemon juice to prevent browning.
5. Arrange the banana slices on top of the set jello in an attractive pattern. Cut the pistachios in half lengthways and carefully place between or around the banana slices.
6. Slowly spoon over the remaining cool jello, taking care not to dislodge the pattern of bananas and pistachios. Chill for 30 minutes until set.
7. Sprinkle the gelatin over the rum and remaining lemon juice in a small bowl. Place the bowl over a saucepan of simmering water and stir until dissolved. (Alternatively, microwave on HIGH for 30 seconds or until dissolved.) Leave to cool for 5 minutes.
8. Whip the cream with the icing sugar. Peel and mash the remaining bananas, then combine with the cream and dissolved gelatin liquid. Spoon on top of the set jello. Chill for about 2 hours until set.
9. To serve, dip the base of the mold briefly in hot water, then invert the banana chartreuse on to a serving plate. Serve chilled.

Not suitable for freezing.

DAMASK CREAM

SERVES 4

This subtly flavored dish, also known as English Devonshire junket, is a far cry from a junket that comes from a packet. Do not serve it until you are ready to eat, as once it is cut the shape will disintegrate. Rose petals make a pretty decoration.

2 cups light cream
3 tablespoons superfine sugar
2 teaspoons rennet
large pinch of nutmeg
1 tablespoon brandy
4 tablespoons heavy cream
1 teaspoon rose water
rose petals, to decorate (optional)

1. Put the cream and 2 tablespoons of the sugar in a saucepan. Heat gently until just warm, stirring until the sugar dissolves. (When the mixture is warm it will register 98.4° on a sugar thermometer, or not feel hot or cold if you put your finger in it.)
2. Stir in the rennet, nutmeg and brandy, then pour into a serving dish. Leave for 2–3 hours until set. It is important not to disturb the junket during this time or it will not set.
3. When the junket is set, mix the remaining sugar, the cream and rose water together and spoon carefully over the top. Decorate with rose petals, if liked.

Not suitable for freezing.

TEA CREAM

SERVES 4

Earl Grey tea, a blended black tea flavored with bergamot oil, gives this unusual tea cream a subtle, perfumed flavor. It isn't essential to use Earl Grey, however, you can use any of your favorite Ceylon or China teas, although aromatic teas are more flavorsome in cooking. Why not try jasmine tea, lapsang souchong or orange pekoe?

1 cup milk
1 tablespoon Earl Grey tea leaves
2 eggs, separated
2 tablespoons sugar
1 tablespoon gelatin
½ cup heavy cream

1. Put the milk into a saucepan, add the tea and bring to to the boil. Remove from the heat and leave to infuse for 10–15 minutes or until the milk is well colored with the tea.

2. Beat the egg yolks and sugar together, then strain on the milk and mix well. Return to the pan and cook gently for 10 minutes, stirring all the time, until the custard thickens slightly and just coats the back of the spoon.

3. Sprinkle the gelatin over 3 tablespoons water in a small bowl and leave to soak for 2–3 minutes. Place the bowl over a pan of simmering water and stir until dissolved. (Alternatively, microwave on HIGH for 30 seconds or until dissolved.)

4. Mix the dissolved gelatin into the tea mixture. Leave for about 2 hours until beginning to set. Stir the mixture occasionally.

5. Whip the cream until thick but not stiff, then fold into the custard. Finally, whisk the egg whites until stiff, then fold into the mixture.

6. Pour the cream mixture into a dampened 2 cup mold. Chill for about 2–3 hours until set. Turn out on to a chilled dish and decorate with grapes and crisp cookies, if liked.

Not suitable for freezing.

Below left: DAMASK CREAM. *Below right:* TEA CREAM.

COFFEE BAVARIAN CREAM

SERVES 6

1 cup roasted coffee beans
3 cups milk
4 egg yolks
scant ½ cup superfine sugar
4 teaspoons gelatin
1 cup heavy cream
2 tablespoons coffee-flavored liqueur

FOR THE DECORATION

coffee dragees
coarsely grated chocolate

1. Lightly grease a 5 cup moule-à-manqué cake pan or soufflé dish.

2. Put the coffee beans in a saucepan and place over low heat for 2–3 minutes, shaking the pan frequently. Remove from the heat, pour all the milk into the pan, then return to the heat and bring to the boil. Remove from the heat, cover and leave to infuse for at least 30 minutes.

3. Beat the egg yolks and sugar together in a bowl until thick and light in color. The beaters should leave a trail on the surface of the mixture when lifted.

4. Strain on the milk and stir well. Pour into the rinsed out pan and stir over low heat for 10 minutes. Do not boil. Strain into a large bowl and leave to cool for 20 minutes.

5. Sprinkle the gelatin over 4 tablespoons water in a small bowl and leave to soak for 2–3 minutes. Place the bowl over a pan of simmering water and stir until dissolved. (Alternatively, microwave on HIGH for 30 seconds or until dissolved.)

6. Stir the dissolved gelatin into the custard. Stand this in a roasting pan of cold water and ice cubes. Stir until the mixture is cool and about to set.

7. Lightly whip ½ cup of the cream to the thick pouring stage, then fold into the custard. Pour into the prepared pan. Chill for at least 3 hours or overnight until completely set.

8. With dampened fingers, gently ease the edges of the cream away from the pan. Turn the cream out on to a flat plate, shaking the pan or dish gently until the cream moves and loosens inside the pan. Carefully ease off the pan and slide the cream into the center of the plate.

9. Whip the remaining cream until stiff, then gradually whisk in the liqueur. Spoon into a pastry tube fitted with a ½ inch star tip and pipe rosettes around the top edge of the cream. Decorate with coffee dragees and grated chocolate. Serve chilled.

Not suitable for freezing.

ZABAGLIONE

SERVES 6

A classic, rich Italian dessert to serve after a light main course. It should be served as soon as it is made so that it remains light, fluffy and slightly warm. Serve with sponge fingers, see the recipe below.

4 egg yolks
⅓ cup superfine sugar
½ cup Marsala

1. Beat the egg yolks and sugar together in a large bowl. Add the Marsala and beat until mixed.

2. Place the bowl over a saucepan of simmering water and heat gently, whisking the mixture until it is very thick and creamy.

3. To serve, pour the zabaglione into six glasses and serve immediately, with sponge fingers.

Not suitable for freezing.

SPONGE FINGERS

MAKES ABOUT 32

scant ½ cup superfine sugar
3 eggs, separated
1 teaspoon vanilla or almond flavoring
¾ cup All Purpose flour
2 tablespoons cornstarch
pinch of salt
icing sugar, for dredging

1. Grease two large cookie sheets.

2. Using an electric mixer, beat half of the sugar and the egg yolks in a bowl until very pale and creamy.

3. Whisk the egg whites until stiff, then gradually add the remaining sugar, whisking between each addition. Fold into the egg yolk mixture, using a large metal spoon. Fold in the vanilla.

4. Sift the flours and salt together, then sift into the mixture. Fold in lightly, using the spoon.

5. Spoon the batter into a pastry tube fitted with a ½ inch plain tip. Pipe 4 inch fingers on to the prepared cookie sheets. Dredge the fingers with icing sugar.

6. Bake in the oven at 300° for about 20 minutes or until crusty on the surface. Transfer to wire racks and cool. Store in an airtight container.

To freeze: wrap and freeze the cooled fingers. Defrost, wrapped, at room temperature.

Opposite: ZABAGLIONE *SERVED WITH* SPONGE FINGERS.

OLD ENGLISH SYLLABUB

SERVES 4

Bring out the full fragrance of the spices by grinding them just before use. Decorate the syllabub with fresh edible flower petals such as nasturtium, geranium and rose, or with borage flowers.

1 clove
1 allspice
1 inch cinnamon stick
little nutmeg
scant ⅓ cup superfine sugar
finely grated peel and juice of 1 lemon
6 tablespoons pale cream sherry
1 cup heavy cream
24 ratafia biscuits

1. Very finely grind the clove, allspice and cinnamon stick with a pestle and mortar, then sift through a fine strainer.
2. Put the ground spices, nutmeg, sugar, lemon peel, lemon juice and sherry into a bowl. Stir well until the sugar dissolves, then cover and leave to stand for 1 hour.
3. Strain the sherry mixture through a fine nylon strainer into a clean bowl. Pour in the cream in a continuous stream, whisking all the time. Whip the heavy cream until it is just thick enough to hold a trail when the whisk is lifted.
4. Place four ratafias in each of four serving glasses, then fill each glass with the spicy syllabub. Chill for about 1 hour. Decorate with the remaining ratafias and a few fresh flower petals.

Not suitable for freezing.

LIME SYLLABUB

SERVES 4–6

Serve this well flavored syllabub with Langues de chat (see page 164). Lemon may be used instead of lime, but if so, use only one.

thinly pared peel and juice of 3 limes
½ cup white wine
2 tablespoons brandy
scant ½ cup superfine sugar
1 cup heavy cream
lime twists, to decorate

1. Put the lime peel and juice, white wine, brandy and sugar into a bowl. Stir well until the sugar has dissolved. Cover and leave to stand for about 2 hours.
2. Remove the peel from the wine mixture with a slotted spoon and discard. Pour the cream into the wine in a continuous stream, stirring with a whisk. Whip the

cream until thick and it holds a trail when the whisk is lifted.
3. Pour the syllabub into serving glasses and chill. Decorate with lime twists.

Not suitable for freezing.

ALMOND BAVAROIS AND PLUM SAUCE

SERVES 6

Add almond flavoring with care, as it can be overpowering.

3 cups milk
6 egg yolks
5 tablespoons superfine sugar
4 teaspoons gelatin
½ cup heavy or whipping cream, lightly whipped
½–1 teaspoon almond flavoring
1 pound ripe red plums
roasted slivered almonds, to decorate

1. Grease a 5 cup ring mold.
2. Place the milk in a pan and bring almost to the boil. Whisk the egg yolks and half the sugar together in a bowl until blended.
3. Add the milk, then return to the pan. Cook gently, stirring all the time, until the custard thickens slightly. Do not boil or the custard will curdle. Strain into a bowl and leave until cold.
4. Sprinkle the gelatin over 4 tablespoons water in a small bowl and leave to soak for 2–3 minutes. Place the bowl over a pan of simmering water and stir until dissolved. (Alternatively, microwave on HIGH for 30 seconds or until dissolved.)
5. Stir the dissolved gelatin into the cold custard. Lightly whip the cream and add to the custard with the almond flavoring. Pour into the prepared mold and chill until set.
6. Meanwhile, slice the plums, discarding the pits. Place in a medium saucepan with ½ cup water and the remaining sugar. Cover and simmer until mushy. Purée in a blender or food processor until smooth. Leave to cool and chill.
7. Turn out the bavarois, decorate with slivered almonds and serve with the plum sauce.

To freeze: pack and freeze the sauce only. Defrost overnight at cool room temperature.

Opposite: OLD ENGLISH SYLLABUB.

STRAWBERRY BAVAROIS

SERVES 6–8

It is essential to use really well flavored strawberries for this bavarois—frozen strawberries may be used, but only as a last resort. This elegant dessert is perfect for summer entertaining.

1½ cups strawberries, hulled
1½ tablespoons gelatin
6 egg yolks
scant ⅓ cup superfine sugar
1 cup milk
1 cup heavy cream

FOR THE STRAWBERRY SAUCE
1 cup strawberries, hulled
scant ⅓ cup superfine sugar
1 tablespoon raspberry-flavored liqueur (optional)

FOR THE DECORATION
½ cup heavy cream, whipped
strawberries

1. Press the strawberries through a very fine nylon strainer to make a purée, over 1 cup.
2. Sprinkle the gelatin over 4 tablespoons water in a small bowl and leave to soak for 2–3 minutes. Place the bowl over a pan of simmering water and stir until dissolved. (Alternatively, microwave on HIGH for 30 seconds or until dissolved.)
3. Lightly whisk the egg yolks and sugar together in a bowl. Bring the milk almost to the boil, then whisk it into the egg yolks. Place the bowl over a pan of simmering water and cook the custard, stirring, until it thickens enough to coat the back of the spoon. (Alternatively, microwave on HIGH for 2½–3 minutes, stirring every 30 seconds with a wire whisk.)
4. Strain the custard through a nylon strainer into a clean bowl and add the dissolved gelatin, stirring. Set the custard aside until cold, but not set, stirring to prevent a skin forming.
5. Whip the cream until it just holds soft peaks. Stir the strawberry purée into the custard, then gently fold in the whipped cream. Pour the mixture into a 5 cup mold. Chill until set.
6. Meanwhile to make the sauce, slice the strawberries and put them into a bowl. Sprinkle with the sugar and liqueur, if using. Cover and leave to stand for about 1 hour. Press through a nylon strainer to form a purée. Pour into a serving container and chill.
7. To unmold the bavarois, quickly dip the mold, right up to the rim, into hot water. Place a serving plate on top, then invert the mold and the plate together, giving the mold a sharp shake to free the bavarois. Decorate with whipped cream and whole, halved or sliced strawberries. Serve the bavarois with the chilled strawberry sauce.

To freeze: pack and freeze the sauce only. Defrost overnight at cool room temperature.

COEURS À LA CRÈME

SERVES 4–6

Light, delicate and refreshing, this may be eaten with cream, or with soft summer fruit, ideally, tiny wild strawberries. This dessert takes its name from the small heart-shaped white porcelain colanders in which it is made.

1 cup curd or ricotta cheese
1 cup crème fraîche
few drops of vanilla
2 tablespoons superfine sugar
2 egg whites

1. Line four small heart-shaped molds with cheesecloth.
2. Press the cheese through a nylon strainer into a bowl. Lightly whip the cream, vanilla and sugar together. Mix into the cheese.
3. Whisk the egg whites until stiff, then fold into the cheese mixture.
4. Turn the mixture into the prepared molds. Leave to drain overnight in the refrigerator. Turn out and serve with strawberries and light cream.

Not suitable for freezing.

CREAM CROWDIE

SERVES 4

In Scotland, crowdie can mean a cream cheese or a kind of oatmeal. This recipe for cream crowdie is so called because it contains oatmeal, which the Scots use for making their famous porridge.

⅔ cup medium oatmeal
1 cup cream
4 tablespoons clear honey
3 tablespoons whisky
1½ cups raspberries, hulled

1. Place the oatmeal in a broiling pan (without the rack) and toast until golden brown, stirring occasionally with a spoon. Leave for 15 minutes until cool.
2. Whip the cream until just standing in soft peaks. Stir in the honey, whisky and cooled toasted oatmeal.
3. Reserve a few raspberries for decoration, then layer up the remaining raspberries and cream mixture in four tall glasses. Cover with plastic wrap and chill for at least 1 hour.
4. Allow to come to room temperature for 30 minutes before serving. Decorate each glass with the reserved raspberries.

Not suitable for freezing.

Opposite: COEURS À LA CRÈME.

Vanilla Bavarian Ring

SERVES 6

This vanilla flavored bavarois is set in a pretty ring mold and served undecorated. However, it can be decorated with cherries or grapes dipped in caramel; piped chocolate scrolls; fresh fruits, or edible flower petals.

1 tablespoon gelatin
6 egg yolks
scant ⅓ cup superfine sugar
1 cup light cream
1 teaspoon vanilla
1 cup heavy cream

1. Sprinkle the gelatin over 3 tablespoons water in a small bowl and leave to soak for 2–3 minutes. Place the bowl over a pan of simmering water and stir until dissolved. (Alternatively, microwave on HIGH for 30 seconds or until dissolved.)

2. Lightly whisk the egg yolks and sugar together in a bowl. Bring the light cream and the vanilla almost to the boil, then whisk into the egg yolks. Place the bowl over a pan of simmering water and cook the custard, stirring, until it thickens enough to coat the back of the spoon. (Alternatively, microwave on HIGH for 2–2½ minutes, stirring every 30 seconds with a wire whisk.)

3. Strain the custard through a nylon strainer into a clean bowl and add the dissolved gelatin, stirring. Leave the custard to cool, stirring frequently to prevent a skin forming.

4. Whip the cream until it just holds soft peaks, then fold into the custard. Pour into a 4 cup ring mold. Chill until set.

5. To unmold the bavarois, dip the mold briefly, right up to the rim, into hot water. Place a serving plate on top, then invert the mold.

Not suitable for freezing.

Illustrated on page 168

Lemon Balm Syllabub

SERVES 6–8

Use freshly picked lemon balm for the best flavor.

2 tablespoons finely chopped lemon balm leaves
2 cups heavy cream
½ cup sweet white wine
grated peel and juice of 2 lemons
1 teaspoon sugar or to taste
sprigs of lemon balm, to decorate

1. Using an electric mixer, whisk together all the ingredients until the consistency of custard is obtained.

2. Chill for 2–3 hours. To serve, spoon the syllabub into tall glasses and decorate with sprigs of lemon balm.

Not suitable for freezing.

Home-Made Yogurt

Home-made yogurt makes a delicious dessert served on its own or as an accompaniment to fruit and fruit pies. It is not necessary to invest in a commercial yogurt machine; a wide-necked insulated container and a thermometer are the only essential equipment. Use either skim or semi-skim milk, skim milk powder, raw, pasteurized milk or sterilized. Condensed and evaporated milks do not always give such good results. You can buy special yogurt starter cultures, but it is simpler at first to use bought plain yogurt. For your next batch, keep back a little from the first yogurt you made. You can do this about three times, then buy a new starter tub of plain yogurt. To obtain a thick, creamy yogurt, add skim milk powder (see recipe). Flavor the finished yogurt with fruit, fruit purée or serve Greek-style with honey and a few chopped nuts.

PLAIN YOGURT

MAKES ABOUT 2 CUPS

2 cups milk
1½ tablespoons plain yogurt
2 tablespoons skim milk powder (optional see above)

1. Use absolutely clean, well rinsed containers and utensils. Warm an insulated container. Pour the milk into a saucepan and bring to the boil. (If you want a thick yogurt, keep the pan on a very low heat after this for 15 minutes.) Remove from the heat and allow to cool to 113°. If you are using sterilized milk, bring them up to 113°.

2. Spoon the plain yogurt into a bowl and stir in a little of the cooled milk. Add the skim milk powder, if using, to make a smooth paste. Stir in the remaining milk.

3. Pour into the warmed insulated container. Cover and leave for 8–9 hours, undisturbed.

4. Transfer the yogurt into small pots or cartons and place in the refrigerator immediately. It will keep for up to 10 days.

Not suitable for freezing.

LEMON CURD CREAMS

SERVES 6

It really is worth making the effort to prepare your own fresh tasting lemon curd but if time is at a premium a good quality bought variety will do!

FOR THE LEMON CURD
finely grated peel and juice of 2 lemons
2 eggs, whisked
½ stick butter, cut into pieces
generous ½ cup superfine sugar

FOR THE CUSTARD
3 eggs, whisked
3 tablespoons superfine sugar
1 cup light cream
½ cup milk
½ cup heavy cream, lightly whipped, to decorate

1. To make the lemon curd, place the lemon peel, 6 tablespoons strained lemon juice, eggs, butter and sugar into a medium heatproof bowl. Place the bowl over a saucepan of simmering water and cook gently, whisking occasionally, until the curd thickens slightly—it should just coat the back of a spoon.

2. Strain the curd into a cold bowl, push a piece of damp wax paper on to the surface of the curd and leave to cool.

3. Spoon about 2 tablespoons lemon curd into the base of six ½ cup custard pots.

4. To make the custard, whisk the eggs, sugar, cream and milk together. Strain, then gently pour into the pots being careful not to disturb the lemon curd.

5. Stand the pots in a roasting pan and pour in hot water to come halfway up the sides. Cover the top of the roasting pan with foil.

6. Bake in the oven at 350° for about 45 minutes or until the custards are just set. Do not overcook or the mixture will curdle and separate.

7. Take the pots out of the roasting pan and cool. When cold, cover and chill well before serving decorated with lightly whipped cream.

Not suitable for freezing.

BAKED SAFFRON YOGURT

SERVES 8

These individual, golden-tinted yogurts make an attractive finale to an Indian meal. They are also excellent for children's desserts, served with fruit.

1 cup milk
pinch of saffron threads
6 green cardamom pods
2 eggs
2 egg yolks
13½ ounce can condensed milk
1 cup plain yogurt
1 large ripe mango, to decorate

1. Bring the milk, saffron and cardamoms to the boil in a pan. Remove from the heat, cover and infuse for 10–15 minutes.

2. Beat the eggs, egg yolks, condensed milk and yogurt together in a bowl.

3. Strain in the milk, stirring gently to mix. Divide between eight custard pots in a roasting pan. Add hot water to come halfway up the sides.

4. Bake in the oven at 350° until firm to the touch.

5. Cool the baked yogurt desserts completely. Chill for at least 2 hours before serving.

6. To serve, carefully run a knife around the edge of each yogurt, then turn out on to individual dishes.

7. Peel the skin off the mango sections. Slice thinly on either side of the central pit. Serve with the yogurts.

Not suitable for freezing.

GERANIUM CREAM WITH RED SUMMER FRUITS

SERVES 8

This rich cream, which is a mixture of heavy cream and full fat soft cream cheese, is delicately scented with geranium leaves. The red summer fruits served with it—a combination of raspberries, strawberries (wild if possible) and redcurrants—look beautiful, with their jewel-like colors surrounding the white cream.

½ cup heavy cream
4 sweet geranium leaves, bruised
2 cups full fat soft cream cheese
scant ½ cup superfine sugar or to taste
1½ pounds red summer fruits, such as raspberries, wild strawberries, small strawberries and redcurrants, chilled
sugar, for sprinkling
sweet geranium leaves, to decorate

1. Gently heat the cream and geranium leaves in the top of a double boiler, or in a bowl placed over a saucepan of hot water, for 10–15 minutes, until it reaches simmering point. Do not allow it to boil. Remove from the heat, cover and leave to cool.

2. Strain the cream, then gradually stir it into the cheese, stirring until smooth. Rinse the geranium leaves, dry them and stir into the cream mixture. Cover and leave in a cool place for 12 hours.

3. Remove the geranium leaves and stir in sugar to taste. Spoon the cream into a mound on a cold serving plate. Spoon the fruits around. Serve sugar for sprinkling over the fruits separately. Decorate with geranium leaves.

Not suitable for freezing.

2. Place the gooseberries in a small saucepan with 4 tablespoons water. Cover and simmer for about 10 minutes until the fruit softens to a pulpy consistency. (Alternatively, microwave, covered, on HIGH for 6 minutes until soft.)

3. Purée the gooseberries in a blender or food processor, then strain to remove the pips. Stir in two-thirds of the sugar.

4. Sprinkle the gelatin over 2 tablespoons water in a small bowl and leave to soak for 2–3 minutes. Place the bowl over a pan of simmering water and stir until dissolved. (Alternatively, microwave on HIGH for 30 seconds or until dissolved.)

5. Meanwhile, make the custard. Beat the egg yolks and remaining sugar together in a bowl until light in color. In a small saucepan, warm the milk, and pour over the eggs and sugar, stirring until blended.

6. Return to the pan and cook over a low heat, stirring all the time, until the custard thickens sufficiently to lightly coat the back of the spoon—do not boil.

7. Remove from the heat and add the dissolved gelatin. Pour the custard out into a large bowl and mix in the gooseberry purée. Leave to cool for 45 minutes.

8. Lightly whip the cream. When the gooseberry mixture is cold, but not set, stir in half the cream until evenly blended. Pour the gooseberry mixture into the prepared plate. Chill for 1–2 hours to set. When firm, turn out on to a flat serving plate.

9. Spread a thin covering of the remaining cream around the edge of the charlotte.

10. Spoon the rest of the cream into a pastry tube fitted with a ½ inch large star tip. Pipe the cream around the top edge of the charlotte. Decorate with angelica. Just before serving, arrange the Langue de chat carefully around the outside.

To freeze: wrap and freeze at the end of step 8. Defrost overnight in the refrigerator, then finish as above.

GOOSEBERRY CHARLOTTE

SERVES 6

There are many varieties of gooseberry, round or long, hairy or smooth, tart or sweet. Their pale green color and unique flavor make them unbeatable for fruit charlottes and fools.

1 pound gooseberries, trimmed
scant ½ cup superfine sugar
2 teaspoons gelatin
2 egg yolks
1 cup milk
1 cup heavy cream
angelica, to decorate
20 Langue de chat (see page 164), trimmed to size

1. Grease a 6 inch soufflé non-metal straight sided dish and line the base with wax paper.

Above: GOOSEBERRY CHARLOTTE. *Below:* GERANIUM CREAM WITH RED SUMMER FRUITS.

BREAD AND BUTTER PUDDING

SERVES 4

This recipe has been made for centuries in England and has always been popular, partly because it is such a good way to use up day-old bread. It can be made with white or brown bread.

6 thin slices bread, crusts removed
½ stick butter or margarine
⅓ cup raisins
3 tablespoons superfine sugar
2 eggs
2 cups milk

1. Grease a 4 cup heatproof dish.

2. Thickly spread the bread slices with the butter. Cut into fingers or small squares. Put half into the prepared dish. Sprinkle with all the fruit and half the sugar.

3. Top with the remaining bread, buttered side uppermost. Sprinkle with the rest of the sugar.

4. Beat the eggs and milk well together. Strain into the dish over the bread. Leave to stand for 30 minutes, so that the bread absorbs some of the liquid.

5. Bake in the oven at 325° for 45 minutes–1 hour until set and the top is crisp and golden.

VARIATION

Osborne Pudding Spread the bread with orange marmalade and flavor the milk with the finely grated peel of 1 orange and 1 tablespoon brandy or rum.

Not suitable for freezing.

Below: BREAD AND BUTTER PUDDING.

ENGLISH TRIFLE

SERVES 6–8

A perfect trifle should be a rich confection of fruit, light sponge, alcohol, real egg custard and whipped cream. The recipe has altered little over the centuries—at one time the custard was topped with syllabub, and fruit has not always been included.

sponge cake, to fit (see recipe)
4 tablespoons cherry jelly
15 ratafia biscuits
4 tablespoons sherry
2 bananas
grated peel and juice of ½ lemon
1½ cups cherries, pitted
1½ cups milk
3 eggs
scant ⅓ cup superfine sugar
½ cup heavy cream

FOR THE DECORATION
candied cherries
¼ cup chopped nuts, roasted

1. Cut the cake sponges in half horizontally and spread with jelly, then sandwich together. Arrange in the base of a glass serving dish.

2. Cover with ratafias and sprinkle with sherry. Peel slice and coat the bananas in lemon juice. Arrange the bananas and cherries on top of the ratafias.

3. Heat the milk in a medium saucepan until almost boiling. (Alternatively, microwave on HIGH for 5 minutes.) Whisk the eggs, lemon peel and sugar together in a bowl until pale. Pour on the hot milk, stirring continuously.

4. Return to the pan and heat gently, stirring continuously, until the custard thickens enough to coat the back of a wooden spoon—about 20 minutes. Do not allow to boil. (Alternatively, microwave the custard on MEDIUM for 7–8 minutes, whisking frequently.) Set aside to cool.

5. Pour the custard over the trifle and leave until cold.

6. Whip the cream until stiff and pipe on the top of the trifle. Decorate with candied cherries and nuts.

Not suitable for freezing.

Above: ENGLISH TRIFLE.

PERFECT SOUFFLÉS AND MERINGUES

Sensational soufflés that rise perfectly to the occasion; crisp, light meringues that melt in the mouth. These are not a far away dream. Follow the recipes in this chapter and you'll find that you can whip up a masterpiece every time.

Awe inspiring soufflés, crisp light meringues and marshmallow soft pavlovas are wonderful creations, guaranteed to bring sighs of delight from dinner guests.

Hot Soufflés

A hot soufflé is the true soufflé. The tiny bubbles of air, trapped within the egg whites, expand as they are heated, puffing up the base mixture, to which they were added, by as much as two thirds of its original size. When making hot soufflés, it is important to follow the recipe precisely; do not try to cut corners.

- All the equipment must be spotlessly clean and dry. This is especially important when whisking the egg whites, as the volume will be poor if there's a trace of grease in the bowl or on the whisk.
- Either a hand whisk or an electric mixer can be used but be careful not to overbeat the whites with an electric mixer. (Egg whites whisked by hand in a copper bowl produce a greater volume, and have a much stronger make up, but as the majority of home cooks do not own a copper bowl this is not practical.)
- The mixture should stand in soft peaks, and the tips of the peaks should flop over gently when held upon the whisk. Overbeaten egg whites look dry and powdery and will be difficult to fold in evenly.
- The basic sauce mixture must still be warm when the whisked whites are folded in. If necessary, the sauce can be prepared in advance and gently reheated before adding the egg whites. Much of the volume of the whites will be lost if they are folded into a cold, stiff mixture.
- Quickly fold in one large spoonful of the egg whites first to loosen the basic sauce. Always add the egg whites with a large metal spoon, using a light cutting and folding action.
- Make sure that the dish is well greased—this helps it rise. Before baking, a hot soufflé dish should be two-thirds to three-quarters full.
- Make sure that the temperature in the oven remains constant and that there are no draughts while the soufflé is baking—which means no peeking! A hot soufflé is cooked when it is risen and golden, and just firm to the touch. Test it in the oven, in case it needs more time. The creamy middle should be a little gooey—if it is dry it tastes like overcooked scrambled egg.
- Finally, a hot soufflé should be served immediately, always keep your guests waiting for the soufflé rather than the soufflé waiting for them.

Cold Soufflés

Cold soufflés are very light mixtures set high above a soufflé dish, as imitations of hot soufflés. They are not true soufflés but mousses set with gelatin. The preparation of the dish is all important. Do not tie the paper collar so tightly as to flute the paper and so spoil the final appearance of the soufflé. It should stand upright and be even all round. To remove the paper from the cold soufflé once the mixture has set, rinse a round bladed knife in hot water and slip it, upright between the paper and the soufflé, peeling away the paper and the knife.

The rules regarding whisking egg whites for hot soufflés apply to cold soufflés too. Similarly, cream should be whipped until it just holds its shape. If it is overbeaten it will be impossible to achieve a smooth mixture. Make sure it is well chilled.

Gelatin

Gelatin sets cold soufflés. It is not difficult to use, providing a few simple rules are followed. Before adding it to a mixture it must be softened, by soaking in cold water, this will make it swell. (Sprinkle the gelatin over the water, never the other way round or you will get lumpy gelatin.) Once soaked it can be added to a hot mixture and stirred until dissolved.

Before gelatin can be added to a cold mixture, it must be dissolved. Do this by standing the bowl over a saucepan of simmering water. Heat gently until it dissolves (just like melting chocolate). Alternatively, dissolve in a microwave. Properly dissolved gelatin will be transparent. To test this, dip a teaspoon in, turn it over and any undissolved granules will show on the back of the spoon. Never allow gelatin to boil.

Always add dissolved gelatin to a mixture which is lukewarm or at room temperature. If added to a cold mixture, it will set on contact, in fine threads. The soufflé will not set properly or will set too quickly before you have a chance to fold in the egg whites or cream.

Allow at least 4 hours for it to set, longe if it contains fruit. For a firm set, allow 12 hours.

Meringues

The light, crisp texture of meringues is the perfect foil to creamy fillings and slices of soft fruit. Meringues are made with whisked egg whites to which sugar is incorporated. They are a perfect way to use up leftover egg whites because meringues will keep in an airtight container for as long as six weeks.

The egg whites must be whisked until they are very stiff and will hold an unwavering peak on the end of the whisk. The sugar can be added in two halves or can be whisked in a little at a time. This type of meringue is known as meringue Suisse. Meringue cuite is made by putting the unwhisked whites and sugar in a bowl, then whisking them over gently simmering water until stiff and thick. As soon as the mixture becomes thick, the bowl should be removed from the heat. This meringue has a smooth texture and wonderful gloss. It also holds its shape well. Italian meringue is made by whisking a hot sugar syrup into egg whites. It is rarely used in home cooking.

HOT VANILLA SOUFFLÉ

SERVES 4

Once used, rinse off the vanilla pod. Leave to dry on kitchen paper, then wrap and refrigerate for use once more. The flavor will not be quite as strong the second time around.

½ *stick butter or margarine, plus extra for greasing*
1 vanilla pod or 1 teaspoon vanilla
1 cup milk
3 tablespoons All Purpose flour
scant ⅓ cup superfine sugar
5 eggs, separated
icing sugar, for dusting

1. Tie a double strip of wax paper around a 5 cup soufflé dish to make a 3 inch collar. Brush the inside of the dish and the paper with melted butter.
2. Split the vanilla pod to reveal the seeds. Place in a saucepan with the milk and bring to the boil. Remove from the heat, cover and leave to infuse for about 20 minutes.
3. Strain the milk. Melt the butter in a large heavy-based saucepan. Add the flour and cook for 1 minute, then blend in the milk. Bring to the boil, stirring all the time, and cook for about 1 minute.
4. Cool slightly, then beat in the sugar, egg yolks and vanilla, if using.
5. Whisk the egg whites until stiff but not dry. Beat one spoonful into the sauce mixture to lighten it, then carefully fold in the remaining egg whites.
6. Gently pour the soufflé mixture into the prepared dish. Level the top with a spatula and make a few cuts through the outer edges of the mixture—this helps it to rise evenly. Stand the dish on a cookie sheet.
7. Bake in the oven at 375° for about 35—40 minutes or until well risen, just set and well browned. Remove the paper and dust lightly with icing sugar. Serve straight away with light cream.

Not suitable for freezing.

ORANGE LIQUEUR SOUFFLÉ

SERVES 4

This soufflé is not quite as light as the plain vanilla one as the liqueur weighs it down. However, it is still wonderful to devour!

½ *stick butter or margarine, plus extra for greasing*
4 tablespoons orange marmalade
3 tablespoons All Purpose flour
1 cup milk
2 tablespoons sugar
5 eggs, separated
5 tablespoons orange-flavored liqueur
icing sugar, to decorate

1. Tie a double strip of wax paper around a 5 cup soufflé dish to make a 3 inch collar. Brush the inside of the dish and the paper with melted butter.
2. Finely chop the marmalade, especially any larger pieces of peel.
3. Melt the butter in a large heavy-based saucepan. Add the flour and cook for 1 minute then blend in the milk. Bring to the boil, stirring all the time, and cook for about 1 minute.
4. Cool slightly, then beat in the marmalade, sugar and egg yolks. Carefully stir in the liqueur until evenly mixed.
5. Whisk the egg whites until stiff but not dry. Beat one spoonful into the sauce mixture to lighten it, then carefully fold in the remaining egg white.
6. Gently pour the soufflé mixture into the prepared dish. Level the top with a spatula and make a few cuts through the outer edges of the mixture—this helps it to rise evenly. Stand the dish on a cookie sheet.
7. Bake in the oven at 375° for about 35—40 minutes or until well risen, just set and well browned. Remove the paper and dust lightly with icing sugar. Serve straight away with light cream.

Not suitable for freezing.

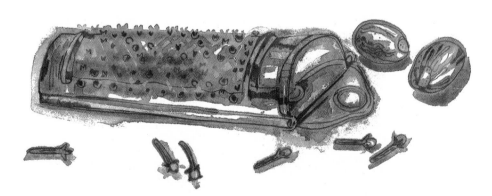

Previous page: PAVLOVA (PAGE 202).

INDIVIDUAL CHOCOLATE MINT SOUFFLÉS

SERVES 4–6

For added luxury, pour in a little light cream to serve.

$\frac{1}{4}$ stick butter or margarine, plus extra for greasing
$\frac{1}{2}$ cup milk
12 wafer thin chocolate mints
scant 2 tablespoons All Purpose flour
2 tablespoons superfine sugar
3 eggs, separated

1. Lightly grease six $\frac{1}{2}$ cup custard pots.
2. Heat the milk and mints in a pan until evenly blended.
3. Melt the butter in a large heavy-based saucepan. Add the flour and cook for 1 minute, then blend in the milk. Bring to the boil, stirring all the time, and cook for 1 minute.
4. Cool slightly, then beat in the sugar and egg yolks.
5. Whisk the egg whites until stiff but not dry. Beat one spoonful into the sauce to lighten it, then carefully fold in the remaining egg white. Spoon into the prepared pots. Stand the dishes on a cookie sheet.
6. Bake in the oven at 375° for 15–20 minutes or until lightly set. Serve straight away.

Not suitable for freezing.

CHOCOLATE CINNAMON SOUFFLÉ

SERVES 4

This soufflé is especially good served with a few sliced strawberries or orange segments.

$\frac{1}{2}$ stick butter or margarine, plus extra for greasing
3 squares semi sweet chocolate
1 cup plus 1 tablespoon milk
3 tablespoons All Purpose flour
$\frac{1}{2}$ teaspoon cinnamon
5 eggs, separated
2 tablespoons superfine sugar
icing sugar, for dusting

1. Tie a double strip of wax paper around a 5 cup soufflé dish to make a 3 inch collar. Brush the inside of the dish and the paper with melted butter.
2. Break the chocolate into small pieces. Place in a heatproof bowl with the 1 tablespoon milk. Stand the bowl over a pan of simmering water and heat gently until the chocolate melts. (Alternatively, microwave on LOW for 3–4 minutes until melted, stirring occasionally.) Remove from the heat.
3. Melt the butter in a large heavy-based saucepan. Add the flour and cook for 1 minute, then blend in the remaining milk and the cinnamon. Bring to the boil, stirring all the time, and cook for about 1 minute.
4. Cool slightly, then beat in the egg yolks, sugar and chocolate.
5. Whisk the egg whites until stiff but not dry. Beat one spoonful into the sauce mixture to lighten it, then carefully fold in the remaining egg whites.
6. Gently pour the soufflé mixture into the prepared dish. Level the top with a spatula and make a few cuts through the outer edges of the mixture—this helps it to rise evenly. Stand the dish on a cookie sheet.
7. Bake in the oven at 375° for about 35–40 minutes or until well risen, just set and well browned. Remove the paper and dust lightly with icing sugar. Serve straight away.

Not suitable for freezing.

MINI LEMON AND RASPBERRY SOUFFLÉS

SERVES 4–6

Small soufflés have the benefit of short cooking making their timing easier.

$\frac{1}{4}$ stick butter or margarine, plus extra for greasing
1 cup raspberries, hulled
$\frac{1}{4}$ cup icing sugar
scant 2 tablespoons All Purpose flour
$\frac{1}{2}$ cup milk
finely grated peel and juice of 2 medium lemons
2 tablespoons superfine sugar
3 eggs, separated

1. Grease six $\frac{1}{2}$ cup custard pots.
2. Purée the raspberries and icing sugar in a blender or food processor. Rub through a nylon strainer. Divide between the prepared pots.
3. Melt the butter in a medium saucepan. Add the flour and cook for 1 minute, then blend in the milk. Bring to the boil, stirring all the time, and cook for about 1 minute.
4. Cool slightly, then beat in the lemon peel, 3 tablespoons lemon juice, the sugar and egg yolks.
5. Whisk the egg whites until stiff but not dry. Beat one spoonful into the sauce to lighten it, then carefully fold in the remaining egg white. Spoon into the prepared pots. Stand the dishes on a cookie sheet.
6. Bake in the oven at 375° for 15–20 minutes or until lightly set. Serve straight away.

Not suitable for freezing.

Opposite: CHOCOLATE CINNAMON SOUFFLÉ.

ORANGE FARINA SOUFFLÉS

SERVES 6

These individual soufflés, baked in orange shells, are good served with thinly sliced oranges sprinkled with a little orange-flavored liqueur or orange flower water.

5 large juicy oranges
2 tablespoons sugar
¼ cup Farina
3 eggs, separated
icing sugar, for dusting

1. Finely grate the peel and squeeze the juice from 2 of the oranges into a measuring container. You will need 1 cup juice. Make up with juice from one of the remaining oranges if there is not enough.

2. Halve the remaining oranges. Scoop out any loose flesh still attached to the skins and eat separately or use in another recipe. You need six clean orange halves to serve the soufflés in. Cut a thin slice from the bottom of each so that they stand flat.

3. Place the orange juice and peel, sugar and Farina in a pan and simmer until thickened, stirring all the time. (Alternatively, microwave on HIGH for 5 minutes, stirring frequently.)

4. Cool slightly, then stir in the egg yolks. Whisk the egg whites until stiff and fold into the mixture. Spoon into the reserved orange shells and stand on a cookie sheet.

5. Bake in the oven at 400° for 15–20 minutes or until risen and golden brown. Dust with icing sugar and serve straight away.

Not suitable for freezing.

APRICOT AND ALMOND SOUFFLÉ

SERVES 4

The dry apricot purée gives a wonderful depth of flavor to this light soufflé. Serve with light cream flavored with a little almond liqueur.

½ stick butter or margarine, plus extra for greasing
1 cup no-soak dry apricots
pared peel of 1 lemon
3 tablespoons All Purpose flour
scant 1 cup milk
3 tablespoons sugar
5 eggs, separated
slivered almonds, to decorate

1. Tie a double strip of wax paper around a 5 cup soufflé dish to make a 3 inch collar. Brush the inside of the dish and the paper with melted butter.

2. Put the apricots and lemon peel in a saucepan with enough water to cover. Cover and simmer for about 20 minutes or until really tender. Drain, reserving the liquid. Purée the apricots with ½ cup of the cooking liquor. Strain to make a really smooth purée.

3. Melt the butter in a large heavy-based saucepan. Add the flour and cook for 1 minute, then blend in the milk. Bring to the boil, stirring all the time, and cook for about 1 minute—the sauce will be very thick.

4. Cool slightly, then beat in the apricot purée, sugar and egg yolks.

5. Whisk the egg whites until stiff but not dry. Beat one spoonful into the sauce mixture to lighten it, then carefully fold in the remaining egg whites.

6. Gently pour the soufflé mixture into the prepared dish. Level the top with a spatula and make a few cuts through the outer edges of the mixture—this helps it to rise evenly. Sprinkle with a few slivered almonds. Stand the dish on a cookie sheet.

7. Bake in the oven at 375° for about 35–40 minutes or until well risen, just set and well browned. Remove the paper and serve straight away.

Not suitable for freezing.

SALZBURGER NOCKERLN

SERVES 4

This soufflé is a speciality of the Salzkammergut region of Austria. The soufflé is baked in a shallow dish, about 1 inch deep, and is mounded in the dish to represent the mountains of the area.

3 egg yolks
finely grated peel of 2 lemons
2 tablespoons lemon juice
2 tablespoons All Purpose flour
4 egg whites
scant ⅓ cup superfine sugar
icing sugar, for sifting

1. Grease a shallow 9 inch round or oval dish.

2. Whisk the egg yolks and lemon peel together until thick. Whisk in the lemon juice, then fold in the flour.

3. Whisk the egg whites until stiff but not dry, then gradually whisk in the sugar, whisking until shiny. Fold a little of the egg whites into the lemon mixture, then carefully fold in the remainder.

4. Spoon the soufflé mixture, in three mounds, in the prepared dish. Place the dish on a cookie sheet.

5. Bake in the oven at 375° for 12–14 minutes until lightly set. Dust with icing sugar and serve straight away.

Not suitable for freezing.

Opposite: ORANGE FARINA SOUFFLÉS.

INDIVIDUAL APPLE SOUFFLÉS

SERVES 6

The apple sauce mixture can be prepared ahead, ready to add the whisked egg whites at the last minute.

icing sugar, for dusting
¾ pound tart apples
½ stick butter or margarine
2 tablespoons superfine sugar
2 tablespoons All Purpose flour
½ cup milk
3 eggs, separated
2 tablespoons apple brandy
apple slices, to decorate (optional)

1. Lightly grease six ½ cup custard pots. Dust them out with icing sugar.

2. Peel, quarter, core and roughly chop the apples. Place in a small saucepan with half of the butter and the sugar. Cover tightly and cook gently until the apples are very soft. Uncover and cook over a moderate heat, stirring frequently until all excess moisture evaporates. (Alternatively, cover and microwave on HIGH for 5 minutes, or until really soft, stirring.) Mash or beat until smooth; cool slightly.

3. Melt the remaining butter in a pan, add the flour and cook for 2 minutes. Remove from the heat and stir in the milk. Cook, stirring, for 2–3 minutes. (Alternatively, put everything in a bowl and microwave on HIGH for 3–4 minutes or until boiling and thickened, whisking.)

4. Remove from the heat, cool slightly, then stir in the apple purée and egg yolks. Gently mix in the apple brandy. Whisk the egg whites until stiff but not dry. Stir one large spoonful into the apple mixture, then gently fold in the remaining egg whites. Divide between the prepared pots so that each is three-quarters full.

5. Bake in the oven at 350° for about 30 minutes or until just set and golden brown. Dust quickly with icing sugar and decorate with apple slices, if using. Serve straight away with light cream.

Not suitable for freezing.

Below: INDIVIDUAL APPLE SOUFFLÉS.

CHILLED LEMON SOUFFLÉ

SERVES 6

Sharp with the tang of lemon, this delicious cold dessert has a creamy, crunchy pistachio casing, making a rich yet beautifully light soufflé.

grated peel and juice of 3 lemons
6 eggs, separated
generous $\frac{1}{2}$ cup superfine sugar
2 tablespoons gelatin
2 cups heavy cream
pinch of salt
generous $\frac{1}{2}$ cup sugar
$\frac{3}{4}$ cup pistachios
slices of star fruit, to decorate

1. Tie a double strip of wax paper around a 3 cup soufflé dish to make a 3 inch collar. Lightly brush the inside of the paper with oil. Lightly oil a cookie sheet.
2. Whisk the lemon peel, egg yolks and two-thirds of the superfine sugar together in a medium bowl until pale and creamy.
3. Sprinkle the gelatin over 7 tablespoons lemon juice and leave to soak for 2–3 minutes. Place the bowl over a pan of simmering water and stir until dissolved. (Alternatively, microwave on HIGH for 30 seconds or until dissolved.) Stir the dissolved gelatin into the egg yolk mixture.
4. Lightly whip three-quarters of the cream until it just begins to hold its shape. (Do not refrigerate or it will become too cold.) Place the gelatin mixture over a bowl of iced water and stir until the mixture is on the point of setting—just beginning to thicken. Remove the bowl from the ice and fold in the cream.
5. Whisk the egg whites in a large bowl with a pinch of salt (to strengthen the whites) until stiff but not dry. Add the remaining superfine sugar and whisk again until very stiff and standing in firm peaks. Stir a spoonful of egg whites into the yolk mixture to loosen it. Then, with a large metal spoon, quickly and carefully fold in the rest of the whites until evenly mixed.
6. Gently pour the mixture into the prepared dish and level the top. Chill for at least 4 hours until set.
7. Meanwhile, melt the sugar very slowly in a small pan until it bubbles and turns golden brown. Stir in the pistachios. Immediately pour on to the prepared cookie sheet and leave to one side to cool.
8. Whip the remaining cream until it holds its shape, reserve 3 tablespoons. Fill a pastry tube fitted with a star tip with the remainder. Keep refrigerated until decorating the soufflé.
9. When set, carefully ease the paper collar away from the soufflé with a knife dipped in hot water.
10. Place the caramel and nut mixture in a plastic bag and lightly crush with a rolling pin or break up into a food processor and roughly chop.
11. Spread a thin layer of the reserved whipped cream around the edge of the soufflé and press the crushed nut mixture on to the sides. Pipe rosettes of cream at regular intervals around the edge of the soufflé then top each one with a slice of star fruit, sitting at an angle almost hiding the rosette. Chill until ready to serve. (No longer than 2 hours or the caramel will start to weep.)

To freeze: remove the paper collar after chilling soufflé mixture for at least 4 hours (see step 6). Open freeze the soufflé, then overwrap loosely. Defrost overnight in the refrigerator, then finish as above.

THREE FRUIT SOUFFLÉ

SERVES 6–8

grated peel and juice of 1 lemon
grated peel and juice of 1 orange
juice of 1 grapefruit
3 teaspoons gelatin
4 eggs, separated
generous $\frac{1}{2}$ cup superfine sugar
1 cup heavy cream
crushed sweet cookies and crystalized oranges and lemon slices, to decorate

1. Tie a double strip of wax paper around a 6 inch soufflé dish to make a 3 inch collar.
2. Pour the fruit juices into a heatproof bowl and sprinkle in the gelatin. Stand the bowl over a saucepan of hot water and heat gently until dissolved. (Alternatively, microwave on HIGH for 30 seconds or until dissolved.) Cool.
3. Put the fruit peel, egg yolks and sugar in a large heatproof bowl and stand over the pan of gently simmering water. Whisk until the mixture is thick and leaves a trail.
4. Remove the bowl from the pan and whisk in the gelatin liquid. Leave until beginning to set, whisking occasionally.
5. Whip the cream until it will stand in soft peaks. Whisk the egg whites until stiff. Fold the cream into the soufflé, then the egg whites, until evenly blended.
6. Pour into the prepared dish and level the surface. Chill until set.
7. Carefully remove the paper. Press the crushed cookies around the exposed edge, then decorate with crystalized fruit.

To freeze: open freeze at the end of step 6, then overwrap loosely. Defrost overnight in the refrigerator, then finish as above.

CHOCOLATE ORANGE SOUFFLÉ

SERVES 6–8

Semi sweet chocolate is the best kind to use for mouth-watering desserts like this one, which call for a good depth of flavor. Cold soufflés and mousses, concocted from whipped cream and egg whites, have been popular desserts in England since the 17th century.

$1\frac{1}{2}$ cups milk
5 squares semi sweet chocolate
3 eggs, separated, plus 1 egg white
scant $\frac{1}{2}$ cup superfine sugar
1 tablespoon gelatin
grated peel and juice of 1 orange
1 cup whipping cream
1 tablespoon chocolate-flavored liqueur
grated chocolate, to decorate

1. Tie a double strip of wax paper around a 3 cup soufflé dish to make a 3 inch collar. Lightly brush the inside of the paper with oil.

2. Put the milk in a saucepan and break the chocolate into it. Heat gently until the chocolate melts, then cook over a high heat until almost boiling.

3. Whisk the egg yolks and sugar together in a bowl until pale and thick. Gradually pour on the chocolate milk, stirring. Return to the pan and cook for about 20 minutes, stirring continuously, until it coats the back of a wooden spoon. Do not boil.

4. Sprinkle the gelatin over 3 tablespoons water in a small bowl and leave to soak for 2–3 minutes. Place the bowl over a saucepan of simmering water and stir until dissolved. (Alternatively, microwave on HIGH for 30 seconds or until dissolved.) Stir the dissolved gelatin into the custard with the orange peel and juice. Leave to cool.

5. Whip the cream until it just holds its shape, then fold most of the cream into the cold mixture. Whisk the egg whites until stiff, then fold into the mixture.

6. Pour the soufflé mixture into the prepared dish and leave to set. Carefully ease away the paper collar just before serving.

7. Stir the liqueur into the remaining cream and use to decorate the soufflé. Sprinkle the top with grated chocolate.

To freeze: open freeze at the end of step 6, then overwrap loosely. Defrost overnight in the refrigerator, then finish as above.

ICED STRAWBERRY SOUFFLÉ

SERVES 8

1 pound strawberries, hulled
4 tablespoons almond-flavored liqueur
2 tablespoons lemon juice
1 tablespoon icing sugar
$\frac{2}{3}$ cup small ratafia biscuits
$1\frac{1}{2}$ cups heavy cream
1 tablespoon gelatin
4 eggs, separated
scant 1 cup superfine sugar

1. Tie a double strip of wax paper around a 4 cup straight sided soufflé dish to make a 3 inch collar. Lightly brush the inside of the paper with oil. Place a straight sided 2 cup glass jar in the center of the dish.

2. Marinate the strawberries in the liqueur, lemon juice and icing sugar for 30 minutes. Purée half the strawberries, then strain to remove the pips.

3. Finely crush half the ratafias. Lightly whip 1 cup of the cream until it just holds its shape. Whip the remaining cream.

4. Sprinkle the gelatin over 3 tablespoons water in a small bowl and leave to soak for 2–3 minutes. Place the bowl over a saucepan of simmering water and stir until dissolved. (Alternatively, microwave on HIGH for 30 seconds or until dissolved.)

5. Meanwhile whisk the egg yolks and sugar together with an electric mixer until very light and creamy. Fold in the strawberry purée, whipped cream and dissolved gelatin.

6. Whisk the egg whites until stiff but not dry, then fold into the strawberry mixture.

7. Pour the mixture into the prepared dish, keeping the glass jar in the center. Chill for 1–2 hours to set. Freeze until firm for at least 3 hours.

8. To serve, about 2 hours before eating, fill the glass jar with hot water. Gently twist and remove it from the center of the dish. Fill the center with the remaining strawberries. Carefully ease away the paper collar and coat the sides with crushed ratafias. Decorate with the remaining whipped cream and the whole ratafias. Refrigerate for about 2 hours before serving.

To freeze: freeze until firm in step 7, then remove the glass jar as step 8. Overwrap and freeze. Finish as above and transfer to the refrigerator for about 2 hours before serving.

FROZEN PASSION FRUIT SOUFFLÉ

SERVES 8

A velvety smooth soufflé to make the perfect ending to a dinner party, it should be made the day before. The soufflé can be decorated with whipped cream and pistachios, but as its impressive qualities are in the texture and fresh flavor, it really doesn't need to be dressed-up.

16 passion fruit
6 egg yolks
scant 1 cup superfine sugar
2 cups heavy cream

1. Tie a double strip of wax paper around a 3 cup soufflé dish to make a 3 inch collar. Lightly brush the inside of the paper with oil.

2. Cut each passion fruit in half and scoop out the flesh and pips into a nylon strainer, placed over a small bowl. Press with a spoon to extract all of the juice—about ½ cup.

3. Whisk the egg yolks in a large bowl with an electric mixer until very thick.

4. Put 4 tablespoons of the passion fruit juice into a small saucepan with the sugar. Stir over a low heat until the sugar has dissolved. Bring to the boil and boil until the temperature reaches 230° on a sugar thermometer.

5. Whisk the syrup in a steady stream into the egg yolks, then continue whisking until the mixture cools and thickens. Gradually whisk in the remaining passion fruit juice, whisking until the mixture is thick and mousse-like.

6. Whip the cream until it just holds its shape. Fold the cream into the passion fruit mixture until no trace of white remains. Pour into the prepared dish, then freeze until firm. Once frozen, cover the top of the soufflé with plastic wrap.

7. To serve, remove the soufflé from the freezer 20–30 minutes before serving and carefully ease away the plastic wrap and paper collar. Decorate the soufflé with whipped cream, if liked.

Above: FROZEN PASSION FRUIT SOUFFLÉ.

ICED ROSE PETAL
SOUFFLÉS

SERVES 8

You can either make individual soufflés or one large one. Do not make more than two or three days in advance.

1 cup well scented rose petals, dry
generous ½ cup superfine sugar
scant 1 cup fromage blanc
scant ½ cup crème fraîche
few drops of rose water (optional)
4 egg whites
small rose petals, to decorate

1. Tie a double strip of wax paper around eight ½ cup custard pots to make 3 inch collars. Lightly brush the inside of the paper with oil.

2. Blend the rose petals and sugar in a blender or food processor until the petals are reduced to very small pieces.

3. Mix the fromage blanc and crème fraîche together. Taste and add a few drops of rose water to increase the flavor, if necessary.

4. Whisk the egg whites until stiff but not dry, then gently fold into the fromage blanc mixture with the sugared rose petals.

5. Divide the mixture between the prepared pots. Freeze until firm, then cover the tops.

6. About 25 minutes before serving, carefully ease away the paper collars. Leave the soufflés in the refrigerator until required. Serve decorated with small rose petals.

APRICOT SOUFFLÉ

SERVES 6–8

This delightful chilled apricot soufflé is flavored with a hint of almond.

⅔ cup no-soak dry apricots
scant 1 cup superfine sugar
2 tablespoons almond-flavored liqueur
1 tablespoon gelatin
4 eggs, separated
1 cup heavy cream

FOR THE DECORATION

ratafia biscuits
whipped cream

1. Tie a double strip of wax paper around a 3 cup soufflé dish to make a 3 inch collar. Lightly brush the inside of the paper with oil.

2. Put the apricots in a saucepan with 8 tablespoons water and one-third of the sugar. Heat gently until the sugar has dissolved, then cover and simmer for about 30 minutes until tender. Leave to cool slightly, then rub through a strainer or purée in a blender or food processor. Stir in the liqueur and leave to cool for about 30 minutes.

3. Sprinkle the gelatin over 4 tablespoons water in a small bowl and leave to soak for 2–3 minutes. Place the bowl over a pan of simmering water and stir until dissolved. (Alternatively, microwave on HIGH for 30 seconds or until dissolved.) Cool slightly.

4. Put the egg yolks and remaining sugar in a large bowl and stand over the pan of gently simmering water. Whisk until the mixture is thick and holds a trail when the whisk is lifted. Remove from the heat and whisk until cold.

5. Whip the cream until it stands in soft peaks. Whisk the egg whites until stiff.

6. Stir the dissolved gelatin into the apricot purée, then fold this into the egg yolk mixture until evenly blended. Next fold in the whipped cream, then egg whites.

7. Pour the soufflé mixture into the prepared soufflé dish and level the surface. Chill for at least 4 hours until set.

8. Carefully ease away the paper collar. Crush some ratafia biscuits and use to press around the exposed edge. Decorate with whipped cream and whole ratafias.

To freeze: open freeze after removing the paper collar, then overwrap. Defrost overnight in the refrigerator. Decorate as above.

CHILLED GINGER WINE SOUFFLÉS

SERVES 6

Brandy snaps make a good accompaniment to these soufflés.

1½ cups milk
4 eggs, separated
scant ⅓ cup brownulated sugar
½ teaspoon ginger
1 tablespoon gelatin
6 tablespoons ginger wine
1 cup whipping cream
¼ cup stem ginger, roughly chopped
slices of stem ginger, to decorate

1. Tie a double strip of wax paper around six ½ cup custard pots to make 3 inch collars.

2. Heat the milk in a pan to almost boiling. Beat the egg yolks, sugar and ginger together in a bowl until well mixed.

3. Pour the milk on to the egg yolk mixture. Return to the pan and cook over gentle heat, without boiling, until the mixture just coats the back of a spoon. Pour into a bowl and leave to cool.

4. Sprinkle the gelatin over 3 tablespoons water in a small bowl and leave to soak for 2–3 minutes. Place the bowl over a saucepan of simmering water and stir until dissolved. (Alternatively, microwave on HIGH for 30 seconds or until dissolved.) Stir the dissolved gelatin into the mixture with the ginger wine. Chill until on the point of setting.

5. Divide the cream in half and lightly whip separately. Stir one portion of cream and the stem ginger into the soufflé mixture.

6. Whisk the egg whites until stiff and fold into the mixture. Spoon into the prepared pots. Chill to set.

7. Gently ease away the paper collars and decorate the soufflés with whirls of cream and slices of stem ginger.

Not suitable for freezing.

Left: PEACH AND WALNUT MERINGUE CAKE (PAGE 208). Right: ICED ROSE PETAL SOUFFLÉS.

MERINGUE MEDLEY

MAKES 44 SMALL MERINGUES

Made with meringue cuite, these little meringues are favorites with adults and children alike.

FOR THE MERINGUE

6 egg whites
1¾ cups superfine sugar
1 tablespoon finely chopped pistachios

FOR THE FILLING

1 cup heavy cream
1 tablespoon orange-flavored liqueur
¼ cup pecans, walnuts or hazelnuts, finely chopped
1 tablespoon raspberry purée
3 squares semi sweet chocolate, melted (see page 78)

1. Line several cookie sheets with non-stick wax paper.
2. To make the meringue, whisk the egg whites and sugar, together in a large bowl standing over a large pan of simmering water until very stiff and shiny. Remove from the heat and continue whisking until the meringue will hold unwavering peaks—on no account let the meringue become too hot.
3. Fill a large pastry tube fitted with a large star tip with meringue and pipe out as follows:
To make whirls: pipe 24 whirls of meringue on the prepared cookie sheets, about 1½ inches in diameter.
To make oblong spirals: pipe the meringue in a spiral fashion to make 24 spirals about 3 inches long. Or, if you find it easier, pipe a joined line of shells to the same length.
To make pistachio fingers: simply pipe 20 straight lines of meringue about 3 inches long on the prepared cookie sheets, then sprinkle with chopped pistachios.
4. Bake in the oven at 275° for 2–2½ hours until dry. Change the sheets around in the oven during cooking to ensure that they all dry evenly. Allow the meringues to cool, then remove from the paper and complete as follows or store in an airtight container until required.
Whirls: Whip ½ cup of the heavy cream with the liqueur until it will hold soft peaks, then fold in the chopped nuts. Sandwich the meringues together, in pairs, with the nut cream, then place in small paper cases for serving.
Spirals: Whip the remaining cream until thick, then fold in the raspberry purée. Put the cream into a pastry tube fitted with a large star tip. Sandwich the meringues together, in pairs, with piped cream. Put the meringues into small paper cases for serving.
Pistachio fingers: dip the base of each meringue in the melted chocolate to coat it evenly, removing excess chocolate by gently pulling the meringue across the back of a knife. Place on wax paper until set.

To freeze: freeze the meringues before filling. Defrost overnight at cool room temperature, then finish as above.

CROQUEMBOUCHE OF MERINGUE

SERVES 8–10

This unorthodox Croquembouche makes a stunning centerpiece for a summer buffet party or a stunning finale to a special meal. The meringues can be made well in advance and stored in an airtight container. The cream can be mixed and flavored, then stored in the refrigerator for several hours before serving. However, once the Croquembouche is assembled, it should be served within 1 hour.

FOR THE MERINGUES

4 egg whites
2 cups icing sugar, sifted
1 tablespoon cocoa

FOR THE FILLING

4 cups full fat soft cream cheese
finely grated peel of 2 oranges
few drops of vanilla
4 tablespoons orange-flavored liqueur
sugar, to taste

FOR THE DECORATION

fresh summer fruits, such as redcurrants, strawberries, blackcurrants
fresh or crystalized flowers or petals

1. Line two large cookie sheets with non-stick wax paper.
2. To make the meringue, place the egg whites and sugar in a large bowl standing over a pan of simmering water. Using a hand held electric mixer, whisk the meringue until thick and standing in stiff peaks. Remove from the heat and continue whisking for 2 minutes.
3. Spoon half of the meringue mixture into a large pastry tube fitted with a star tip and pipe small star shapes, about 1 inch in diameter, on to one of the prepared cookie sheets.
4. Sift the cocoa into the remaining meringue mixture. Fold in, using a large metal spoon. Spoon into the pastry tube and pipe star shapes as above.
5. Bake all the meringues at 225° for 2½–3 hours or until dry. Leave to cool on a wire rack.
6. To make the filling, beat the soft cheese, orange peel, vanilla, liqueur and sugar to taste together. Pile most of the mixture in a pyramid shape on a cake stand or large serving plate.
7. Stick meringues on to the soft cheese pyramid until completely covered. Spread a little of the reserved cheese mixture on to the flat side of the remaining meringues and attach to the first meringues, forming a tall, thin pyramid about 8 inches high. Decorate with fresh fruits and flowers.

To freeze: freeze the meringues. Defrost at cool room temperature, then finish as above.

Opposite: MERINGUE MEDLEY.

MERINGUE BASKET

SERVES 6–8

The unfilled basket will keep well for several days in an airtight container.

FOR THE MERINGUE

4 egg whites
2 cups icing sugar

FOR THE FILLING

1 cup whipping cream
2 tablespoons kirsch
about 1 pound prepared fresh fruit in season, such as strawberries, raspberries, blackberries, starfruit

1. Line three cookie sheets with non-stick wax paper (turn rimmed cookie sheets upside down and use the bases) and draw a 7½ inch circle on each. Turn the paper over so that the pencilled circle is visible but does not come into contact with the meringues.
2. To make the meringue, place 3 of the egg whites in a large bowl standing over a pan of simmering water. Sift in three-quarters of the icing sugar. Whisk the egg whites and sugar until the mixture stands in very stiff peaks. Do not allow the bowl to get too hot or the meringue will crust around edges.
3. Spoon one third of the meringue mixture into a pastry tube fitted with a large star tip. Secure the paper to the cookie sheets with a little meringue. Pipe rings of meringue, about ½ inch thick, inside two of the circles on the paper. Fill the bag with the remaining meringue and, starting from the center, pipe a continuous coil of meringue on the third sheet of paper to make the base of the basket.
4. Bake all in the oven at 200° for 2½–3 hours until dry. Change over the positions of the meringues during this time so that they cook evenly.
5. Use the remaining egg white and sugar to make meringue as before and put into the pastry tube. Remove the cooked meringue rings from the paper and layer up on the base, piping a ring of fresh meringue between each. Return to the oven for a further 1½–2 hours.
6. Leave to cool, then slide on to a wire rack and peel off the base paper. Just before serving, stand the meringue shell on a flat serving plate.
7. To make the filling, lightly whip the cream and fold in the kirsch. Spoon half into the base of the meringue basket and top with fruit. Whirl the remaining cream over the top and decorate with more fruit.

To freeze: freeze the meringue basket before filling. Defrost overnight at cool room temperature, then finish as above.

VARIATION

Mini Meringue Baskets Prepare the cookie sheets as above, but draw sixteen 2 inch circles or eight 4 inch circles on the paper. Make the meringue as above, using 3 egg whites and ¾ cup icing sugar. Pipe a continuous coil of meringue on each circle to make the bases, then pipe a ring on top of each circle. Bake as step 4 above for 2½ hours to dry out.

PAVLOVA

SERVES 8

This luscious meringue is generally believed to have been created in Australia in the 1930s to celebrate the visit of Anna Pavlova, the great prima ballerina.

FOR THE MERINGUE

3 egg whites
scant 1 cup superfine sugar
1 teaspoon cornstarch
1 teaspoon vinegar
½ teaspoon vanilla

FOR THE FILLING

2 passion fruit
2 kiwi fruit
1 cup strawberries
1 cup fresh pineapple
1½ cups heavy cream or Greek yogurt and double cream, mixed
walnuts, pecans or almonds, to decorate

1. Line a cookie sheet with greased foil or non-stick wax paper.
2. To make the meringue, whisk the egg whites in a large bowl until very stiff. Add one-third of the sugar and whisk until very stiff. Add another third sugar and whisk once more until the mixture returns to its stiff texture. Spoon in the remaining sugar and whisk again until shiny and standing in stiff peaks. Do not rush this process or the meringue will become too soft.
3. Fold in the cornstarch, vinegar and vanilla.
4. Pile or pipe the meringue in a 9 inch round or oval on to the prepared cookie sheet, making sure there is a substantial dip or hollow in the center to hold the filling. It should look rather like a nest.
5. Bake in the oven at 250° for 1¼–1½ hours or until pale brown and dry but a little soft in the center. Press lightly with a finger to test if the meringue is cooked. Leave to cool slightly, then peel off the foil or paper and place on a serving dish to cool completely. At this stage the meringue will probably crack and sink a little—this is to be expected with a Pavlova. (When completely cold, the meringue can be overwrapped in foil and stored for a couple of days if wished.)
6. To make the filling, halve the passion fruit and scoop out the pulp. Peel and slice the kiwi fruit. Halve the strawberries. Slice the pineapple, discard skin and core, and roughly chop the flesh. Whip the cream until it just holds its shape and, if using, mix with the yogurt.
7. Either fold the fruit into the cream and spoon into the Pavlova or fill the center with cream—it may have to be whipped a little longer if used in this way—and arrange the fruit on top. Scatter with nuts to decorate and serve immediately, or within an hour or so.

Not suitable for freezing.

Illustrated on pages 186–187

CHOCOLATE CHIP MERINGUES

SERVES 6

Serve these chocolate speckled meringues with a bowl of strawberries or a fresh fruit salad.

---

4 egg whites
generous 1 cup superfine sugar
4 squares semi sweet chocolate, grated
1 cup heavy or whipping cream

1. Line a cookie sheet with non-stick wax paper.
2. Whisk the egg whites in a bowl until stiff but not dry. Whisk in 4 teaspoons of the sugar, keeping the mixture stiff. Fold in the remaining sugar with the grated chocolate.
3. Spoon out 12 meringues on to the prepared cookie sheet, allowing them room to spread.
4. Bake in the oven at 250° for about 1½ hours until dry. Peel off the paper and cool on a wire rack. Store, if wished, in an airtight container.
5. To serve, whip the cream until softly stiff and use to sandwich together the meringues.

To freeze: freeze the meringues before filling. Defrost overnight at cool room temperature, then finish as above.

MERINGUE AND ICE CREAM EXTRAVAGANZA

SERVES 10–12

A more elaborate version of the meringue basket on page 202, filled with ice cream and decorated with frosted fruits, flowers and leaves.

FOR THE MERINGUE

1 meringue basket, made with 3 egg whites and 1½ cups icing sugar to the end of step 4 (see page 202)
3 egg whites
1½ cups icing sugar

FOR THE FILLING AND DECORATION

1 quantity ice cream of your choice (see pages 216–224)
Frosted fruits, flowers and leaves (see page 10)

1. Line a cookie sheet with non-stick wax paper.
2. Using the egg whites and sugar, make a stiff meringue mixture as page 202.
3. To assemble the meringue basket, stand the rings of meringue on the base. Stand on the prepared cookie sheet.
4. Using a spatula, spread a little of the uncooked meringue mixture around the outside of the basket, filling in the gaps between the rings.
5. Spoon the remaining meringue into a pastry tube fitted with a large star tip. Working from the base to the top of the basket, pipe vertical lines of meringue to cover the sides completely. Pipe scrolls or rosettes around the top to neaten the edge.
6. Bake in the oven at 200° for about 2 hours until dry. Leave the basket to cool completely.
7. To make the filling, leave the ice cream at room temperature to soften slightly. When the basket is cold, quickly fill with the ice cream. Return to the freezer for 1 hour until firm. Decorate and serve.

To freeze: pack the meringue basket in a rigid container and freeze. Defrost at cool room temperature.

CHOCOLATE MERINGUE GÂTEAU

SERVES 6–8

FOR THE MERINGUE

3 egg whites
scant 1 cup superfine sugar

FOR THE FILLING

2 egg yolks
scant ⅓ cup superfine sugar
2 squares semi sweet chocolate, melted (see page 78)
½ stick sweet butter, softened
¼ cup heavy cream
Chocolate curls (see page 78), to decorate

1. Draw two 8 inch circles on non-stick cookie paper and place on separate wax sheets.
2. To make the meringue, whisk the egg whites in a large bowl until stiff. Whisk in half of the sugar. Whisk again for 5 minutes until stiff. Carefully fold in the remaining sugar.
3. Spoon the mixture into a pastry tube fitted with a large star tip and pipe the mixture on to the circles on the cookie sheets. Or, using a spatula, spread the mixture evenly.
4. Bake in the oven at 225° for about 1¾ hours until dry. Cool on the sheets for 30 minutes.
5. To make the filling, beat the egg yolks in a bowl. Put the sugar and 3 tablespoons water into a small pan and heat to dissolve the sugar.
6. Bring to the boil and boil to 230° on a sugar thermometer, or until the mixture reaches the soft ball stage. Check by plunging a teaspoonful into a bowl of iced water. It should form a ball in your fingers.
7. Pour the syrup on to the egg yolks in a steady stream, whisking all the time. Continue to whisk until thick and mousse-like.
8. Cool the chocolate for 5 minutes. Gradually beat the butter and melted chocolate into the syrup mixture.
9. Carefully peel the paper from the meringues, then use the chocolate filling to sandwich the rounds together. Whip the cream until stiff and pipe on to the gâteau. Decorate with chocolate curls.

To freeze: freeze the meringues before filling. Defrost overnight at cool room temperature, then finish as above.

Brown Sugar and Hazelnut Meringues

MAKES ABOUT 40

Meringues made with brown sugar have a rich flavor and are a delicate pale brown in color. Serve them sandwiched together with ice cream or cream, or as an accompaniment to fruit salads or compotes.

$\frac{1}{4}$ cup hazelnuts
3 egg whites
$\frac{3}{4}$ cup light brown soft sugar
FOR THE FILLING
Ice cream (see pages 216–224)

1. Line two large cookie sheets with non-stick wax paper.
2. Roast the hazelnuts under the grill until golden brown. Tip on to a clean cloth and rub off the loose skins. Chop roughly.
3. Whisk the egg whites in a bowl until stiff. Whisk in the sugar, 1 tablespoon at a time. Spoon the meringue mixture into a pastry tube fitted with a large star tip and pipe about 40 small swirls on to the prepared cookie sheets. Sprinkle with the hazelnuts.
4. Bake in the oven at 225° for about 2–3 hours or until dry. Change over the position of the sheets halfway through the cooking time to ensure even browning. Leave to cool.
5. Sandwich the meringues together in pairs with a little ice cream. Arrange on a freezerproof plate or a cookie sheet and freeze for up to 2 hours before serving. Serve with a sauce, if liked.

Queen of Puddings

SERVES 4

A delicate old English favorite.

4 eggs
2 cups milk
2 cups fresh breadcrumbs
3–4 tablespoons raspberry jelly
scant $\frac{1}{2}$ cup superfine sugar

1. Separate 3 of the eggs and beat together the 3 egg yolks and one whole egg. Add to the milk in a bowl and mix well. Stir in the breadcrumbs.
2. Spread the jelly on the base of a pie plate. Pour over the milk mixture and leave for 30 minutes.
3. Bake in the oven at 300° for 1 hour until set.
4. Whisk the egg whites in a bowl until stiff. Fold in the sugar. Pile on top of the custard and return to the oven for a further 15–20 minutes until the meringue is set.

Not suitable for freezing.

Meringue and Ganache Gâteau

SERVES 14–16

This very rich gâteau makes a lovely party-time special.

FOR THE MERINGUE
4 egg whites
generous 1 cup superfine sugar
FOR THE FILLING
12 squares semi sweet chocolate
2 cups heavy cream
2–3 tablespoons orange-flavored liqueur, brandy or rum
icing sugar, for sifting

1. Line four cookie sheets with non-stick wax paper. Draw an 8 inch circle in the center of each sheet of paper.
2. To make the meringue, whisk the egg whites in a bowl until stiff, but not dry. Gradually whisk in the sugar, a little at a time, whisking well until very stiff and shiny. Divide the meringue equally between the prepared cookie sheets, then spread evenly to form neat rounds.
3. Bake in the oven at 275° for 1–1$\frac{1}{4}$ hours until dry, changing over the cookie sheets during cooking to ensure that they dry out evenly. Leave to cool.
4. Meanwhile to make the filling, break the chocolate into small pieces. Put into a large saucepan with the cream. Heat gently, stirring, until the chocolate melts and blends with the cream to form a smooth rich cream. Do not allow to boil.
5. Pour the chocolate cream into a bowl and leave to cool, stirring frequently to prevent a skin forming. When cold, add the liqueur and whisk well until light and fluffy.
6. Place one of the meringue layers on a flat serving plate, then spread with a generous layer of the whipped chocolate cream. Continue until the meringue rounds are sandwiched together.
7. Spread the remaining chocolate cream all over the meringue to cover completely. Mark the cream into swirls with a spatula. Sift the icing sugar lightly over the gâteau. Chill until slightly chilled, but do not let the chocolate cream set too hard. Serve the gâteau still slightly chilled.

To freeze: freeze the meringues before filling. Defrost overnight at cool room temperature, then finish as above.

Opposite: BROWN SUGAR AND HAZELNUT MERINGUES.

VACHERIN AU CHOCOLAT ET AUX MARRONS

SERVES 10–12

The meringues can be made in advance and stored in an airtight container. Do not sandwich them with the filling more than 2 hours before serving.

FOR THE MERINGUE
1½ cups hazelnuts
6 egg whites
1¾ cups superfine sugar

FOR THE FILLING AND DECORATION
8 squares semi sweet chocolate
4 tablespoons dark rum
12 ounces sweetened chestnut paste
1 cup heavy or whipping cream
Chocolate caraque (see page 78) or grated chocolate, to decorate

1. Grease three 8 inch layer cake pans and line the bases with non-stick wax paper.
2. To make the meringue, first roast the hazelnuts lightly under the broiler, shaking the pan frequently. Transfer the nuts to a clean cloth and rub gently while still hot to remove the skins. Grind until very fine.
3. Put the egg whites in a large bowl and whisk until very stiff and standing in peaks. Whisk in half of the sugar until the meringue is glossy. Fold in the remaining sugar with the hazelnuts. Spoon the meringue into the prepared pans. Level the tops.
4. Bake in the oven at 350° for 35–40 minutes until crisp.
5. Invert the pans on to a wire rack and turn out the meringues. Peel off the lining papers carefully. (Don't worry if the meringues are cracked.) Leave to cool.
6. To make the filling, break the chocolate in small pieces. Place in a heatproof bowl standing over a pan of simmering water. Add the rum and heat gently until the chocolate melts. Remove from the heat and gradually blend in three-quarters of the chestnut purée.
7. Put the meringue round, soft side uppermost, on a serving plate. Spread with half of the chocolate and chestnut mixture, then top with the second meringue round, crisp side uppermost. Spread with the remaining mixture, then top with the last round.
8. Whip the cream until it holds its shape. Reserve 2 tablespoons of the cream and swirl the remainder all over the gâteau to cover the top and sides completely.
9. Blend the remaining chestnut purée into the reserved cream, then pipe around the edge. Decorate with chocolate caraque or grated chocolate. Chill before serving.

Not suitable for freezing.

HAZELNUT MERINGUE GÂTEAU

SERVES 6–8

This simple gâteau is perfect for the novice meringue-maker. The sharp flavor of the raspberries contrasts well with the nutty meringue.

FOR THE MERINGUE
3 egg whites
scant 1 cup superfine sugar
½ cup hazelnuts, peeled, roasted and finely chopped

FOR THE FILLING
1 cup heavy cream
1½ cups raspberries, hulled
icing sugar, for sifting
finely chopped pistachios, to decorate

1. Line two cookie sheets with non-stick wax paper, then draw an 8 inch circle on each one.
2. To make the meringue, whisk the egg whites in a bowl until very stiff, but not dry. Gradually whisk in the sugar, a little at a time, whisking well between each addition until stiff and very shiny. Carefully fold in the chopped hazelnuts.
3. Divide the meringue equally between the prepared sheets, then spread neatly into rounds. With a spatula, mark the top of one of the rounds into swirls—this will be the top meringue.
4. Bake in the oven at 275° for about 1½ hours until dry. Turn the oven off, and allow the meringues to cool in the oven.
5. To make the filling, whip the cream until it will hold soft peaks. Carefully remove the meringues from the paper. Place the smooth meringue round on a large flat serving plate, then spread with the cream. Arrange the raspberries on top of the cream, then place the second meringue on top. Sift icing sugar over the top of the gâteau, then sprinkle with the nuts. Serve the gâteau as soon as possible.

To freeze: freeze the meringues before filling. Defrost at cool room temperature, then finish as above.

Opposite: HAZELNUT MERINGUE GÂTEAU.

PEACH AND WALNUT MERINGUE CAKE

SERVES 8

FOR THE MERINGUE

4 egg whites
generous 1 cup superfine sugar
1 tablespoon cinnamon
2 cups walnut pieces, finely chopped

FOR THE FILLING

2 tablespoons sugar
1⅓ cups ripe peaches, thinly sliced
pared peel of 1 lemon
⅔ cup redcurrants
2 tablespoons kirsch
1½ cups heavy cream
icing sugar, for dusting
Frosted redcurrants (see page 10), to decorate

1. Line three cookie sheets with non-stick wax paper.
2. To make the meringue, whisk the egg whites in a bowl until stiff but not dry. Gradually whisk in half of the sugar, keeping the mixture stiff. Fold in the remaining sugar with the cinnamon and half of the walnuts.
3. Divide the meringue between the prepared cookie sheets and, with a spatula, spread the mixture into three 7 inch rounds.
4. Bake in the oven at 375° for 5 minutes. Reduce the oven temperature to 275° and bake for a further 1–1¼ hours until dry. Cool in the oven, then carefully ease off the paper.
5. To make the filling, dissolve the sugar in a scant ½ cup water in a pan over a very gentle heat. Add the peaches, lemon peel and redcurrants. Bring to the boil, then cover and simmer for 5 minutes until the juices begin to run. Uncover and simmer for about 5 minutes.
6. Cool, then purée in a blender or food processor. Strain the fruit into a bowl and stir in the kirsch.
7. Lightly whip the cream until it just holds its shape. Place one meringue round on a serving plate. Spread a quarter of the whipped cream over the meringue. Spread half of the peach purée over the cream. Top with another round and cover with cream and fruit purée as before. Finish with the remaining round.
8. With a spatula, cover the sides of the meringue cake with cream. Press on the remaining walnuts. Decorate with whirls of cream. Cover loosely and chill for at least 1 hour before serving, but no longer than 3–4 hours. Dust with icing sugar and decorate.

To freeze: freeze the meringues before filling. Defrost at cool room temperature, then finish as above.

Illustrated on page 198

LEMON MERINGUE PIE

SERVES 6–8

Lemon meringue pie comes in various forms. This delicious version has a lemon filling which is cool, smooth and tangy.

1 quantity Pâte sucrée (see page 43)

FOR THE FILLING

peel and juice of 4 large lemons
generous ½ cup cornstarch
4–6 tablespoons superfine sugar
3 egg yolks

FOR THE MERINGUE

3 egg whites
scant 1 cup superfine sugar

1. Roll out the pastry on a lightly floured work surface to a round 1 inch larger than a 9 inch fluted pie plate. Line the dish with the pastry, pressing it well into the flutes. Trim the edge, then prick the pastry well all over with a fork. Chill for 30 minutes.
2. Bake blind at 425° for 25–30 minutes until cooked and lightly browned. Leave to cool. Leave the oven on.
3. Meanwhile to make the filling, put the lemon peel and 2 cups water in a saucepan. Bring to the boil, then remove from the heat, cover and leave to stand for at least 30 minutes.
4. Remove all of the lemon peel from the pan, then stir in the lemon juice. Blend the cornstarch with a little of the lemon liquid to form a smooth paste, pour it into the pan and stir well. Bring the lemon mixture to the boil, stirring continuously. Reduce the heat and continue cooking until thickened. Stir in the sugar to taste, then beat in the egg yolks. Pour the lemon filling into the pastry case.
5. To make the meringue, whisk the egg whites in a bowl until stiff, but not dry. Gradually whisk in the sugar, a little at a time, whisking well between each addition, until very stiff and shiny.
6. Put the meringue into a large pastry tube fitted with a large star tip, then pipe it attractively on top of the lemon filling. Alternatively, spoon the meringue on to the filling and shape it into swirls with a spatula.
7. Bake in the oven for 5–10 minutes until the meringue is very lightly browned. Remove the pie from the oven and leave to cool, then refrigerate until cold.

Not suitable for freezing.

Opposite: LEMON MERINGUE PIE.

208

KEY LIME PIE

SERVES 8

A favorite pie from the Florida Keys. It can also be made with a Graham Cracker crust.

1½ quantity Sweet pastry (see page 43)

FOR THE FILLING
1 cup sugar
¼ stick butter
¼ cup cornstarch
finely grated peel and juice of 4 limes
3 egg yolks
2 tablespoons milk
grated lime peel, to decorate

FOR THE MERINGUE
3 egg whites
6 tablespoons superfine sugar

1. Roll out the pastry and use to line a 9 inch fluted pie plate. Chill for 30 minutes.
2. Bake blind in the oven at 400° for 10–15 minutes. Remove the beans and bake for a further 10 minutes or until pale brown. Leave to cool.
3. To make the filling, put the sugar, butter and 1 cup water in a saucepan and heat gently until the sugar has dissolved, stirring all the time. Do not boil.
4. Meanwhile, blend the cornstarch to a smooth paste with the lime peel and juice. Stir a little of the sugar mixture into the blended cornstarch, then return to the pan. Heat gently, stirring all the time, until boiling and thickened. Cool slightly, then stir in the egg yolks, one at a time, and the milk. Leave to cool.
5. Pour the cold filling into the pastry case.
6. To make the meringue, whisk the egg whites in a bowl until stiff. Continue whisking, adding the sugar 1 tablespoon at a time. Spoon the meringue on to the filling. Using a spatula, spread it to the edges of the pastry case to seal in the filling. Pull the meringue into peaks with a teaspoon.
7. Bake in the oven at 400° for about 15 minutes or until the meringue is lightly browned. Leave to cool, then sprinkle with the lime peel.

Not suitable for freezing.

ALMOND MERINGUE WITH NECTARINES

SERVES 6

Almonds ground at home from whole almonds have a stronger flavor than store-bought, ready ground ones.

FOR THE MERINGUE
¾ cup whole almonds
4 egg whites
generous 1 cup superfine sugar
pinch of cream of tartar

FOR THE FILLING
scant ⅓ cup sugar
4 ripe nectarines
1 cup whipping cream
2–3 tablespoons peach brandy
icing sugar, for dusting

1. Line two cookie sheets with non-stick wax paper.
2. To make the meringue, first blanch the almonds in boiling water to remove the skins. Dry well, then finely grind in a nut mouli or food processor.
3. Whisk the egg whites in a bowl until stiff. Add 1 tablespoon of the sugar and the cream of tartar and whisk again for about 1 minute. Fold in the remaining sugar with the ground almonds.
4. Spread the mixture evenly into two 8 inch rounds on the prepared cookie sheets.
5. Bake in the oven at 275° for 1–1½ hours until firm and golden. Leave to cool.
6. Meanwhile to make the filling, dissolve the sugar in ½ cup water in a pan. Boil for 1 minute. Halve 2 of the nectarines. Add to the syrup, cover and poach until tender. Lift out of the liquid and discard the liquid. Remove the pits and purée the nectarines in a blender or food processor until smooth. (If wished, press through a nylon strainer.) Cool.
7. Pit and slice the remaining nectarines. Carefully remove the paper from the meringue rounds. Whip the cream until stiff and fold in the fruit purée, adding peach brandy to taste. Use to fill the meringues, layering with the nectarine slices. Dust with icing sugar.

To freeze: freeze the meringue before filling. Defrost overnight at cool room temperature, then finish as above.

BAKED ALASKA

SERVES 6–8

A spectacular dessert for a special dinner party, the recipe for Baked Alaska originated here in the United States, and is also sometimes called Norwegian Omelet or *omelette norwégienne* in French. Although impressive to serve, Baked Alaska is in fact surprisingly easy to make; the essential thing is to allow yourself unhurried time in the kitchen before serving — Baked Alaska cannot be kept waiting once it is cooked!

---

1 cup fresh or frozen raspberries

2 tablespoons orange-flavored liqueur

8 inch Basic whisked sponge (see page 125)

2 cups vanilla ice cream

FOR THE MERINGUE

4 egg whites

scant 1 cup superfine sugar

---

1. Place the raspberries on a shallow dish and sprinkle over the liqueur. Cover and leave to macerate for 2 hours, turning occasionally.

2. Place the sponge on a large heatproof serving dish and spoon the raspberries and juice into the center.

3. To make the meringue, whisk the egg whites in a bowl until stiff, but not dry. Add 4 teaspoons of the sugar and whisk again, keeping the mixture stiff. Sprinkle over the remaining sugar and fold through gently.

4. Fit a pastry tube with a large star tip and fill with the meringue mixture.

5. Place the ice cream on top of the raspberries, then immediately pipe the meringue on top. Start from the sponge base and pipe the meringue around and over the ice cream until it is completely covered, leaving no gaps.

6. Immediately bake in the oven at 450° for 3–4 minutes. At this stage the meringue should be nicely tinged with brown. Watch the meringue carefully as it burns easily. Do not overcook or the ice cream will become too soft. Serve at once, before the ice cream begins to melt.

Not suitable for freezing.

Below: BAKED ALASKA.

spoons as molds. Slide about six or eight at a time into the liquid and poach gently for 2–3 minutes. The meringue will puff up then shrink back a little. When cooked, it will be firm if lightly touched. Remove with a slotted spoon and drain on kitchen paper. Poach the remaining mixture. Store in a cool place for not more than 2 hours.

5. To serve, spoon a little blackcurrant sauce on to individual serving dishes. Float a few 'islands' on top and sprinkle with nutmeg.

To freeze: pack and freeze the sauce at the end of step 1. Defrost overnight at cool room temperature, then chill.

MERINGUE ROULADE
MAKES 10 SLICES

FOR THE MERINGUE ROULADE
3 egg whites
scant 1 cup superfine sugar

FOR THE FILLING
1 cup raspberries, hulled
1 tablespoon icing sugar
1 cup heavy cream

FOR THE DECORATION
$\frac{1}{2}$ cup heavy cream
cocoa
few raspberries, hulled
mint, chervil or geranium leaves

1. Grease a 13 × 9 inch jelly roll pan and line with wax paper.
2. To make the meringue, using a hand held mixer, whisk the egg whites in a bowl until stiff. Gradually whisk in the sugar, whisking after each addition until thoroughly incorporated. The mixture should be thick and glossy. Spoon the meringue into the prepared pan and level the surface.
3. Bake in the oven at 375° for 10–15 minutes or until risen and firm to the touch.
4. Turn the roulade out on to a sheet of wax paper. Peel away the lining paper and leave until cold.
5. To make the filling, mix half of the raspberries with the sugar and crush lightly with a fork. Whip the cream until stiff then fold in the crushed raspberries. Spoon the cream evenly over the cold meringue. Sprinkle with the remaining raspberries.
6. Starting at one of the narrow ends of the meringue, roll up, using the wax paper to help. Transfer to a serving plate.
7. To make the decoration, whip the remaining cream until stiff and spoon into a pastry tube fitted with a large star tip. Pipe the cream down the center of the roulade. Sift over a little cocoa, then decorate with the raspberries and herb leaves.

Not suitable for freezing.

FLOATING SPICE ISLANDS
SERVES 8
Poached meringues are floated on a blackcurrant sauce.

FOR THE SAUCE
1$\frac{1}{2}$ cups blackcurrants, stalks removed
scant $\frac{1}{2}$ cup sugar
2 tablespoons blackcurrant-flavored liqueur

FOR THE MERINGUE
2 egg whites
scant $\frac{1}{3}$ cup superfine sugar
nutmeg
pinch of salt

1. To make the sauce, place the blackcurrants, sugar and 4 tablespoons water in a small saucepan. Cover tightly and cook gently until the fruit softens. Rub through a nylon strainer, then leave to cool. Stir in the liqueur. Cover and chill.
2. Meanwhile to make the meringue, whisk the egg whites in a bowl until stiff, but not dry. Gradually whisk in the sugar, keeping the mixture stiff. Fold in $\frac{1}{4}$ teaspoon nutmeg.
3. Pour $\frac{3}{4}$ inch water into a large skillet and bring to a gentle simmer. Add the salt.
4. Shape the meringue into small egg shapes, using two

Above: FLOATING SPICE ISLANDS.

SWISS TART

SERVES 6–8

The tip of every meringue star in this dessert is dotted with a bead of redcurrant jelly to give a jeweled effect. Therefore, a little skill with a pastry tube is needed as each star must have a clean point.

1 quantity Pâte sucrée (see page 43)

FOR THE FILLING
generous 1 cup sugar
juice of 1 lemon
2 pounds sweet apples

FOR THE MERINGUE
3 egg whites
scant 1 cup superfine sugar
2 tablespoons redcurrant jelly or seedless raspberry jelly

1. Roll out the pastry on a lightly floured work surface to a round 1 inch larger than a 9 inch fluted pie plate. Line the plate with the pastry, pressing it well into the flutes. Trim the edge, then prick the pastry well, all over, with a fork. Chill for 30 minutes.

2. Bake blind in the oven at 425° for 20–25 minutes until cooked and lightly browned. Cool. Reduce the temperature to 275°.

3. To make the filling, put the sugar and lemon juice into a wide saucepan with the water. Heat gently until the sugar has dissolved, then bring to the boil and simmer gently for 5 minutes.

4. Peel, quarter, core and slice the apples about $\frac{1}{4}$ inch thick. Add the apple slices, in batches, to the sugar syrup and poach until just tender. Lift out with a slotted spoon and drain on kitchen paper.

5. Leaving the pastry case in the pie plate, arrange the apple slices neatly inside the tart case.

6. To make the meringue, put the egg whites and sugar into a bowl standing over a pan of simmering water. Whisk until stiff. Remove from the heat and continue whisking until the meringue forms stiff peaks.

7. Put the meringue into a pastry tube fitted with a large star tip, then pipe stars over the top of the apple-filled tart, making sure that each star is finished with a clean point. Continue to pipe the meringue, in decreasing circles, until it builds up to a point.

8. Bake in the oven for 1 hour until the meringue is set, but not browned—it must remain as white as possible.

9. Put the redcurrant jelly into a small paper pastry tube and cut a small hole in the base of the tube. Pipe a small bead of jelly on the tip of every meringue star. Serve the tart warm or cold.

Not suitable for freezing.

Below: SWISS TART.

FROZEN DESSERTS

A simple, refreshing sherbet, a rich, velvety ice cream, or
an elaborate iced dessert, make a superb finale for almost
any meal. Here, you will find some delectable desserts
that are real frozen assets.

There is nothing to beat the rich flavor and creamy texture of home-made ice cream, or the mouthwatering fruitiness of home-made sherbet.

The knack of successfully making smooth frozen desserts largely involves making sure that no large ice crystals form during freezing. This means that it is necessary to periodically beat the freezing mixture by hand, if you do not own an ice cream machine, which will do the job for you.

To Freeze Ice Cream By Hand

The following freezing times based on 3 cups ice cream are given as a guide. If making a larger quantity of ice cream, the times should be increased.

1. Set the freezer to maximum or fast freeze about 1 hour before you intend to freeze the mixture.
2. Make the ice cream as directed in the recipe.
3. Pour the mixture into a shallow non-metal, freezer container. Cover and freeze for about 3 hours or until just frozen all over. It will have a mushy consistency.
4. Spoon into a bowl and mash with a fork or flat whisk to break down the ice crystals. Work quickly so that the ice cream does not melt completely.
5. Return the mixture to the shallow container and freeze again for about 2 hours or until mushy.
6. Mash again as step 4. If any other ingredients are to be added, such as, nuts, chocolate chips, then fold it in at this stage.
7. Return to the freezer and freeze for about 3 hours or until firm.
8. Remove from the freezer and leave at room temperature for 20–30 minutes to soften before serving. (Do not forget to return the freezer setting to normal.) Ice cream can be stored in the freezer for up to 3 months.

Ice Cream Machines

An ice cream machine will freeze an ice cream or sherbet mixture and churn it at the same time, thus eliminating the physical effort. The results will be smooth and even textured.

There are several types of ice cream machine available, some use a salt solution and others a disc which needs to be frozen before use. Always follow manufacturer's instructions.

Generally speaking, the cooled mixture should be poured into the machine when the paddles are moving, otherwise it tends to freeze on to the base and sides of the bowl, stopping the paddles working. When making ice cream this way, if the recipe calls for whipped cream, it should be ignored. The cream can simply be added from the carton with the custard. When making sherbet, any egg white should be lightly whisked with a fork and added at the start of the churning process. Freezing time is usually about 20–30 minutes. The ice cream or sherbet should then be transferred to the freezer and frozen for 1–2 hours to allow the flavors to develop before serving. Soften them slightly at room temperature before serving.

It is vital to clean ice cream machines thoroughly after using to prevent development of bacteria. Wash bowls, tops, paddles and spatulas in the hottest water temperature possible. Be sure to wash and dry all parts which come into contact with salt to prevent corrosion.

VANILLA ICE CREAM

SERVES 4–6

This recipe is the basis for many ice creams. If preferred, cook custard in a bain marie or a bowl standing over a pan of simmering water.

1 vanilla pod or vanilla flavoring
1 cup milk
3 egg yolks
4–6 tablespoons superfine sugar
1 cup heavy cream

1. Split the vanilla pod to reveal the seeds. Put the milk and vanilla pod into a heavy-based saucepan and bring almost to the boil. (Alternatively, put the ingredients in a large bowl and microwave on HIGH for 3 minutes or until almost boiling.) Remove from the heat, cover and leave to infuse for about 20 minutes. (If using vanilla flavoring, add during step 3 below.)

2. Beat the egg yolks and sugar together in a bowl until well blended. Stir in the milk and strain back into the pan. Cook the custard over a gentle heat, stirring all the time, until it thickens very slightly. (Alternatively, microwave on LOW for 12–15 minutes or until slightly thickened, stirring frequently.) It is very important not to let the custard boil or it will curdle. Pour out into a bowl and leave to cool.

3. Whisk the cream into the cold custard mixture, with about $\frac{1}{4}$ teaspoon vanilla flavoring, if using (omit if vanilla pod already used).

4. Freeze the ice cream mixture by hand or in an ice cream machine (see opposite). Leave at cool room temperature for 20–30 minutes to soften before serving.

Previous page: BUTTERSCOTCH AND GINGER ICE CREAM (PAGE 220). Opposite, from left to right: STRAWBERRY AND MINT ICE CREAM, MANGO ICE CREAM (PAGE 218), BANANA AND DATE ICE CREAM, CHOCOLATE AND ORANGE LIQUEUR ICE CREAM.

VARIATIONS

Fruit Ice Cream   Add 1 cup fruit purée, sweetened to taste, to the cooled custard. Complete as before. Serves 4–6.

Chocolate and Orange Liqueur Ice Cream   Prepare Vanilla ice cream to the end of step 3, omitting the vanilla. Break up 4 squares semi sweet chocolate. Place in a bowl with 2 tablespoons orange-flavored liqueur and melt over a pan of simmering water. (Alternatively, microwave on LOW for 4–6 minutes, stirring occasionally.) Stir occasionally until smooth. Cool slightly. Add the chocolate to the custard mixture and complete as before. Serves 4–6.

Double Chocolate Ice Cream   Put the milk in a saucepan with 4 squares semi sweet chocolate and heat gently until the chocolate melts, then cook over high heat until almost boiling. Complete as for Vanilla ice cream to step 3. Freeze by hand to the end of step 5 (see page 216). Mash again, then stir in 2 squares semi sweet chocolate drops. Freeze until firm. Serves 4–6.

Chocolate Flake Ice Cream   Grate 2 squares chocolate. Stir half into the cooled custard with the cream. Complete as before. Stir in the remaining chocolate just before the ice cream is completely frozen. Serves 4–6.

Cinnamon Ice Cream   Add 2 teaspoons cinnamon and a cinnamon stick to the milk instead of the vanilla pod. Complete as before. Serves 4–6.

Gooseberry and Orange Ice Cream   Prepare Vanilla ice cream to the end of step 3, omitting the vanilla. Stew 1 pound gooseberries with 3 tablespoons icing sugar, the grated peel of 1 orange and 4 tablespoons orange juice. Purée, strain and cool. Add gooseberry purée and complete as before. Serves 6.

Banana and Date Ice Cream   Prepare Vanilla ice cream to the end of step 3, omitting the vanilla. Peel 1 pound bananas and purée in a blender or food processor with 3 tablespoons lemon juice and 2 tablespoons honey. Add the banana purée to the custard mixture. Freeze by hand to the end of step 5 (see page 216). Mash 1 cup roughly chopped dates (either fresh or dry), add to the banana mixture and complete as before. Serves 6–8.

Coconut Ice Cream   Finely chop 1 cup creamed coconut. Add to the milk and warm until dissolved, whisking until smooth, then add 2 tablespoons lemon juice. Complete as for Vanilla ice cream, omitting the vanilla. Serves 4–6.

Strawberry and Mint Ice Cream   Slice 1 pound strawberries. Sprinkle over 2 tablespoons icing sugar with 2 tablespoons lemon juice. Cover and macerate for about 1 hour. Purée in a blender or food processor, then press through a nylon strainer. For the custard, bring the milk to the boil with a handful of fresh mint. Cover and leave to infuse for at least 30 minutes. Strain. Complete as for Vanilla ice cream, omitting the vanilla and adding the strawberry mint purée at the end of step 3. Serves 6–8.

Mango Ice Cream   Cut the flesh from 2 medium ripe mangoes, discarding the skin and pit. Purée in a blender or food processor until smooth with the juice of 1 large lime, then press through a nylon strainer. Chill. Prepare Vanilla ice cream to the end of step 3, omitting the vanilla. Add the mango purée and complete as before. Serves 8.

Avocado and Pistachio Ice Cream   Prepare Vanilla ice cream to the end of step 3. Purée 1 medium ripe avocado with the finely grated peel and juice of 1 lime, 3 tablespoons icing sugar and the cream. Stir into the cooled custard. Fold in $\frac{1}{2}$ cup chopped pistachios, if freezing in an ice cream machine. If freezing by hand, freeze to the end of step 5 (see page 216), then mash and fold in the nuts. Freeze as before. Serves 6.

Peanut and Toffee Ice Cream   Put the milk in a saucepan with 3 tablespoons corn syrup and 2 tablespoons soft dark brown sugar. Heat gently until the sugar has dissolved, stirring occasionally. Complete the custard as before, then stir in 3 tablespoons crunchy peanut butter. Serve straight from the freezer. Serves 4–6.

Coffee Ice Cream   Add $\frac{1}{2}$ cup strong fresh coffee to the cooled custard or 2 teaspoons instant coffee granules to the milk instead of the vanilla pod. Complete as before. Serves 4–6.

BLACKCURRANT RIPPLE ICE CREAM

SERVES 8

Follow this basic method to make other ripple ice creams.

2 cups milk
1 vanilla pod
6 egg yolks
1$\frac{3}{4}$ cups sugar
2 cups whipping cream
1 pound blackcurrants, stalks removed

1. Put the milk and vanilla pod in a heavy-based pan and bring almost to the boil. Remove from the heat, cover and leave to infuse for at least 20 minutes.
2. Beat egg yolks and half of the sugar together in a bowl. Stir in the milk and strain back into the pan. Cook the custard over a gentle heat, stirring all the time, until thickened slightly. Do not boil. (Alternatively, microwave on LOW for 12–15 minutes, stirring occasionally. Do not boil.)
3. Pour into a chilled, shallow freezer container and leave to cool. Freeze by hand to the end of step 3 (see page 216).
4. Whip the cream until stiff. Mash the ice cream, then fold in the cream. Freeze for 2 hours until mushy.
5. Cook the blackcurrants, remaining sugar and 8 tablespoons water in a pan until soft. Purée in blender or food processor, the strain to remove the pips. Leave to cool.

6. Whisk the ice cream to a spreading consistency. Spoon a layer into freezer container. Pour over some of the blackcurrant purée. Continue to layer. Freeze until firm.
7. Leave at cool room temperature for 20–30 minutes to soften before serving.

PISTACHIO AND ALMOND ICE CREAM

SERVES 6

This is a very special ice cream, traditionally served at wedding banquets in India. It is best reserved for dinner parties, but only serve it after a fairly light main course as it is very rich.

5 cups milk
1 tablespoon rice flour
scant 1 cup sugar
$\frac{1}{4}$ cup pistachios
$\frac{2}{3}$ cup ground almonds
few drops of rose water
$\frac{1}{2}$ cup heavy cream
shredded pistachios, to decorate

1. Pour the milk into a large, heavy-based saucepan. Bring to the boil, then simmer gently for about 45 minutes or until the milk reduces by half. Cool slightly.
2. Mix the rice flour with a little of the cooled milk until smooth. Return to the pan and bring to the boil, stirring. Cook for 15 minutes, stirring frequently until the consistency of thin batter. Strain, add the sugar and stir until dissolved. Leave to cool.
3. Cover the pistachios with boiling water. Leave to stand for 1–2 minutes, then drain. Ease the skins off the pistachios with the fingers. Shred the nuts finely.
4. Stir the pistachios, ground almonds and rose water into the milk mixture. Whip the cream lightly, then fold into the mixture. Pour into a shallow freezer container.
5. Freeze the ice cream mixture by hand (see page 216) or in an ice cream machine.
6. Leave at cool room temperature for 20–30 minutes to soften before serving. Serve in scoops or cut into slices, decorated with shredded pistachios.

Opposite: PISTACHIO AND ALMOND ICE CREAM.

GRAPEFRUIT AND MINT ICE CREAM

SERVES 4–6

The ice cream will be smoothest if you can freeze the mixture in an ice cream machine, because it breaks down the ice crystals as it mixes the ice cream. Custard powder can be bought at specialist stores.

½ cup mint leaves
2 cups milk
scant ¼ cup custard powder
scant ½ cup superfine sugar
finely grated peel and juice of 2 pink grapefruit
½ cup heavy cream, lightly whipped

1. Reserve a few sprigs of mint for decoration and refrigerate these in a plastic bag. Roughly chop the remainder.

2. Put 1½ cups of the milk and the chopped mint into a heavy-based saucepan and bring almost to the boil. Remove from the heat, cover and leave to infuse for about 10 minutes.

3. Whisk the custard powder, sugar and remaining milk together in a bowl until smooth. Strain the milk on to the mixture, then return to the pan. Bring to the boil, stirring constantly, and cook for 1–2 minutes. (Alternatively, microwave on HIGH for 4–5 minutes, stirring frequently.) Pour into a bowl and leave to cool, whisking occasionally to prevent a skin forming.

4. Stir the grapefruit peel and 1 cup juice into the cold custard with the cream.

5. Freeze by hand (see page 216) or in an ice cream machine.

6. Leave at cool room temperature for 20–30 minutes to soften before serving. Scoop into individual serving dishes and decorate with the reserved mint sprigs.

GOOSEBERRY MARSHMALLOW ICE CREAM

SERVES 6

This ice cream is easy to make as it doesn't need churning.

2 cups white marshmallows
6 ounce can evaporated milk
1 pound fresh or frozen gooseberries, trimmed
scant ½ cup superfine sugar
½ cup heavy cream, lightly whipped
¼ cup corn syrup

1. Place the marshmallows and evaporated milk in a small heatproof bowl standing over a pan of simmering water to melt the marshmallows. (Alternatively, micro-

wave on HIGH for 1–2 minutes, stirring occasionally.) Stir until smooth, then leave to cool.

2. Place half the gooseberries and 2 tablespoons water in a pan. Cover and cook gently for about 5 minutes, or until the skins burst and the fruit softens. (Alternatively, microwave, covered, on HIGH for 4–5 minutes.)

3. Stir the sugar into the warm fruit, then purée in a blender or food processor until just smooth. Strain and leave to cool. Stir into the marshmallow mixture with the cream.

4. Spoon the ice cream mixture into a deep freezer container. Cover and freeze for about 5 hours until required. Do not churn.

5. Meanwhile, prepare the sauce. Place the remaining gooseberries, syrup and 2 tablespoons water in a small pan. Cover and cook gently until the gooseberries are soft. (Alternatively, microwave on HIGH, covered, for 4–5 minutes.) Strain and return to the pan.

6. Serve the ice cream straight from the freezer with the warm sauce.

BUTTERSCOTH AND GINGER ICE CREAM

SERVES 6–8

1 vanilla pod or vanilla
1 cup milk
scant ⅓ cup superfine sugar
3 tablespoons dark brown soft sugar
¼ stick butter
1 cup heavy cream
¼ cup stem ginger, finely chopped
⅓ cup meringues, roughly crushed
1 tablespoon brandy

FOR THE DECORATION
⅔ cup ratafia biscuits
slices of stem ginger

1. Follow the basic Vanilla ice cream recipe to the end of step 2. Divide the custard in half. Leave to cool.

2. Warm the brown sugar and butter together in a small pan until both have melted, then cook for 1 minute. Mix with half of the custard and leave to cool.

3. Freeze by hand (see page 216) to step 6, keeping the mixtures separate.

4. Lightly whip the cream. Fold half into the vanilla ice cream with the ginger and meringues. Freeze for about 1 hour until firm but not solid.

5. Fold the remaining cream and the brandy into the butterscotch mixture. Spoon into a 3½ cup loaf pan. Freeze for about 1¼ hours until firm.

6. Spoon the vanilla ice cream mixture evenly over the butterscotch layer and freeze until firm.

7. Dip the pan in warm water and unmold on to a freezerproof serving plate, mopping up any runny ice cream. Decorate with ratafias and stem ginger. Leave in the refrigerator for 10–15 minutes to soften before serving. Serve sliced.

Illustrated on pages 214–215

BLACKBERRY ICE CREAM

SERVES 6–8

Choose a mild honey like clover rather than one of the scented varieties.

1 pound blackberries, fresh or frozen
2 tablespoons thick honey
14½ ounce can evaporated milk, chilled
½ cup whipping cream
2 tablespoons orange-flavored liqueur
3 tablespoons lemon juice

1. Pick over the fresh blackberries, wash and drain well.
2. Place the blackberries and honey in a small saucepan. Cover and cook gently until the fruit is soft and pulpy. Purée in a blender or food processor, then rub through a nylon strainer. Leave to cool.
3. Whip the evaporated milk until thickened slightly. Whip the cream to the same consistency, then fold gently together. Stir in the cold fruit purée with the liqueur and lemon juice.
4. Freeze by hand (see page 216) or in an ice cream machine.
5. Leave at cool room temperature for 20–30 minutes to soften before serving. Scoop into individual glass dishes and serve with light cream and crisp cookies.

TUTTI FRUTTI ICE CREAM

SERVES 8–10

If you are making the ice cream with children in mind, use orange juice instead of rum and add ¼ cup chocolate chips to the mixture in step 5, when adding the macerated fruit.

6 tablespoons dark rum
½ cup white raisins
⅓ cup pitted dates
⅓ cup candied cherries
⅓ cup no-soak dry apricots
2 cups milk
1 vanilla pod or few drops of vanilla
6 egg yolks
scant 1 cup superfine sugar
2 cups heavy cream, whipped

1. Pour the rum into a jar or a bowl with a secure top. Add the raisins, then roughly snip the dates, cherries and apricots into the jar or bowl. Make sure all the fruit is coated with rum. Cover and leave to macerate for 2–3 hours, shaking or tossing occasionally until the rum is absorbed.
2. Put the milk and vanilla pod or flavoring into a heavy-based saucepan and bring almost to the boil. Remove from the heat, cover and leave to infuse for 15 minutes.

3. Beat the egg yolks and sugar together in a bowl until pale and thick. Stir in the milk and strain back into the pan. Cook the custard over a gentle heat, stirring all the time, until it coats the back of a wooden spoon. Do not boil. (Alternatively, microwave on LOW for 12–15 minutes, stirring occasionally. Do not boil.) Cover and leave to cool.
4. Pour into a chilled, shallow freezer container and freeze by hand to the end of step 5 (see page 216).
5. Whip the cream. Mash the ice cream, then fold in the cream and macerated fruit. Freeze until firm. (If using an ice cream machine, put the custard, cream and macerated fruit into the machine together.)
6. Leave at cool room temperature for 20–30 minutes to soften before serving.

QUICK RHUBARB ICE CREAM

SERVES 6

A pretty, pink ice cream made with kitchen ingredients. It is easy too because it doesn't need churning.

1¼ pounds can rhubarb in syrup
2 tablespoons redcurrant jelly
14 ounce can condensed milk
½ cup Greek yogurt

1. Purée the rhubarb, syrup and redcurrant jelly in a blender or food processor until really smooth. Stir the condensed milk and yogurt into the rhubarb mixture until evenly blended.
2. Pour into a shallow freezer container, don't use a metal dish. Freeze until firm, then overwrap and return to the freezer until required.
3. Leave at cool room temperature for 20–30 minutes to soften before serving.

PRUNE AND BRANDY ICE CREAM

SERVES 8

Serve this sumptuous ice cream with small, crisp cookies such as Langues de chats (see page 164).

1⅓ cups no-soak dry prunes
6 tablespoons brandy
2 tablespoons lemon juice
generous ½ cup superfine sugar
1½ cups milk
1 vanilla pod
5 egg yolks
generous ¼ stick butter
1 cup fresh brown breadcrumbs
2 tablespoons brownulated sugar
1½ whipping cream, whipped

1. Cut all the prune flesh off the pits, then snip into small pieces. Place in a bowl with the brandy, lemon juice and quarter of the sugar. Stir well to mix, then cover and leave to soak.

2. Put the milk and vanilla pod into a heavy-based pan and bring almost to the boil. Remove from the heat, cover and leave to infuse for 10 minutes.

3. Beat the egg yolks and remaining sugar together in a bowl until pale and frothy. Stir in the milk and strain back into the pan. Cook the custard over a gentle heat, stirring all the time, until thickened slightly. Do not boil. (Alternatively, microwave on LOW for 11–13 minutes, stirring occasionally. Do not boil.) Leave to cool.

4. Melt the butter in a small skillet, add the breadcrumbs and brownulated sugar and cook over a moderate heat, stirring frequently until the crumbs turn golden brown and become crisp. Immediately, spoon the mixture out on to a plate. Leave to cool.

5. Freeze the ice cream mixture by hand to the end of step 5 (see page 216). Mash the ice cream, then fold in the whipped cream, the soaked prunes with any juices, and the crumb mixture. Freeze until firm.

6. Leave at cool room temperature for 20–30 minutes to soften before serving.

VARIATION

Fig and Port Ice Cream Use 1⅓ cups no-soak dry figs in place of the prunes and 6 tablespoons port in place of the brandy.

SNOWCAP ICED PUDDING

SERVES 6–8

½ cup kirsch
4 tablespoons water
about 15 lady fingers
¾ quantity Chocolate flake ice cream (see page 217)
1½ cups ripe cherries, pitted and roughly chopped
¾ quantity Vanilla ice cream (see page 216)
½ cup heavy cream

1. Cut out a circle of wax paper and use it to line the base of a 5 cup ceramic bowl.

2. Mix the kirsch with the water and dip the lady fingers one at a time into the mixture. Use to line the sides of the bowl, trimming them to fit so that there are no gaps in between. Fill the base with leftover pieces. Refrigerate for 15 minutes.

3. Stir any remaining kirsch liquid into the chocolate ice cream and mash the ice cream well with a fork to soften it slightly and make it smooth without any ice crystals.

4. Spoon the chocolate ice cream into the bowl and work it up the sides of the fingers to the top of the bowl so that it forms an even layer. Freeze for about 2 hours until firm.

5. Mix the cherries into the vanilla ice cream and mash well with a fork as in step 3.

6. Spoon the vanilla ice cream into the center of the bowl and smooth it over the top so that it covers the chocolate ice cream and lady fingers. Cover with foil and freeze overnight.

7. To serve, whip the cream until it will just hold its shape. Run a knife around the inside of the bowl, then turn the ice cream out on to a well chilled serving plate.

8. Spoon the cream over the top and let it just start to run down the sides, then freeze immediately for about 15 minutes or until the cream has frozen solid. Serve straight from the freezer.

Opposite: PRUNE AND BRANDY ICE CREAM.

ROSE PETAL ICE CREAM

SERVES 4–6

A delicious ice cream scented with the fragrance of rose petals. To make a rose petal infusion, pick off the white bases, then clean, but do not wash, the petals from 2–4 fragrant roses. Bruise them with a scant ⅓ cup sugar, then pour on ½ cup boiling water. Leave overnight to infuse. Strain and use or freeze for use later.

1½ cups whpping cream
strip of lemon peel
1 egg
3 egg yolks
scant ⅓ cup superfine sugar
rose petal infusion (see recipe introduction)

1. Put the cream and strip of lemon peel in a pan and slowly bring to boiling point.
2. Beat the whole egg, egg yolks and sugar together in a bowl. Stir in the cream and strain back into the pan. Cook the custard over a gentle heat, stirring all the time, until it coats the back of a spoon. (Alternatively, microwave on LOW for 10–12 minutes, stirring occasionally.) Leave to cool.
3. Mix the ice cream mixture with the rose petal infusion. Freeze by hand or in an ice cream machine (see page 216).
4. Leave at cool room temperature for 20–30 minutes to soften before serving.

BROWN BREAD ICE CREAM

SERVES 6

The addition of lemon in this recipe for brown bread ice cream adds a pleasing tang.
Custard powder can be bought at specialist stores.

2 tablespoons custard powder
⅔ cup light brown soft sugar
1 cup milk
finely grated peel and juice of 1 lemon
½ cup heavy cream
½ cup light cream
1 egg white
2 tablespoons oil
¼ cup butter
2 cups fresh brown breadcrumbs

1. Mix the custard powder and half of the sugar to a smooth paste with a little milk. Bring the remaining milk almost to the boil in a pan. Stir into the custard powder, then return to the pan. Bring to the boil, stirring all the time, and cook for 2 minutes. (Alternatively, microwave on HIGH for 4–5 minutes, stirring frequently.) Pour out into a bowl and cool slightly.

2. Whisk in the lemon peel and 3 tablespoons juice. Leave to cool completely.
3. Whip the creams together until they just begin to hold their shape. Whisk the custard until smooth, then gently whisk in the creams. Stiffly whisk the egg white and fold in.
4. Freeze by hand up to step 5 (see page 216).
5. Meanwhile heat the oil and butter in a skillet, add the breadcrumbs and remaining sugar and cook over a moderate heat, stirring occasionally, until the crumbs brown well and begin to crisp. This can take as long as 15 minutes. Turn out into a bowl and leave to cool.
6. Mash the ice cream, then stir in the cold crumbs. Freeze until firm.
7. Leave at cool room temperature for 20–30 minutes to soften before serving.

DEEP FRIED ICE CREAM

SERVES 12

A fun dessert for children to enjoy. Do not attempt it with soft scoop ice cream!

3½ cups vanilla ice cream, cut into squares
2 eggs, beaten
3½ cups Graham Cracker crumbs
oil, for deep frying

1. Cut the ice cream into 2 inch squares.
2. Working quickly, coat the ice cream pieces in the beaten egg, then cover completely in crumbs.
3. Place on a cookie sheet and freeze for about 2 hours or until firm. Repeat step 2. Return to the freezer and freeze for at least 5 hours or overnight until really hard.
4. Heat the oil to 375°. Remove the ice cream from the freezer. Deep fry in batches for about 30 seconds. Serve immediately with a fruit sauce.

LEMON GERANIUM ICE CREAM

SERVES 4–6

Not only do lemon-scented geraniums provide a marvellous display of color all through the summer, but their leaves can be used to add a deliciously aromatic flavor to this unusual ice cream.

1 cup milk
10–12 lemon-scented geranium leaves, crushed
3 egg yolks
1 cup icing sugar, sifted
1 cup whipping cream
lemon-scented geranium leaves, to decorate

1. Put the milk and geranium leaves in a heavy-based pan and bring almost to the boil. (Alternatively, microwave on HIGH for 2–3 minutes until boiling.) Remove from the heat and leave to infuse for 30 minutes. Remove the geranium leaves.

2. Whisk the egg yolks and sugar together in a bowl until pale and frothy. Stir in the milk and strain back into the pan.

3. Cook the custard over a gentle heat, stirring all the time, until it coats the back of a wooden spoon. Do not boil. This takes about 20 minutes. (Alternatively, microwave on LOW for 10–12 minutes, stirring occasionally. Do not boil.)

4. Freeze by hand up to step 5 (see page 216).

5. Whip the cream until stiff. Mash the ice cream, then fold in the cream. Complete step 6, then freeze until firm.

6. Leave at cool room temperature for 20–30 minutes to soften before serving. Decorate with geranium leaves.

Below: LEMON GERANIUM ICE CREAM.

HERB SCENTED HONEY ICE CREAM

SERVES 4–6

This ice cream, with a luxurious velvety, smooth texture, is very rich, so serve in small portions after a light main course.

⅓ cup herb or wild flower honey
1½ cups heavy cream
sprig of rosemary
1 bay leaf
4 egg yolks

1. Put the honey, cream, rosemary and bay leaf in a pan and heat very gently until just boiling, stirring occasionally. (Alternatively, microwave in a large bowl on HIGH for 3–4 minutes.) Leave to infuse for 15 minutes.
2. Using an electric whisk, whisk the egg yolks in a bowl until pale and frothy.
3. Quickly bring the honey and cream mixture to boiling point again in the saucepan, or on HIGH for 1½–2 minutes. Remove the herbs, then pour on to the eggs, whisking all the time. Return to the pan and heat gently until thick enough to coat the back of a spoon. (Alternatively, microwave on LOW for 12–15 minutes until thickened, stirring frequently.) Leave to cool.
4. Freeze by hand or in an ice cream machine (see page 216). Serve straight from the freezer.

ORANGES EN SURPRISE

SERVES 6

An extremely easy and quick frozen pudding.

6 large oranges
1 cup heavy cream
½ cup icing sugar
6 tablespoons orange-flavored liqueur
6 tablespoons thick cut orange marmalade
fresh bay leaves or Chocolate rose leaves (see page 78), to decorate

1. Cut a slice off the top of each orange and reserve. Scoop out all the flesh, pips and juice from the oranges and discard (the juice can be used for drinking or in other recipes). Wash, then dry thoroughly. Set aside.
2. Whip the cream and icing sugar together in a bowl until standing in stiff peaks. Mix the liqueur and marmalade together, then fold into the cream until evenly distributed.
3. Spoon the cream mixture into the orange shells, mounding it up over the top. Freeze for at least 4 hours, preferably overnight (to allow the flavors to develop).
4. Serve straight from the freezer, decorated with reserved orange tops, bay leaves or chocolate rose leaves.

FROZEN YOGURT

SERVES 4–6

This ice will be more granular if made by hand rather than in an ice cream machine.

2 egg whites
2–4 tablespoons superfine sugar
2 cups Greek yogurt or thick Home-made plain yogurt (see page 181)
2 tablespoons milk
1 teaspoon vanilla

1. Whisk the egg whites and sugar together until stiff.
2. Mix the yogurt, milk and vanilla together in a bowl, then fold in the egg whites.
3. Freeze in an ice cream machine or by hand (page 216).

VARIATIONS

Frozen Fruit Yogurt   Add 1 cup fruit purée to the yogurt mixture, then complete as above.

Frozen Muesli Yogurt   Blend 1 cup muesli, 2 tablespoons milk and 2 tablespoons clear honey with the yogurt, then complete as above.

MAPLE AND PECAN ICE CREAM

SERVES 6

Serve this rich ice cream in small portions.

1¼ cups milk
½ cup maple syrup
5 egg yolks
scant ⅓ cup superfine sugar
¾ cup pecans
1 cup sour cream

1. Put the milk and maple syrup in a heavy-based pan and bring almost to the boil, stirring occasionally. (Alternatively, microwave on HIGH for 3–4 minutes.)
2. Using an electric mixer, whisk the egg yolks and sugar in a bowl until very pale and fluffy. Pour on the hot milk, whisking all the time.
3. Return to the pan and cook the mixture over a gentle heat, stirring all the time, until thick enough to coat the back of a spoon. (Alternatively, return to the bowl and microwave on LOW for 12–15 minutes, until thickened, stirring frequently.) Leave to cool.
4. Meanwhile, lightly roast the pecans under a hot broiler. Cool, then chop finely.
5. When the custard is cold, fold in the sour cream. If using an ice cream machine, fold in the nuts and freeze. If freezing by hand, freeze up to the end of step 5 (see page 216). Mash the ice cream, then stir in the nuts. Freeze until firm. Leave at cool room temperature for 20–30 minutes to soften before serving.

QUENELLES OF PRALINE ICE CREAM WITH APRICOT COULIS

SERVES 2

If you have difficulty in shaping the ice cream into quenelles, shape into scoops instead using an ice cream scoop.

FOR THE ICE CREAM

⅔ cup unblanched almonds
scant ¾ cup superfine sugar
3 eggs, separated
1 cup whipping cream
½ teaspoon vanilla

FOR THE APRICOT COULIS

1½ cups fresh apricots, halved
2 tablespoons Southern Comfort
sugar, to taste

1. Lightly oil a cookie sheet.

2. To make the praline, put the almonds and scant ⅓ cup of the sugar in a heavy-based saucepan. Heat gently until the sugar melts and caramelizes to a rich golden brown. Turn on to the prepared sheet and leave until cold and set. Break up with a rolling pin, then crush to a fine powder in a nut mill or food processor.

3. Put the egg yolks in a bowl over a pan of gently simmering water. Put the remaining sugar in a clean heavy-based pan. Add ½ cup cold water and heat gently until the sugar has dissolved. Increase the heat and boil for 3–5 minutes, without stirring, until a light syrup is formed. Remove from the heat and whisk into the egg yolks until thick, using an electric mixer.

4. Remove the bowl from the heat and whisk until cold. Stir in the cream, vanilla and praline. Stiffly whisk the egg whites, then fold into the mixture until evenly incorporated.

5. Freeze by hand or in an ice cream machine (see page 216).

6. To make the apricot coulis, put the apricots in a heavy-based pan with just enough water to cover the bottom. Cover and poach until soft. Press the flesh through a nylon strainer into a bowl. Stir in the Southern Comfort and sugar to taste. Cover and chill.

7. Leave the ice cream in the refrigerator for 30 minutes to soften. Shape into six quenelles with dessertspoons. Arrange three quenelles on each individual plate and return to the freezer. When ready to serve, remove the plates from the freezer and flood with the chilled apricot coulis.

Above: QUENELLES OF PRALINE ICE CREAM WITH APRICOT COULIS.

COMPLETE BOOK OF DESSERTS

Meringue Surprise Cassis

SERVES 6–8

Use store-bought meringues or make your own following the recipe on page 200, using half the ingredients.

1 tablespoon arrowroot
6 egg yolks
scant ⅓ cup vanilla sugar
1 cup milk
1 cup heavy cream
2 egg whites
16 baby meringues

FOR THE SAUCE

3 cups frozen blackcurrants
juice of 1 lemon
½ cup icing sugar or to taste
3 tablespoons blackcurrant-flavored liqueur

1. Line the base of a 6 inch charlotte mold, soufflé dish or cake pan with non-stick wax paper.
2. Put the arrowroot in a bowl and blend to a paste with the egg yolks and vanilla sugar.
3. Put the milk in a pan and bring almost to the boil. Stir slowly into the egg yolk mixture.
4. Stand the bowl over a pan of simmering water and stir until the custard is thick enough to coat the back of a wooden spoon. Remove from the heat, cover the surface of the custard closely with plastic wrap, to prevent a skin forming, and leave for 1 hour.
5. Whip the cream until it just holds its shape, then fold into the cold custard. Whisk the egg whites until stiff, then fold in until evenly incorporated.
6. Crush ten of the meringues roughly and fold into the custard mixture until evenly distributed.
7. Pour the custard mixture into the prepared mold. Cover, then freeze for at least 4 hours or overnight until solid.
8. To make the sauce, reserve a few whole frozen blackcurrants for decoration. Put the remaining frozen blackcurrants and the lemon juice in a heavy-based pan and heat gently until defrosted, shaking the pan constantly. Cook gently for 10 minutes, then tip into a strainer and press with the back of a spoon to extract as much juice as possible.
9. Sift the icing sugar into the blackcurrant juice, then stir in the liqueur. Leave until cold, taste and add more sugar if liked.
10. To serve, run a knife around the dessert in the mold, then carefully turn out on to a serving plate. Remove the paper.
11. Pour a little of the sauce over the dessert, then decorate with the reserved blackcurrants and the remaining meringues. Serve at once, with the remaining sauce handed separately.

Christmas Pudding Ice Cream

SERVES 4–6

All the nicest things that go into an English Christmas pudding—dry fruit, rum, port and spices—are used in this unusual recipe.

1 cup mixed no-soak dry fruit
4 tablespoons light or dark rum
2 tablespoons port
finely grated peel and juice of 1 orange
1½ cups light cream
3 egg yolks
generous ½ cup superfine sugar
½ cup whipping cream
1 teaspoon mixed spice

1. Mix the dry fruit, rum, port and orange peel and juice together in a bowl. Leave to macerate overnight.
2. Gently heat the light cream in a small saucepan to simmering point. (Alternatively, microwave on HIGH for 5 minutes.)
3. Whisk the egg yolks and sugar together in a bowl until pale and thick. Gradually pour on the hot cream, stirring continuously.
4. Strain the mixture into a medium heavy-based or double saucepan and cook for about 20 minutes over a gentle heat, stirring all the time, until it coats the back of a wooden spoon. Do not boil. (Alternatively, microwave on LOW for 12–15 minutes, stirring frequently.) Leave to cool.
5. Whip the cream until stiff, then fold into the cold custard with the dry fruit mixture and mixed spice.
6. Freeze by hand to the end of step 6 (see page 216) or in an ice cream machine.
7. Beat the ice cream again, then turn into a 4 cup bombe mold. Cover and freeze for a further 2 hours until firm.
8. Dip briefly in hot water to unmold, then turn out on to a cold serving plate. Transfer to the refrigerator to soften for 30 minutes before serving.

Opposite: CHRISTMAS PUDDING ICE CREAM.

RASPBERRY REDCURRANT FREEZE

SERVES 4–6

Serve this pretty ice cream with a red fruit salad and crisp cookies.

3 cups fresh or frozen raspberries

8 ounce jar redcurrant jelly

1 cup sour cream

1. Put the raspberries and jelly in a saucepan and heat gently, stirring frequently, until the fruit is soft. (Alternatively, microwave on HIGH for 4–5 minutes, stirring occasionally.)

2. Purée in a blender or food processor, then strain to remove the pips. Chill for about 1 hour until cold.

3. Whisk in the sour cream. Freeze by hand or in an ice cream machine (see page 216).

4. Leave at cool room temperature for 20–30 minutes to soften before serving.

ICED RASPBERRY MOUSSE

SERVES 6–8

2 cups raspberries, hulled

2 egg yolks

scant ⅓ cup superfine sugar

1½ teaspoons gelatin

½ cup whipping cream

1 egg white

1 tablespoon orange-flavored liqueur

FOR THE DECORATION

mint leaves

raspberries, hulled

1. To purée the raspberries, press through a strainer.

2. Using an electric mixer, whisk the egg yolks and sugar together in a bowl until very thick. Slowly add the raspberry purée and continue whisking until the mixture is very thick again.

3. Sprinkle the gelatin over 2 tablespoons water in a small bowl and leave to soak for 2–3 minutes. Place the bowl over a saucepan of simmering water and stir until dissolved. (Alternatively, microwave on HIGH for 30 seconds or until dissolved.)

4. Lightly whip the cream. Whisk the egg white. Stir the dissolved gelatin, cream, egg white and liqueur into the raspberry mixture.

5. Divide between six to eight small freezerproof serving dishes and freeze for at least 5 hours until firm.

6. Transfer to the refrigerator for 30–45 minutes to soften before serving. Decorate with mint leaves and surround with raspberries.

To freeze: pack at the end of step 5.

ICED LEMON MOUSSE

SERVES 6

1 teaspoon gelatin

3 eggs, separated

generous ½ cup superfine sugar

finely grated peel and juice of 2 lemons

½ cup plain yogurt

FOR THE DECORATION

lemon twists

chopped pistachios

1. Sprinkle the gelatin over 2 tablespoons water in a small bowl and leave to soak for 2–3 minutes. Place the bowl over a pan of simmering water and stir until dissolved. (Alternatively, microwave on HIGH for 30 seconds or until dissolved.)

2. Whisk the egg yolks, sugar and lemon peel together in a bowl until thick, using an electric mixer if possible.

3. Gradually add the lemon juice, about 6 tablespoons to the egg yolk mixture, whisking well between each addition. Keep the mixture as thick as possible. Stir the dissolved gelatin into the lemon mixture.

4. Stand the bowl in a roasting pan of iced water and stir occasionally until the lemon mixture begins to set.

5. Whisk one egg white until stiff. Add to the lemon mixture with the yogurt.

6. Gently pour the mixture into six small custard pots and freeze. When firm, overwrap and return to the freezer.

7. Ten minutes only before serving, transfer the lemon mousse to the refrigerator to soften. Decorate with lemon twists and chopped pistachios.

ICED ORANGE SABAYON

SERVES 6

6 egg yolks

⅔ cup brownulated sugar

6 tablespoons orange-flavored liqueur

scant 1 cup unsweetened orange juice

Chocolate leaves (see page 78), to decorate

1. Beat the egg yolks and sugar together in a bowl until pale and creamy. Stir in the liqueur and orange juice.

2. Transfer the mixture to a medium heavy-based saucepan and stir over low heat until the mixture thickens and just coats the back of the spoon. Do not boil. (Alternatively, microwave on LOW for 4–6 minutes or until just thickened, stirring frequently. Do not boil.)

3. Pour the mixture into six individual freezerproof soufflé dishes or custard pots and leave to cool for at least 30 minutes. Freeze for 3–4 hours until firm. Wrap in plastic wrap and return to the freezer.

4. Serve straight from the freezer, decorated with chocolate leaves.

CASSATA

SERVES 8

Recipes for Cassata are confusing, because there are two different types. The recipe given here is for Cassata Gelata, which is an ice cream bombe. The other type is known as Cassata Siciliana and is a chilled dessert made from layers of ricotta cheese and sponge cake. Making Cassata is not difficult but it does take several hours. Start the recipe at least 2 days before you intend to serve it; complete up to the end of step 6 on day one, then complete the remaining steps on day two. Freeze the Cassata overnight ready for serving the next day.

1 cup milk
3 egg yolks
scant $\frac{1}{2}$ cup sugar
2 squares semi sweet chocolate
1 cup ripe strawberries, hulled
$\frac{1}{4}$ teaspoon vanilla
1 cup heavy cream
red food coloring
$\frac{1}{8}$ cup pistachios
4 candied cherries, cut into small pieces
2 tablespoons candied fruit
2 tablespoons orange-flavored liqueur

1. Set the freezer to fast freeze. Bring the milk to boiling point in a pan. Beat the egg yolks and sugar together in a bowl until thick and pale in color.

2. Stir in the milk and strain back into the pan. Cook the custard over a gentle heat, stirring all the time, until it thickens slightly. Do not boil. Leave to cool for 30 minutes.

3. Break the chocolate into small pieces. Place in a bowl standing over a pan of simmering water and heat until the chocolate melts. (Alternatively, microwave on LOW for 2–3 minutes or until melted, stirring occasionally.) Add two thirds of the cool custard to the chocolate, stirring to blend.

4. Purée the strawberries in a blender or food processor. Strain into the remaining custard and stir in the vanilla.

5. In a separate bowl, lightly whip half of the cream. Stir two thirds of this through the cold chocolate mixture and the remainder into the strawberry, adding red food coloring to the latter if necessary.

6. Pour the mixtures into separate shallow freezer containers and freeze by hand to step 5 (see page 216).

7. Put a 4 cup ceramic bowl or bombe mold in the freezer. Leave the chocolate ice cream at cool room temperature for 20 minutes to soften slightly. Line the bowl evenly with chocolate ice cream, using a round-bowled spoon. Freeze for about 1 hour until firm.

8. Take the strawberry ice cream out of the freezer and leave at cool room temperature for 20–30 minutes to soften slightly. Work the strawberry ice cream with a spoon to make it more pliable (it will be firmer than the chocolate ice cream), then use to make a second lining of ice cream in the bowl. Freeze, covered, for 1–2 hours until firm.

9. Meanwhile pour boiling water over the pistachios. Leave to stand for 10 minutes, then skin and chop roughly. Place the cherries, nuts, fruit and liqueur in a bowl. Cover and macerate for 2 hours.

10. In a separate bowl, whip the remaining cream until stiff, then fold in the cherry mixture. Spoon into the centre of the cassata. Cover and freeze for 4 hours or until firm.

11. Dip the bowl briefly in hot water to loosen the cassata. Slip a knife around the top edge to ensure it is loose and invert on to a serving plate. Leave in the refrigerator for about 40 minutes to soften before serving. Serve the cassata in wedges.

FROZEN BRANDY CREAMS

SERVES 4

This works equally well with other liqueur flavors, such as almond or coffee.

4 egg yolks
$\frac{3}{4}$ cup superfine sugar
6 tablespoons brandy
$\frac{1}{2}$ cup heavy cream
coffee dragées, to decorate

1. Mix the egg yolks, sugar and brandy together in a medium bowl, stirring well.

2. Place the bowl over a pan of simmering water. Stir the mixture all the time for about 15 minutes until it thickens slightly and will just coat the back of the spoon. Do not overheat or the eggs may curdle. Remove from the heat and leave to cool for 30 minutes. (Alternatively, microwave on LOW for 4–6 minutes or until thickened. Cool.)

3. Lightly whip the cream and stir half into the cold brandy mixture. Pour into four small freezerproof soufflé dishes or custard pots. Cover and freeze for at least 5 hours until firm.

4. To serve, decorate each pot with a whirl of the remaining whipped cream, then top with a coffee dragée. Serve immediately.

PERNOD PARFAIT

SERVES 8

Small molds of frozen cream flavored with aniseed and topped with a crisp, lacy cookie.

4 egg yolks
1 cup Stock syrup (see page 237)
2 tablespoons Pernod
1½ cups whipping cream
½ cup whipping cream, to decorate

FOR THE COOKIES
¼ stick butter or margarine
2 tablespoons sugar
1 tablespoon corn syrup
¼ cup All Purpose flour
½ teaspoon Pernod

1. Using an electric mixer, beat the egg yolks in a bowl until pale and fluffy. Meanwhile, bring the syrup back up to boiling point. Pour the hot syrup in a thin stream on to the egg yolks and continue beating. Beat until the mixture is cool. Beat in the Pernod.

2. Whip the cream until it just holds its shape, then fold into the egg mixture. Pour into eight freezerproof serving bowls or custard pots. Cover and freeze for 5 hours or overnight until firm.

3. Meanwhile to make the cookies, line 2 cookie sheets with non-stick wax paper. Melt the butter, sugar and syrup over a low heat in a small pan. Remove from the heat and stir in the flour and Pernod.

4. Put about 16 small spoonfuls of the mixture, spread well apart on the prepared cookie sheets.

5. Bake in the oven at 350° for 7–10 minutes until bubbly and golden. Leave to cool slightly, then remove from the paper and pinch into petal shapes. Store in an airtight container until ready to serve.

6. To serve, whip the cream until it just holds its shape, then pipe a swirl on to each parfait. Top each with a cookie. Serve immediately with the remaining cookies.

INDIVIDUAL COFFEE BOMBES WITH TRUFFLE CENTERS

SERVES 6

These delicious bombes with a surprise center will not fail to impress. Substitute the coffee ice cream with any of the others on pages 217–218, if preferred.

1½ quantity Coffee ice cream (see page 218)

FOR THE FILLING
½ cup cake crumbs
scant ⅓ cup ground almonds
2 squares semi sweet chocolate
3 tablespoons heavy cream
2 tablespoons rum or brandy
Chocolate leaves or caraque, to decorate (see page 78)

1. Set the freezer to fast freeze. Put six ¾ cup individual freezerproof pie or pudding molds in the freezer to chill.

2. Leave the ice cream at room temperature for 20–30 minutes or until soft enough to spread.

3. Meanwhile, to make the truffle filling, mix the cake crumbs and almonds together in a bowl. Put the chocolate and cream in a small bowl standing over a pan of simmering water and stir until melted. (Alternatively, microwave on LOW for 3–4 minutes or until melted, stirring occasionally.) Add the chocolate mixture to the crumb and almond mixture with the rum. Mix well.

4. Spread the softened ice cream around the base and sides of the pie molds, leaving a cavity in the center for the truffle mixture. Freeze for 1 hour or until firm.

5. Fill the center of each mold with the truffle mixture and level the surface. Cover and freeze for 1 hour or until firm.

6. To serve, dip the molds briefly in hot water, then unmold on to serving plates. Return to the freezer for 10 minutes to firm up. Decorate and serve.

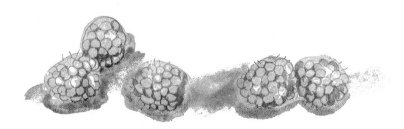

Above: INDIVIDUAL COFFEE BOMBE WITH TRUFFLE CENTER.
Below: PERNOD PARFAIT.

APRICOT AND RAISIN BOMBE

SERVES 8

A delicious fruit and nut filled bombe served with an apricot sauce.

FOR THE BOMBE

⅓ cup no-soak dry apricots
¾ cup raisins, roughly chopped
½ cup whole blanched almonds, roughly chopped
4 tablespoons medium dry sherry
1½ cups milk
3 eggs
scant ½ cup superfine sugar
1 cup whipping cream
½ cup meringues, lightly crushed

FOR THE SAUCE

1 cup no-soak dry apricots
1 cup orange juice
1 bay leaf
1 teaspoon lemon juice

1. Line the base of a 5½ cup ceramic bowl with wax paper.

2. Snip the apricots into small pieces and place in a bowl. Add the raisins, almonds and sherry. Cover and leave to soak for 2–3 hours.

3. Meanwhile gently heat the milk in a pan. Lightly whisk the eggs and sugar together in a bowl. Stir in the milk and strain back into the pan. Cook the custard over a gentle heat, stirring all the time, until it thickens slightly and just coats the back of the spoon. Do not boil. Leave to cool.

4. Lightly whip the cream and fold into the cool custard. Freeze by hand up to step 5 (see page 216). Mash the ice cream, then stir in the fruit mixture and liquor and crushed meringue.

5. Spoon the mixture into the prepared bowl. Return to the freezer and freeze for about 4½ hours or until firm.

6. Meanwhile to make the apricot sauce, place the apricots, orange juice and bay leaf in a small pan. Bring to the boil, cover and simmer gently for about 10 minutes. Cool slightly, remove the bay leaf, then purée in a blender or food processor until smooth. Add the lemon juice and pour into a container to cool. Chill.

7. To serve, dip the bowl briefly in hot water, then invert on to a serving plate. Serve with the chilled apricot sauce.

To freeze: pack the bombe and sauce separately. Defrost the sauce overnight at cool room temperature. Chill before use.

FROZEN CHESTNUT BOMBE

SERVES 8–10

It is important to return the unmolded bombe to the freezer for 10 minutes (see step 5), it helps the cream to adhere to the sides of the bombe.

FOR THE BOMBE

1 quantity Vanilla ice cream (see page 216)
10 ounce can whole chestnuts, drained
2 tablespoons icing sugar
½ cup sour cream
1⅓ cups macaroons
3 tablespoons rum

FOR THE DECORATION

1 cup whipping cream
1 tablespoon rum
marrons glacés or dragées
herb leaves

1. To make the bombe, remove the ice cream from the freezer and leave at cool room temperature for 45 minutes to soften.

2. Purée the chestnuts, icing sugar and sour cream in a blender or food processor until smooth. Add the ice cream and purée.

3. Roughly crush the macaroons and sprinkle with the rum. Fold into the ice cream mixture.

4. Pour into a 4 cup bombe mold or ceramic bowl. Cover and freeze for at least 5 hours or until firm.

5. To serve, dip the mold or bowl briefly in hot water, then unmold on to a serving plate. Return to the freezer for 10 minutes.

6. To make the decoration, whip the cream and rum until stiff. Spoon into a pastry tube fitted with a large star tip. Pipe around the base of the bombe and up and over the sides. Decorate with marrons glacés or dragées and herb leaves. Leave in the refrigerator for 1 hour to soften before serving.

Above: FROZEN CHESTNUT BOMBE. Below: FROZEN CHOCOLATE AND MANGO CAKE (PAGE 236).

FROZEN CHOCOLATE AND MANGO CAKE

SERVES 8–10

Use this as a basic recipe to make other ice cream cakes of your choice.

---

1 chocolate jelly roll sponge, made with 2 eggs (see page 125)

½ quantity Mango ice cream (see page 218)

¼ quantity Chocolate flake ice cream (see page 217)

FOR THE DECORATION

Chocolate caraque (see page 78)

mango slices

---

1. Trim the jelly roll and cut into three pieces the width and length of a 4 cup loaf pan.
2. Take the ice creams out of the freezer and leave at room temperature for 30 minutes or until soft enough to spread. Spread half the mango ice cream into the loaf pan and level the surface.
3. Place one piece of roll on top of the mango ice cream in the loaf pan. Spread with the chocolate flake ice cream. Return to the freezer for 15 minutes to firm.
4. Place a second piece of roll on top of the chocolate flake ice cream. Spread with the remaining mango ice cream. Top with the last piece of roll. Cover and freeze for at least 3 hours or until firm.
5. One hour before serving, dip the pan briefly in hot water then unmold on to a serving plate. Leave in the refrigerator for 1 hour before serving. Decorate with chocolate caraque and slices of mango. Serve sliced.

Illustrated on page 234

FROZEN CHOCOLATE TERRINE WITH BRANDIED PRUNES

SERVES 14

1⅓ cups no-soak pitted, dry prunes

½ cup cold tea

3 tablespoons brandy

8 squares semi sweet chocolate

4 eggs, separated

¾ cup icing sugar, sifted

⅓ cup cocoa, sifted

1 cup heavy cream

---

1. Place the prunes, tea and brandy in a bowl and leave to soak for 3–4 hours or overnight. Drain, reserving the liquid, then roughly chop the prunes.
2. Break the chocolate into small pieces. Place in a small bowl standing over a pan of simmering water and heat until the chocolate melts. (Alternatively, microwave on LOW for 6–8 minutes or until melted, stirring occasionally.) Leave to cool.
3. Using an electric mixer, whisk the egg whites and icing sugar together in a bowl to make a stiff meringue. Fold in the cocoa.
4. Whip the heavy cream until it just holds soft peaks. Whisk the egg yolks until pale and fluffy, then whisk in the chocolate.
5. Carefully fold the egg yolk and chocolate mixture into the meringue, followed by the cream. Fold in the soaked prunes and the reserved liquid.
6. Pour the mixture into a 4 cup terrine. Cover and freeze for at least 5 hours or until firm.
7. To serve, dip the terrine briefly in hot water, then turn out on to a serving plate. Serve cut into slices with light cream.

ICED BLACK FOREST GÂTEAU

SERVES 8

The cake quickly softens at room temperature to give a delicious base for the gâteau.

FOR THE SPONGE

2 eggs

scant ½ cup superfine sugar

½ cup All Purpose flour

⅓ cup cocoa, sifted

FOR THE FILLING AND DECORATION

16 ounce can pitted cherries

2 tablespoons kirsch

1 quantity Vanilla ice cream (see page 216) or 2 cups soft vanilla ice cream

⅓ cup roasted slivered almonds

Chocolate curls (see page 78)

---

1. Grease an 8 inch round cake pan and line the base with wax paper. Dust out with a little sugar and flour.
2. To make the sponge, using an electric mixer, beat the eggs and sugar in a bowl until pale and thick. Gently fold in the flour and cocoa. Spoon into the pan.
3. Bake in the oven at 350° for about 30 minutes or until firm to the touch. Turn out on to a wire rack to cool.
4. To make the filling, drain the cherries, reserving the juice. Mix 6 tablespoons juice with the kirsch. Finely chop the cherries.
5. Cut the cake into two layers and place the base on a flat plate. Spoon on half the kirsch juices and all the cherries. Top with spoonfuls of ice cream, then the second layer of cake and remaining juices. Sprinkle with slivered almonds and chocolate curls.
6. Return immediately to the freezer and freeze for at least 3 hours. Overwrap once firm. Leave at cool room temperature for about 40 minutes to soften before serving. Cut into wedges.

Granita All' Arancia

(ORANGE WATER ICE)

SERVES 6

This light, refreshing iced dessert makes the perfect finale to a rich entertaining menu.

scant 1 cup sugar
1½ cups water
10 large oranges
1½ lemons

1. To make the sugar syrup, place the sugar and water in a medium saucepan. Heat gently until the sugar dissolves, then boil gently for 10 minutes without stirring.
2. Meanwhile, using a potato peeler, thinly pare off the peel from four of the oranges and the lemons. Add the orange and lemon peel to the sugar syrup and leave until cold.
3. Squeeze the juice from the four oranges and the lemons. Strain into a measuring container—there should be 1¼ cups.
4. Strain the cold syrup into a shallow freezer container and stir in the fruit juices. Mix well. Cover and freeze for about 4 hours until mushy in texture.
5. Remove from the freezer and turn the frozen mixture into a bowl. Beat well with a fork to break down the ice crystals. Return to the freezer container and freeze for at least 4 hours or until firm.
6. Meanwhile, using a serrated knife, cut away the peel and pith from the remaining oranges.
7. Slice the oranges down into thin rings, ease out and discard any pips. Place the oranges in a serving bowl, cover tightly with plastic wrap and refrigerate until serving time.
8. Place the water ice in the refrigerator for 45 minutes to soften before serving. Serve with the fresh orange slices.

VARIATIONS

Granita al Limone (*Lemon Water Ice*) With 6–8 lemons as a basis, follow the recipe using the pared peel of four lemons and enough juice to give 1¼ cups.

Granita di Fragole (*Strawberry Water Ice*) With 1½ pounds strawberries, puréed and strained, and the pared peel and juice of 1 orange as a basis, follow the recipe, using the strawberry purée and orange juice instead of the orange and lemon juices in step 3.

Granita di Caffé (*Coffee Water Ice*) Put 2 tablespoons sugar and ⅔ cup finely ground Italian coffee in a jug. Pour over 2 cups boiling water and leave to stand for 1 hour. Strain the coffee through a filter paper or cheesecloth, then follow the recipe after the straining in step 4.

Granita di Pescanoce (*Nectarine Water Ice*) Poach 2 pounds halved ripe nectarines in the syrup. Remove the pits, then purée until smooth. Press through a strainer. Freeze as step 4 above, then add 2 tablespoons peach brandy. Finish as above.

Sherbets

Stock Syrup Put generous ½ cup sugar in a heavy-based saucepan. Add 1 cup water and heat gently until the sugar dissolves. Do not stir the ingredients but occasionally loosen the sugar from the base of the pan to help it dissolve. Bring to the boil and boil for 2 minutes. Cool and use as required in the following recipes. *Makes about 1¼ cups.*

Lemon Sherbet

SERVES 3–4

1¼ cups Stock syrup (see above)
pared peel and juice of 3 lemons
1 egg white

1. Prepare the stock syrup as far as dissolving the sugar. Add the lemon peel and simmer gently for about 10 minutes. Leave to cool completely.
2. Stir in the lemon juice and strain into a shallow freezer container. Cover and freeze for about 3 hours until mushy.
3. Whisk the egg white until stiff. Turn the sherbet into a bowl and beat gently to break down the ice crystals. Fold in the egg white.
4. Return to the freezer container, cover and freeze for 4 hours or until firm.
5. Leave in the refrigerator for about 40 minutes to soften slightly before serving.

To freeze in an ice cream machine, see page 216.

VARIATION

Orange or Lime Sherbet Make as above, using the pared peel and juice of 2 oranges or 5 limes instead of the lemons.

Pear Sherbet

SERVES 6

A little kirsch spooned over this sherbet at serving time enhances the subtle flavor of the pears.

1½ pounds ripe pears, peeled and cored
1¼ cups Stock syrup (see above)
1 cup sour cream

1. Poach the pears in the stock syrup in a pan for 15–20 minutes or until tender. Leave to cool. Purée in a blender or food processor.
2. Freeze as for Lemon sherbet, adding the sour cream when you would add the egg whites. Serve straight from the freezer.

VARIATION

Apple Sherbet Make as above using 1½ pounds sweet apples.

MIXED BERRY SHERBET

SERVES 6

Frozen redcurrants can be used instead of fresh and they do not need defrosting beforehand.

1 cup redcurrants, stalks removed
1 cup strawberries, hulled
$\frac{1}{2}$ cup Stock syrup (see page 237)
$\frac{1}{2}$ cup sparkling white wine
2 egg whites

1. Place the redcurrants, strawberries and 2 table-spoons water in a pan. Cover and cook for about 10 minutes until soft. Press the blackcurrants and strawberries through a strainer to form a purée.
2. Stir the stock syrup and wine into the fruit purée. Freeze as Lemon sherbet, adding the egg whites as directed.

PLUM SHERBET

SERVES 6

Any variety of sweet plum can be used.

$1\frac{1}{4}$ pounds purple plums, halved and pitted
$1\frac{1}{2}$ cups Stock syrup (see page 237)
1 tablespoon lemon juice
1 egg white

1. Add the plums to the stock syrup in a pan. Cover and simmer for about 20 minutes or until very soft. Cool, then purée in a blender or a food processor. Press through a nylon strainer to remove the skins.
2. Stir in the lemon juice. Freeze as for Lemon sherbet, adding the egg white as directed.

PASSION FRUIT SHERBET

SERVES ABOUT 6

This sherbet has a very exotic taste.

10 medium passion fruit
4 tablespoons orange juice
$1\frac{1}{2}$ cups Stock syrup (see page 237)
2 egg whites

1. Halve the passion fruit and scoop out the flesh and pips. Purée briefly in a blender or food processor with the orange juice. Press through a nylon strainer—there should be about 1 cup juice.
2. Add to the stock syrup. Freeze as for Lemon sherbet, adding the egg whites as directed.
3. After 1 hour, check and refold in the egg whites, if necessary, as the mixture tends to separate.

PINEAPPLE SHERBET

SERVES 4

Stock syrup made with a generous $\frac{1}{2}$ cup sugar and $\frac{1}{2}$ cup water (see page 237)
$1\frac{1}{2}$ cups pineapple juice
juice of 1 orange
1 egg white

1. Mix the stock syrup, pineapple juice and orange juice together.
2. Freeze as for Lemon sherbet, adding the egg white as directed.

POMEGRANATE SHERBET

SERVES 4

A marvelously fragrant sherbet.

4–5 pomegranates
$1\frac{1}{2}$ cups Stock syrup (see page 237)
1 egg white

1. Squeeze the juice from the pomegranates. You need at least 1 cup.
2. Mix with the stock syrup. Freeze as for Lemon sherbet, adding the egg white as directed.

MANGO SHERBET

SERVES 8

2 large ripe mangoes
$1\frac{1}{2}$ cups Stock syrup (see page 237)
juice of 1 large lime
1 egg white

1. Peel the mangoes and remove the flesh from the pit. Purée the flesh in a blender or food processor. Press through a strainer. Mix with the stock syrup and lime juice.
2. Freeze as for Lemon sherbet, adding the egg white as directed. Serve straight from the freezer.

Above: RASPBERRY SHERBET (PAGE 241). Center: MANGO SHERBET. Below: PINEAPPLE SHERBET.

ROSE GERANIUM SHERBET

SERVES 4

You will only need a small handful of rose geranium leaves. Do not use too many—they have a strong flavor.

small handful rose geranium leaves
1½ cups Stock syrup (see page 237)
juice of 1–2 small lemons
1 egg white

1. Add the rose geranium leaves to the stock syrup in a pan. Bring quickly to the boil, then leave to infuse.
2. When the syrup is cold, remove the leaves and add lemon juice to taste. Freeze as for Lemon sherbet, adding the egg white as directed.

BLACKCURRANT SHERBET

SERVES 8

One of the strongest flavored sherbets, this is ideal after spicy curries.

1 pound blackcurrants, stalks removed
2 tablespoons blackcurrant-flavored liqueur
2 tablespoons lemon juice
1½ cups Stock syrup (see page 237)
2 egg whites

1. Blend the blackcurrants, liqueur, lemon juice and half the stock syrup together in a blender or food processor. Press through a nylon strainer.
2. Add the remaining stock syrup. Freeze as for Lemon sherbet, adding the egg whites as directed.

GUAVA SHERBET

SERVES 4–6

The pink fleshed variety of guava has the best flavor and color for sherbets.

about 1¼ pounds ripe guavas
1¼ cups Stock syrup (see page 237)
juice of 1 lime
1 egg white

1. Peel the guavas and roughly chop the flesh. Purée the flesh in a blender or food processor. Press through a nylon strainer to remove the pips.
2. Mix with the stock syrup and lime juice. Freeze as for Lemon sherbet, adding the egg white as directed. Serve straight from the freezer.

KIWI FRUIT SHERBET

SERVES 6

Serve this sherbet decorated with slices of kiwi fruit.

6 kiwi fruit, peeled
½ cup Stock syrup (see page 237)
2 egg whites

1. Purée the kiwi fruit and syrup in a blender or food processor. Press through a strainer to remove the pips.
2. Freeze as for Lemon sherbet, adding the egg whites as directed.

MINT SHERBET

SERVES 4–6

Serve this as a cool, refreshing dessert or as a palate cleanser between courses.

4 sprigs of mint
1½ cups Stock syrup (see page 237)
juice of 2 lemons
1 tablespoon finely chopped fresh mint
1 egg white

1. Add the mint sprigs to the stock syrup in a pan. Bring to the boil, then leave to infuse.
2. When the syrup is cold, strain it then add the lemon juice and chopped mint. Freeze as for Lemon sherbet, adding the egg white as directed.

APRICOT AND MINNEOLA SHERBET

SERVES 8

Minneolas are one of the new varieties of 'easy peelers'. You can also use tangerines.

two 15 ounce cans apricot halves in syrup
pared peel and juice of 1 minneola
2 egg whites

1. Drain the apricots, reserving the syrup. Simmer the minneola peel in the apricot syrup for 2–3 minutes. Leave to cool, then strain.
2. Purée the apricots with 4 tablespoons minneola juice in a blender or food processor. Press through a nylon strainer. Add the apricot syrup.
3. Freeze as for Lemon sherbet, adding the egg whites as directed.

Left: Apricot and Minneola Sherbet. Right: Melon and Ginger Sherbet.

MELON AND GINGER SHERBET

SERVES 6

Ginger lovers thought this sherbet was delicious; others weren't so keen! The type of melon used determines the color of the sherbet.

1 medium green or orange-fleshed melon
¼ cup stem ginger
2 tablespoons lemon juice
1½ cups Stock syrup (see page 237)
2 egg whites

1. Purée the melon flesh, ginger and lemon juice in a blender or food processor. Press through a nylon strainer.
2. Add the stock syrup. Freeze as for Lemon sherbet, adding the egg whites as directed.

RASPBERRY SHERBET

SERVES ABOUT 6

This full flavored sherbet is a favorite with both adults and children alike. It works equally well with loganberries or strawberries. The hint of kirsch adds a touch of luxury to this dessert.

1 pound raspberries
2 tablespoons lemon juice
2 tablespoons kirsch
1½ cups Stock syrup (see page 237)
2 egg whites

1. Purée the raspberries with the lemon juice and kirsch in a blender or food processor. Press through a nylon strainer.
2. Add to the stock syrup. Freeze as for Lemon sherbet, adding the egg whites as directed.

COLA SHERBET

SERVES 4–6

1½ cups Stock syrup (see page 237)
1 cup cola
1 egg white

1. Mix the stock syrup with the cola.
2. Freeze as for Lemon sherbet, adding the egg white as directed.

CHAMPAGNE SHERBET

SERVES 4–6

A refreshing way to end a special occasion meal.

1½ cups Stock syrup (see page 237)
juice of 1 lemon
1½ cups champagne
1 egg white

1. Mix the stock syrup, lemon juice and champagne together.
2. Freeze as for Lemon sherbet, adding the egg white as directed.

LYCHEE SHERBET

SERVES 6

This sherbet has a wonderful fragrant taste, even though the lychees used are canned ones.

1 pound 4 ounce can lychees in syrup
2 tablespoons lemon juice
1 egg white

1. Purée the lychees, their syrup and the lemon juice in a blender or food processor. Press through a nylon strainer.
2. Freeze as for Lemon sherbet, adding the egg white as directed.

SAUCES AND CREAMS

Enliven the plainest pancake or enhance a simple ice cream with our tempting selection of hot and cold sauces and creams. Ignore the fear and mystique surrounding sauce making, with our easy-to-follow recipes you will never fail to create a luscious, glistening topping for all your desserts.

Sweet White Sauce
MAKES 1 CUP

1½ tablespoons cornstarch

---
1 cup milk

1½ tablespoons sugar or to taste

---

1. Blend the cornstarch with 1–2 tablespoons of the milk to a smooth paste.
2. Heat the remaining milk until almost boiling in a saucepan. (Alternatively, microwave on HIGH for 1½ minutes.) Add to the cornstarch mixture, stirring.
3. Return to the pan and bring to the boil, stirring. Cook for 1–2 minutes after the mixture has thickened to a glossy sauce. (Alternatively, microwave on HIGH for 3–4 minutes, stirring every minute.) Add sugar to taste.

VARIATIONS

When adding extra liquid to the sauce, make a thicker sauce by increasing the cornstarch to 2 tablespoons.
  Flavor with any of the following when sauce has thickened:
1 teaspoon mixed spice
2 tablespoons jelly
grated peel of ½ orange or lemon
2 tablespoons light cream
2 tablespoons rum.
Chocolate Sauce Blend 1 tablespoon cocoa with the cornstarch.

To freeze: pack in a rigid container. Defrost at cool room temperature overnight. Reheat gently in a saucepan or microwave on HIGH for 2–3 minutes.

Fruit Purée Sauce
MAKES ABOUT 1¼ CUPS, DEPENDING ON FRUIT
Serve poured over sherbets or mousses or flood a flat plate with the sauce and lay slices of ice cream or gâteau on top.

---
1 pound ripe fruit, prepared, such as raspberries, blackcurrants, redcurrants, strawberries, mango, papaya, apricots, kiwi, passion fruit pulp

---
Stock syrup (see page 237), to taste

---
lime or lemon juice, to taste

---
fruit liqueur or brandy (optional)

---

1. Purée the fruit in a blender or food processor. Add enough sugar syrup and lime or lemon juice until the sauce has the desired consistency and flavor.
2. Press through a fine strainer to remove pips, then stir in liqueur to taste, if using.

To freeze: pack in a rigid container. Defrost overnight in the refrigerator.

Orange Sabayon Sauce
SERVES 4
This deliciously light and fluffy sauce may be served hot or cold. If serving cold, serve within 1 hour of making or it will separate.

---
5 egg yolks

---
scant ½ cup superfine sugar

---
scant ½ cup orange-flavored liqueur

---

1. Put all the ingredients in a bowl placed over a saucepan of simmering water and whisk constantly until the sauce is thick and creamy.
2. Remove from the heat, place the bowl in a bowl of cold water and whisk constantly until the sauce cools to lukewarm.
3. Serve warm, or cool completely, whisking occasionally and serve cold.

Not suitable for freezing.

Chocolate Fudge Sauce
MAKES ABOUT 1½ CUPS
Serve this rich, sticky sauce with profiteroles, ice cream and bananas.

---
5 tablespoons light cream

---
scant ¼ cup cocoa

---
generous ½ cup superfine sugar

½ cup light molasses

¼ stick butter or margarine

---
pinch of salt

½ teaspoon vanilla

---

1. Combine all the ingredients, except the vanilla, in a saucepan over low heat and mix well. Slowly bring to the boil, stirring occasionally. Boil for 5 minutes, then add the vanilla.
2. Cool the sauce slightly before serving.

To freeze: pack in a rigid container. Defrost at cool room temperature. Reheat gently, stirring all the time. Alternatively, reheat from frozen, in a heavy-based saucepan, stirring all the time.

Previous page: FRUIT PURÉE SAUCE USING RASPBERRIES.

EGG CUSTARD SAUCE

MAKES 1 CUP

The classic accompaniment to hot and cold puddings.
The sauce can be flavored with vanilla or lemon.

2 eggs
1 tablespoon sugar
1 cup milk
1 vanilla pod, split, or 1 teaspoon vanilla or few strips of thinly pared lemon peel

1. Beat the eggs, sugar and 3 tablespoons of the milk together in a bowl.
2. Heat the rest of the milk with the vanilla pod or lemon peel, if using, in a pan until lukewarm. (Alternatively, microwave on HIGH for 2 minutes or until hot.) Beat into the eggs.
3. Pour the mixture into a double saucepan or bowl standing over a pan of simmering water. Cook, stirring continuously, until the custard thickens enough to thinly coat the back of a spoon. Do not boil. (Alternatively, microwave on HIGH for 1 minute, then on LOW for $4\frac{1}{2}$ minutes, whisking frequently.) Remove the vanilla pod or lemon peel, if using.
4. Pour into a cold container and stir in the vanilla, if using. Serve hot or cold. The sauce thickens slightly on cooling.

To freeze: pack in a rigid container. Defrost in the refrigerator overnight. Serve cold. Do not reheat.

BUTTERSCOTCH NUT SAUCE

MAKES ABOUT $\frac{1}{2}$ CUP

Serve with steamed or baked puddings and ice cream.

2 teaspoons custard powder
1 tablespoon light molasses
1 tablespoon soft dark brown sugar
$\frac{1}{8}$ stick butter or margarine
few drops of lemon juice
2 tablespoons chopped nuts

1. Blend the custard powder with $\frac{1}{2}$ cup water in a bowl.
2. Put the syrup, sugar and butter in a saucepan and heat gently until melted. Remove from the heat and mix in the custard powder mixture. Bring to the boil, stirring, and add a little lemon juice and the nuts.
3. Serve the sauce hot or cold.

To freeze: pack in a rigid container. Defrost at cool room temperature. Reheat gently, stirring all the time. Alternatively, reheat from frozen in a heavy-based saucepan, stirring all the time.

LEMON SAUCE

MAKES ABOUT $1\frac{1}{2}$ CUPS

juice and grated peel of 1 large lemon
1 tablespoon cornstarch
2 tablespoons sugar
knob of butter
1 egg yolk

1. Make up the lemon juice to 1 cup with water. Add the lemon peel.
2. Blend a little of the liquid with the cornstarch and sugar until smooth.
3. Bring the remaining liquid to the boil and stir into the cornstarch mixture. Return all the liquid to the pan and bring to the boil, stirring until the sauce thickens and clears. Add the butter.
4. Cool, then beat in the egg yolk. Reheat without boiling, stirring all the time.

Not suitable for freezing.

COFFEE CREAM SAUCE

MAKES ABOUT 1 CUP

2 teaspoons instant coffee powder
$\frac{1}{2}$ cup heavy cream
1 tablespoon milk
2 tablespoons sugar
few drops of vanilla

1. Dissolve the coffee powder in 2 teaspoons hot water in a bowl. Leave to cool slightly.
2. Stir in the cream, milk, sugar and vanilla. Whisk until the cream begins to hold its shape.

Not suitable for freezing.

APRICOT SAUCE

MAKES ABOUT 1 CUP

Serve this speedy sauce with poached fruit or ice cream.

15 ounce can apricots in natural juice
2 teaspoons brandy

1. Drain the apricots, reserving the juice. Purée the apricots with 4 tablespoons of the juice in a blender or food processor until smooth.
2. Pour the purée into a saucepan and add the brandy. Heat gently for 2–3 minutes. (Alternatively, microwave on HIGH for 1–2 minutes.)

To freeze: pack in a rigid container. Defrost at cool room temperature. Serve cold.

MELBA SAUCE

MAKES 1½ CUPS
Serve hot or cold with ice cream and fresh fruit.

1 pound raspberries, hulled
4 tablespoons redcurrant jelly
1 tablespoon icing sugar
2 teaspoons arrowroot

1. Rub the raspberries through a strainer into a saucepan. Add the jelly and icing sugar and bring to the boil.
2. Blend the arrowroot with 1 tablespoon cold water to a smooth cream. Stir in a little of the raspberry mixture. Return the mixture to the pan and bring to the boil, stirring with a wooden spoon, until it thickens and clears.

To freeze: pack in a rigid container. Defrost at cool room temperature.

WALNUT RUM SAUCE

MAKES ABOUT 1½ CUPS
This sauce is equally good hot or cold. Serve with vanilla, coffee or chocolate ice cream.

generous 1 cup dark brown soft sugar
2 teaspoons instant coffee powder
6 tablespoons light cream or evaporated milk
¼ stick butter or margarine
1 tablespoon corn syrup
1 tablespoon rum
½ cup walnuts, roughly chopped

1. Combine the sugar, coffee, cream, butter and syrup together in a saucepan. Cook over a low heat to dissolve the sugar.
2. Bring to the boil and simmer, stirring, for 2–3 minutes or until thickened. Stir in the rum and walnuts.

To freeze: pack in a rigid container. Defrost at cool room temperature. Serve cold.

MOUSSELINE SAUCE

MAKES ABOUT ½ CUP
Serve with fruit desserts, chocolate gâteau or light steamed puddings.

1 egg
1 egg yolk
3 tablespoons sugar
1 tablespoon sherry
4 tablespoons light cream

1. Place all the ingredients in a bowl over a pan of boiling water and whisk until pale, frothy and a creamy thick consistency. Serve at once.

Not suitable for freezing.

CARAMEL SAUCE

MAKES ABOUT 1 CUP
Serve with poached apples or pears.

scant 1 cup light brown soft sugar
½ cup light cream
¼ cup stem ginger, cut into thin strips

1. Melt the light soft brown sugar in a small, heavy-based saucepan over a gentle heat.
2. Take the pan off the heat, cover your hand with a cloth and carefully stir in ½ cup water. Cook gently for another minute, stirring continually to make a smooth sauce.
3. Cool slightly, stir in the cream and ginger and serve immediately.

Not suitable for freezing.

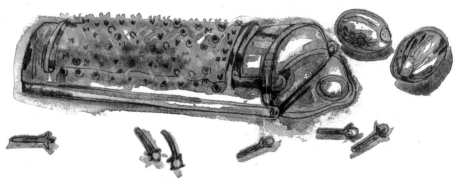

Opposite: MELBA SAUCE.

CRÈME PÂTISSIÈRE

MAKES ABOUT 2 CUPS

A rich, thick, custard used as a filling for cakes, small pastries and pies. Its light, smooth, cool texture contrasts and complements both sponge cakes and pastries alike. The basic mixture is flavored with vanilla, but it can also be flavored with liqueurs, chocolate, coffee, orange or lemon peel. Add liqueurs, such as kirsch or brandy, to the cold custard, but do not add too much or the custard will become thin. Chocolate, coffee, orange or lemon peel should be heated with the milk. It is always best to make the custard the day before required, to ensure that it is thoroughly chilled.

1 cup milk
1 teaspoon vanilla
3 egg yolks
scant $\frac{1}{3}$ cup superfine sugar
2$\frac{1}{2}$ tablespoons All Purpose flour
1 egg white
$\frac{1}{2}$ cup heavy cream

1. Put the milk and vanilla into a saucepan and bring almost to the boil.
2. Whisk the egg yolks and 1 tablespoon of the sugar together in a bowl until pale and thick. Fold in the flour. Gently whisk in the milk and strain back into the pan.
3. Cook the custard over a gentle heat, stirring all the time, until thickened. Pour the hot custard into a clean bowl, then cover the surface closely with plastic wrap to prevent a skin forming. Allow the custard to cool completely, but not to set too firmly.
4. Whisk the egg white until stiff, then gradually whisk in the remaining sugar. Whip the cream until thick.
5. Whisk the cooled custard until smooth, gradually fold in the egg white mixture, then the cream. Cover the crème pâtissière with plastic wrap and thoroughly chill before using.

Not suitable for freezing.

2. Heat the rest of the milk in a pan until almost boiling. (Alternatively, microwave on HIGH for 2–2$\frac{1}{2}$ minutes until almost boiling.) Pour on to the egg mixture, stirring all the time.
3. Return the custard to the pan and stir over a low heat until the mixture boils. Add vanilla to taste and cook for a further 2–3 minutes until thickened. (Alternatively, microwave on HIGH for 1$\frac{1}{2}$–2 minutes until very thick, stirring frequently.) Cover and leave to cool before using.

Not suitable for freezing.

CRÈME CHANTILLY

MAKES 1 CUP

The addition of sugar and vanilla before whipping, turns heavy cream into crème Chantilly, making the cream smoother and more flavorful. It is used extensively for filling and decorating cakes, large and small pastries, and desserts, or as an accompaniment to fruit salads or poached fruit.

1 cup heavy cream, well chilled
1 tablespoon icing sugar, sifted
$\frac{1}{2}$–1 teaspoon vanilla

1. Put the cream, sugar and vanilla to taste into a well chilled bowl.
2. Whip until the cream forms soft peaks, or a little thicker if required for piping. Take care not to overwhip the cream or it will turn buttery and be unusable.

Not suitable for freezing.

QUICK CRÈME PÂTISSIÈRE

MAKES 1 CUP

2 eggs
scant $\frac{1}{3}$ cup superfine sugar
2 tablespoons All Purpose flour
2 tablespoons cornstarch
1 cup milk
few drops of vanilla

1. Whisk the eggs and sugar together in a large bowl, using an electric mixer, until pale and creamy and the mixture leaves a trail when the whisk is lifted. Sift the flour and cornstarch into the bowl and beat in with a little of the milk until smooth.

Opposite: ORANGE SABAYON SAUCE.

TOFFEE SAUCE

MAKES ABOUT 1 CUP

Serve with bananas and ice cream.

scant ⅓ cup superfine sugar
1 stick butter or margarine
½ cup heavy cream
2 tablespoons corn syrup
vanilla

1. Put the sugar, butter or margarine, cream and syrup in a bowl, and add vanilla to taste.
2. Stand over a saucepan of water and heat gently. Stir until the butter and sugar have melted and the ingredients are well mixed. (Alternatively, microwave on HIGH for 3—5 minutes, or until melted, stirring frequently.) Serve hot.

Not suitable for freezing.

SYRUP SAUCE

MAKES ABOUT ½ CUP

Serve with steamed puddings and baked desserts.

4—5 tablespoons light molasses
juice of ½ lemon

1. Put the syrup and 3 tablespoons water in a saucepan. Stir over gentle heat until blended.
2. Simmer for 3—4 minutes. (Alternatively, microwave on HIGH for 2—3 minutes, stirring occasionally.) Add the lemon juice. Serve hot.

To freeze: pack in a rigid container. Defrost at cool room temperature. Reheat gently, stirring all the time. Alternatively, reheat from frozen in a heavy-based saucepan, stirring all the time.

CRÈME AU BEURRE

MAKES ABOUT 1¼ CUPS

Use this rich butter cream to fill gâteaux, pastries and choux puffs.

scant ½ cup superfine sugar
2 egg yolks, beaten
1½ sticks butter

1. Place the sugar and 4 tablespoons water in a heavy-based saucepan. Heat very gently to dissolve the sugar, without boiling. When completely dissolved, bring to boiling point and boil steadily for 2—3 minutes, to reach a temperature of 225°.
2. Put the egg yolks in a bowl. Pour the syrup in a thin stream on to the egg yolks, whisking all the time. Continue to whisk until the mixture is thick and cold.
3. In another bowl, cream the butter until very soft and gradually beat in the egg yolk mixture.

VARIATIONS

Chocolate Melt 2 squares semi sweet chocolate with 1 tablespoon water. Cool slightly and beat in.

Coffee Beat in 1—2 tablespoons coffee flavoring.

Fruit Crush 1 cup fresh strawberries, raspberries etc, or defrost, drain and crush frozen fruit. Beat into the basic mixture.

Orange or Lemon Add grated peel and juice to taste.

To freeze: pack in a rigid container. Defrost in the refrigerator. Beat thoroughly before using.

Opposite: SYRUP SAUCE.

BRANDY OR RUM BUTTER

SERVES 8

A favorite English accompaniment to hot Christmas pudding and equally delicious served with fruit pies.

$\frac{2}{3}$ cup light brown soft sugar
$\frac{3}{4}$ cup icing sugar
$1\frac{1}{2}$ sticks softened butter
about 2 tablespoons brandy or rum

1. Gradually beat the sugars into the butter in a bowl until evenly blended.

2. Add the brandy or rum, about 1 teaspoon at a time, beating well between each addition. Spoon into a serving bowl, cover tightly and chill.

3. Take the brandy butter out of the refrigerator 30 minutes before serving.

VARIATIONS

Lemon Butter Omit the brandy or rum. Use superfine sugar in place of brown sugar. Add the finely grated peel and juice of 1 lemon.

Orange Butter Make as above using the grated peel and juice of 1 orange.

Lime Butter Make as above using the grated peel and juice of 1–2 limes.

To freeze: pack and freeze. Defrost overnight at cool room temperature. Chill again before serving.

ALMOND BUTTER

SERVES 4

This works equally well with roasted and finely ground hazelnuts. Serve with warm apple or pear pies or hot waffles and pancakes.

1 stick butter, softened
generous $\frac{1}{2}$ cup superfine sugar
$\frac{1}{3}$ cup ground almonds, lightly roasted
1 tablespoon almond-flavored liqueur

1. Cream the butter and sugar together in a bowl until light and fluffy.

2. Stir in the almonds and liqueur.

3. Pile into a small dish and chill well before serving.

To freeze: pack and freeze. Defrost overnight at cool room temperature. Chill again before serving.

CHOCOLATE NUT BUTTER

SERVES 4

Serve with hot pancakes and waffles.

1 stick butter
2 teaspoons superfine sugar
1 tablespoon grated chocolate
2 tablespoons chopped walnuts, hazelnuts or pecans

1. Beat the butter until very light and fluffy, then beat in the remaining ingredients.

To freeze: pack and freeze. Defrost overnight at cool room temperature. Chill again before serving.

Opposite: BAKED CHOCOLATE MARBLE SPONGE *(PAGE 102)* WITH CHOCOLATE FUDGE SAUCE.

INDEX